Jurists: Profiles in Legal Theory

General Editors:
William Twining
Neil MacCormick

Émile Durkheim
Law in a Moral Domain

Roger Cotterrell

EDINBURGH UNIVERSITY PRESS

© Roger Cotterrell, 1999

Edinburgh University Press Ltd
22 George Square, Edinburgh

Typeset in Plantin Light
by The Florence Group, Stoodleigh, Devon,
and printed and bound in Great Britain by
The Cromwell Press, Trowbridge

A CIP Record for this book is available from
the British Library

ISBN 0 7486 0700 5 (hardback)
ISBN 0 7486 1339 0 (paperback)

Contents

For Frank and Zillah

Preface

Émile Durkheim's legal theory, taken as a whole, is little known and, where known, often much misunderstood. This may seem a strange statement to make about a central part of the work of a writer now universally seen as one of the classic social theorists and whose ideas are endlessly discussed. Durkheim has, indeed, long been recognised as a founding father of the sociological study of law. Yet, even in this field, he is usually associated with theories that represent only a limited, somewhat misleading aspect of his work on law. The Durkheim known to much of the literature of legal scholarship is a shadow of his real intellectual self. Even more remarkably, his ideas about law are rarely explored in depth as part of modern sociology. For Durkheim, the study of law was an absolutely essential and central part of sociological work. Yet law tends to be marginalised as a subject for study in sociology as an academic discipline. Thus, the strange consequence is that Durkheim, revered as one of the greatest figures in sociology's history, is often studied in a way that largely ignores his own major contribution to what he himself regarded as one of the central foci of the sociological enterprise.

Why read Durkheim on law today? He never wrote systematically about legal phenomena and his insights are scattered through many sources. So understanding his legal theory involves a task of elaborate reconstruction. More fundamentally, his approach to law raises the kinds of problems that critics often find in his sociological outlook as a whole. Above all, it is unashamedly moralistic. For Durkheim the idea that law and morality should be analytically separated is unrealistic. But this separation dominates much modern Western legal and sociological thinking. And Durkheim is unlikely to appear allied even with legal philosophers who deny that law and morality are analytically separable. Typically they seek abstract moral principles, procedures, or insights, as groundings for law. But Durkheim sees morality as set by the conditions of social life, or by popularly shared beliefs in particular historical circumstances. Morality is to be understood sociologically, in relation to the empirical contexts of moral actions in particular times and places. So he gives little comfort to those seeking a basis for law in moral absolutes or philosophical first principles.

Even for more sociologically inclined legal observers Durkheim poses challenges. Modern sociology of law has tended to focus on law's character as an expression of power. It has examined law's practical techniques and effects as a means of government. But questions about power seem as absent from Durkheim's discussions of law, on first encounter, as from other aspects of his sociology. Indeed, one of the most frequent criticisms of Durkheim's work as a whole (a criticism I shall challenge in this book in relation to his legal theory) is that it ignores the phenomena of power and coercion in social life.

The central task in expounding Durkheim's ideas on law must therefore be to explain the integrity of those ideas and the purpose that inspires them. I aim to show in this book that Durkheim's view of law is important and illuminating. Much contemporary law seems a mass of technical regulation remote from moral concerns. But many lawyers and other citizens are not content to think of it in this way. The search for principle, for intelligible values that law embodies, never ceases; the aspiration is for law that expresses the moral commitments of people living in relationships of community of many kinds, reflecting values that are real in the experience of those whose lives it regulates. The question is how, today, law can fulfil this role.

Durkheim's writings embody this aspiration. They use history, ethnography and social theory to unearth law's intricate, shifting moral foundations. They suggest ways in which, in modern complex Western societies, relationships between law and morality can be reformulated. The approach does not try to legislate philosophically a moral authority for law. The moral groundings of law are to be found by empirically studying social phenomena and understanding their conditions of existence.

This book seeks to present Durkheim's legal theory systematically and critically. As sources, I have often used existing translations of the original texts, but have substituted my own translation of quoted passages in many instances where this seemed justifiable. In fact, much material important for the study of Durkheim's legal ideas and those of his juristic followers remains untranslated into English. In all cases, translations from cited French texts are mine.

Durkheim's legal theory cannot be isolated from the general themes of his sociology. The chapters in Part 1 emphasise this by introducing his outlook on law in relation to its essential contexts. Throughout all parts of the book the legal focus is strictly maintained. But explaining Durkheim's legal thought necessarily entails examining his view of the nature of morality, which is a concern throughout the text. Further, his ideas on law are intimately linked with a very distinctive conception of the state. Hence central aspects of Durkheim's political theory are discussed, especially in the chapters in Part 4. The final part of the book offers a general assessment and overview of Durkheim's approach in the light of contemporary concerns in legal theory.

My purpose is not to wrench Durkheim's writings on law from their proper context, as part of one of the most ambitious, sophisticated and influential systems of sociological thought. It is to illustrate that his social theory can be approached from what has previously been a neglected standpoint. This book is the first detailed analysis in English of the entirety of Durkheim's legal theory. It tries to explain his ideas in a manner accessible to readers previously unfamiliar with his sociology, and to show the significance of his work for students of law. Above all, it assumes that Durkheim's ideas on law are fundamentally important to his sociology as a whole.

In part the reasons for reading Durkheim on law today are those that inspire interest in the rest of his work. His social theory is systematic, combative, bold and imaginative, engaged with issues of enduring social concern, expressed with passion and directness, and insightful on a very wide range of topics. His work has a moral vision. It burns with a faith that society can be more just and cohesive than in the past. It rejects utopianism but finds ideals – of individual autonomy and dignity, solidarity and mutual concern – demanded by the very structure of social life. It traces its insights through inquiries into the distant past and follows them through to predictions of the future. All these qualities are strongly present in Durkheim's writings about law.

To enter his world of legal understanding is, however, to enter what must seem, for many students of law today, a strange territory, one where familiar nostrums are inverted and wholly different assumptions from those of most contemporary legal thought apply. Some of Durkheim's ideas may seem naive, with omissions or distortions too serious to be forgiven. Also, although I assume in this book that his thought must be presented and judged as a unity, matters are complicated by changes in his views over time. But his writings on law offer new insight and restate much neglected wisdom. I try to show here why despite all problems with his work he remains a great theorist of law in society. A century after he wrote, many of his ideas remain profoundly relevant for contemporary legal theory.

Over the long period during which I have researched Durkheim's ideas, I have accumulated many debts, especially to: Paul Hirst, Sami Zubaida and Suzanne MacGregor who first helped me to explore Durkheim's work systematically; Tim Murphy, Simon Roberts and, particularly, David Nelken, with all of whom I have discussed Durkheim's work frequently over the years; Jean Carbonnier, André-Jean Arnaud, Peter Fitzpatrick, Geraldine Van Bueren and Christoph Eberhard for assistance on specific matters; William Twining and Neil MacCormick who encouraged the writing of this book; Bob Burns and

Susan Richards of Queen Mary and Westfield College library, and staff of other university libraries in London, Paris and Brussels, for their help in locating materials and making my research visits productive. I am grateful also to my college and its Faculty of Laws for giving me research funding and a period of leave to work on this project; to David and Linda, for their interest and enthusiasm; and to Ann for all the support and critical stimulus she gives.

Roger Cotterrell
Queen Mary and Westfield College
University of London
August 1998

Part 1

The context of Durkheim's legal thought

1

A sociological project

Visiting the Sorbonne – the old University of Paris – today, it is still possible to imagine the charismatic figure of Émile Durkheim there nearly a century ago. One can visualise him, serious and somewhat stern, walking the corridors of the university and into a packed lecture theatre. Perhaps he would be striding to the lectern, as usual, with a copy of *L'Humanité*, the French radical newspaper of the day, tucked rather conspicuously under his arm (cf. Clark, 1968: 84). From the surviving notes of his lectures and the testimony of colleagues and students, one gains some sense of this 'orator without equal' (Davy, 1919: 194) and of the presence that fascinated students who heard him. These sources suggest something of the zeal that drove his teaching. And the ideas he presented in his lectures at the beginning of the twentieth century are studied today – more widely than ever, it seems – through his published writings and a vast body of secondary literature devoted to the theories of this French scholar.

In the last two decades of the nineteenth century and the first two of the twentieth Durkheim worked to promote a new science. His compatriot Auguste Comte, some decades earlier, had named it 'sociology' (Giddens, 1975). Although the science was in its infancy, Durkheim saw it as having the potential to change not merely the public policies of his own country, but all aspects of social understanding in the modern world. Among much else it would offer a new understanding of law – showing its nature and significance in complex modern societies and the pattern of its development through history. Indeed, the study of law would be central to this science.

Durkheim's writings have received extensive and continuous critical attention in the century since he wrote. This book addresses his ideas on law. In Parts 2 to 4 these ideas are examined in detail. Initially, however, they have to be put in their broader intellectual setting. It is important to see how they take shape in the context of concerns and conditions that colour his sociological thinking more generally. This and the following two chapters are intended to locate his legal studies in this context. This chapter considers the place of law in the general project of Durkheim's sociology.

Sociology's ambition

Early contributions had been made to sociology, especially in Germany, France and England, before Durkheim wrote. But he presents the aspirations of the discipline in a new way in his writings. Sociology, he insists, is to contribute to an understanding of the rights and duties of citizenship. It will inform the actions of legislators and the educational philosophy of schools. Scholars, and through them other citizens, will use it to make sense of history and social change, and of changes in mores and ethical beliefs. It will replace purely abstract philosophical speculation about social matters with a scientific respect for the observable, variable, empirical detail of social life.

Sociology, according to this agenda, resists reactionary celebrations of the status quo no less than utopian flights of fancy about possible futures for mankind. Through comparative study of social phenomena, scholars, in Durkheim's view, will recognise how and why society evolves in particular ways. They will understand the nature of social crises and analyse objectively how society's problems may best be addressed. Sociology will make it possible to see which values and ideals are in harmony with the broad tendencies of social evolution, and which are at odds with them. It will show which features of social life may be considered normal and inevitable in a particular kind of society and which abnormal or pathological, requiring clear-sighted policies and actions to redress problems.

Thus, Durkheim's new science carried immense ambitions. But his writings stress the caution with which its claims should be made. A science in its infancy has to acknowledge the provisional, limited character of its knowledge. Durkheim admits that sociology cannot answer many questions. The data are not to hand; researches remain to be done; analyses have not been attempted. And these researches and analyses will require the efforts of many hands. The time of renaissance scholars who could range over many fields has gone (Durkheim, 1984: 3–4). Understanding society requires teamwork between specialists and careful, laborious inquiries: the piecing together of information and insight from many sources. It involves collective effort to observe and report, interpret and synthesise, and to reinterpret and revise ideas continually as observation and experience provide more evidence.

 Thus, sociology reaches out to other disciplines of social inquiry, asking for their aid. It allies itself, for example, with the work of jurists, historians and ethnographers. It is the synthesising social science, taking the findings of other disciplines and reinterpreting them in a broader picture (Durkheim, 1982a: 260). In return it offers its evolving frameworks of understanding as guides for scholars working in particular fields of social study, such as law.

At sociology's heart is a concern for morality. For Durkheim, society cannot exist without moral bonds (1984: 13; 1961: 6), whether these are bonds of shared belief or of mutual commitment reflecting the interdependence of individuals or social groups. Moral ideas are neither innate in the individual nor to be deduced from abstract first principles. They are inspired by the empirical conditions of social life in particular times and places. To understand those conditions and the forces that shape social development is, for Durkheim, rationally to appreciate morality's demands. Morality provides the normative framework of stable social relationships. In modern society these relationships are primarily domestic, economic and occupational, and the political relationships of citizenship. It follows, therefore, that these are modern morality's concerns. Morality expresses the requirements of living together in particular environments; 'the domain of the moral begins where the domain of the social begins' (Durkheim, 1961: 60).

This focus on morality informs all discussion in this book, because for Durkheim, morality and law cannot be firmly separated. 'Moral ideas are the soul (*l'âme*) of the law,' he declares (1909: 150; cf. 1978a: 80). Law expresses what is fundamental in any society's morality. So the study of law, like that of morality, is central to sociology. Indeed 'sociology of law was an essential component of . . . [Durkheim's] work, so much so that his sociology cannot be fully understood without considering it' (Vogt, 1993: 71).

A career

Who was this champion of the sociological study of law? Before examining his ideas further, it is appropriate to sketch an outline of the career in which they were formed. Durkheim was born in 1858 in Épinal, near the Alsace border in eastern France. He was descended from a line of rabbis, but there is no clear evidence that he was expected to follow in this family tradition. In fact, during his youth, he broke not only with Judaism but with all religious faith. Nevertheless, a secular sociological concern with the nature of religion later became central to his work and, as will appear, it is important to his legal theory.[1]

After studying at the prestigious École Normale Supérieure in Paris, he gained his *aggrégation* (teaching qualification) in philosophy in 1882. By then he had decided to become a sociologist (Davy, 1919: 186). Few appropriate models for such a career existed and there seems to be no information about the circumstances in which Durkheim's decision was reached. He taught philosophy in schools for five years, apart

1. See Chapter 4, below.

from a break in 1885–6 including a six-month visit to Germany funded by a government grant. German scholarship in legal philosophy and ethics particularly impressed him (Lukes, 1973: 87), and he wrote lengthy reports of his academic impressions on returning to France (see Durkheim, 1887). By 1886 he had produced a first draft of the doctoral thesis that would inspire his most famous book, *The Division of Labour in Society*, the work containing his most extensive discussions of law.

Government interest in new ideas for social science led to his being appointed in 1887 to a lecturing post (*chargé de cours*) in sociology and education at the University of Bordeaux. In the fifteen years he taught there, he published, together with many papers, three works that are now social science classics: *The Division of Labour in Society* in 1893, *The Rules of Sociological Method* in 1895 and *Suicide* in 1897 (Durkheim, 1952, 1982a, 1984).

Thereafter his career was one of uninterrupted success and recognition. In 1896 he was named professor of social science at Bordeaux, the holder of the first such chair in France. The following year he founded an annual publication, the *Année sociologique*, which, under his editorship, became a focus of activity for the band of academic co-workers attracted to his project of a science of sociology. Jean Duvignaud (1965: 8) remarks: 'Between his thirtieth and fortieth years, Durkheim thus invented a science by teaching it, opened up new perspectives and realised part of his first vocation: to found a positive understanding of society.' In 1902 he moved to Paris to take up a teaching post in education and sociology at the Sorbonne. Four years later he succeeded to the Chair of Education there and in 1913 the University of Paris gave him the title of Professor of the Science of Education and Sociology. From this position he exerted great influence on the institutional development of sociology in France.

Durkheim's ideas dominated much of French educational thinking in the first two decades of the twentieth century. And he attracted many followers. Durkheimian sociology reached out – if strictly on its own terms – to all academic disciplines concerned with social inquiry. It welcomed collaborators whatever their disciplinary training might be. And it offered frameworks of understanding that could be used in many different fields. Scholars of law, history, ethics and other disciplines found that Durkheim's ideas could give direction to their own researches.

This initial flowering of Durkheimian sociology turned out to be short-lived. Many of Durkheim's followers and co-workers, including his only son, died on First World War battlefields. Durkheim never recovered psychologically from the effect of his son's death at the end of 1915. He himself died on 15 November 1917, 'though far from the field of battle, a victim of the war', as his friend Georges Davy noted

(Davy, 1919: 181). Thereafter Durkheimian sociology lost the leadership and unity that had made it a ferment of collective activity. Eventually it became defined as the theoretical legacy of Durkheim's own work. After his death, it gradually ceased to be an open, collective project involving many co-workers but became, mainly, a settled canon of insights largely focused on Durkheim's works, explored endlessly by later commentators as a system of social theory.

Law in sociology, sociology in law

Durkheimian sociology, applied to special fields such as law, is both an aspiration and a set of methods. In the opening lecture of his first sociology course at Bordeaux in 1887, Durkheim claimed: 'I am able to pose with some precision a certain number of special questions which are related to each other in such a way as to form a science set among the other positive sciences' (1978b: 43). What links these questions is that they are asked from a 'social' perspective. Thus, for Durkheim, it is not a matter of considering – as philosophers and jurists had in the past – for what purposes mankind creates societies in which to live, or how, and to what extent, society or particular forms of social organisation can be justified from the standpoint of individual interests. Instead, sociology treats society as a natural phenomenon. The task is not to *justify* society from the standpoint of the individual, as though the individual can somehow stand apart from it. It is to *explain* society's nature, to show by what processes social life has developed into its modern forms, and what moral implications the existence of this phenomenon – society – has for individuals living in it.

The Durkheimian aspiration, then, is to unite or, at least, interpret systematically and consistently, in an evolving sociological perspective, all the major findings of the various disciplines concerned with studying social phenomena. Durkheim writes that the 'specialised sciences' – for example, political economy, comparative history of law and of religion, demography and political geography – have been treated as separate wholes

> whereas, on the contrary, the facts they are concerned with are just different manifestations of the same collective activity ... By not linking social facts to the social environment in which they are rooted, these studies hang in the air unrelated to the rest of the world, so that the bond that connects them to each other and unites them cannot be seen ... It is not necessary to show at length how this drawback is removed when these different sciences are thought of as branches of a single science, called sociology, embracing them all.

The consequence is that one of them cannot be developed in isolation from the others, because the facts that they study interconnect,
like the functions of a single organism . . . At the same time . . . [these
facts] take on a different aspect. Being products of society, they
appear as functions of society, not of the individual, and as such
they can be explained. (Durkheim, 1900a: 32–4; cf. 1960a: 370–2)

Durkheimian sociology's methods are dictated by these aims. They
imply a 'certain kind of eclecticism' (Durkheim, 1978b: 52). 'We are
not looking for new facts,' writes Durkheim's follower Paul Fauconnet
(1928: 22), in the context of his own sociological study of the nature
of legal and moral responsibility. 'All those we shall use are well known
and, we believe, will not be contested.' However, 'in their interpretation we may distance ourselves from the historians who described them.'
Paul Huvelin, another Durkheimian, hoped 'to encourage . . . [histo-
rians] to bring to sociologists a series of tested and verified results all
ready for a synthesis' (Huvelin, 1907: 5). In one view, sociology is 'less
a new science than the application of a new method . . . to some old
studies' (Gaston Richard quoted in Vogt, 1983: 189). Such an outlook
could seem modest or arrogant depending on the natural sympathies
of the scholars to whom Durkheimian sociology reached out. Sociology
offered partnership and willingly acknowledged its dependence on the
findings of other sciences. But it also gave the impression that these
sciences were underworkers, fated to operate with inadequate frameworks of explanation until sociology offered help. Durkheim's writings
hardly dispel the impression of sociological imperialism. 'My aim', he
declared in 1907, 'has been precisely to introduce . . . [the sociological]
idea into those disciplines from which it was absent and thereby to
make them branches of sociology' (Durkheim, 1982a: 260).

These approaches to method explain why some of Durkheim's ideas
about law are set out not in books or articles but in relatively obscure
comments in the *Année sociologique* and elsewhere, often in brief reviews
and critical notes on the work of other scholars. It has been said that
'Durkheimian method, perhaps more so in studies of law than in other
fields, amounted to writing series of connected book reviews, to a sort
of *explication de texte*' (Vogt, 1983: 189). This exaggerates, because
the main elements of Durkheim's legal theory are found in his books,
lectures and essays developing original themes. Nevertheless, book
reviews, which made up a large part of the *Année*, were an important
means of putting a different (sociological) gloss on writings that were
not necessarily sociological. The *Année*, the 'laboratory' of Durkheim's
method (Davy, 1919: 196), was a forum in which non-sociological or
only peripherally sociological works could be considered for their sociological use, and ideas built out of them. In this way the Durkheimians

drew the products of jurists into their sociological orbit. By showing the sociological significance of these works they encouraged legal specialists to take account of and develop sociological ideas and concerns. The Roman law scholar Huvelin and his colleague at the University of Lyons, Emmanuel Lévy, were prominent among the law professors drawn into Durkheim's sociological circle by this outreach policy. Their ideas feature prominently in discussion later in this book.

Thus, for Durkheim, a main means of developing sociology's place alongside law and other disciplines is to reinterpret systematically the findings of these disciplines and synthesise them in an evolving sociological perspective. He and most of his co-workers did not carry out empirical studies of their own. They relied on other scholars' research. Specialisation was required. There would be 'as many branches of sociology, as many specialised social sciences, as there are different species of social fact' (Durkheim, 1909: 147; cf. 1978a: 79). Law, for example, provides 'the subject matter for an entire science' in its own right (Durkheim and Fauconnet 1982: 184), but it is also one of sociology's special fields. And, from Durkheim's perspective, it does not matter whether those promoting sociological understanding of law call themselves jurists or sociologists. Durkheimian sociology 'does not pay a great attention to who is carrying on this approach' (Lévi-Strauss, 1945: 508).

[margin note: Sociology and Law]

Functional analysis

What is a sociological perspective on law? Sociology's distinctive object of study is society. Mankind no more invented society than the physical world. On the contrary, Durkheim claims in his early writings on sociological method that society, like nature, is subject to scientific laws. Sociology's task is to discover these and make them available as useful knowledge, as the physical scientist reveals the laws of nature for mankind's use (see Durkheim, 1895; 1982a).

Sociology is a unique science, but it needs models to guide it. Like some earlier writers, Durkheim often invokes biology – 'a veritable treasure trove of perspectives and hypotheses' (1978b: 56) – as a primary model. The biologist studies component parts of an organism in terms of the function that each component (organ) fulfils within the organism as a whole. So functional analysis looks not to inherent qualities of the thing studied, but to its usefulness in some larger structure of which it forms part. Applying the biological analogy to sociology, this larger structure is society. Social phenomena can be studied in terms of the part they play – their function – in relation to society, the larger social whole, or to other components of it. Thus, one could ask what is the social function of religion, education, marriage, property, law in general or a particular kind of law such as contract law. This would be to explore their *sociological* nature.

Functional analysis is not Durkheim's sole concern. The biological analogy is a limited device. He often considers social phenomena – for example, the institutions of contract, property or punishment – in terms of their history or patterns of development. Much effort was invested by the Durkheimians in studying very early forms of social institutions. But historical inquiry is often aimed at clarifying the most basic functions of a particular social institution, or how it came to fulfil them. The most rudimentary or earliest known forms of a particular social institution might be specially instructive foci for studies with this aim (Durkheim, 1898: 37). Historical study can suggest the social needs that a particular social phenomenon – for example, the transmission of property on death according to inheritance laws and customs – met in earlier times. In this way it might help to show whether the early need is still being met in the same way, whether, therefore, the particular phenomenon still has the same social character, judged in terms of its functions.

This method has profound consequences. The function of an institution is not necessarily the same as its perceived purpose. The sociologist can deduce functions that are latent or hidden. The consciously understood or intended purposes of an institution may be entirely different from its social functions. The original purpose of establishing a monarchy, for example, might have been to secure the political power of an individual or an elite. But long after that purpose has become redundant a monarchy might function as a symbol of national unity. This is not to claim that monarchy is essential to such a function, for some other institution might serve the same function instead, or more effectively. Neither is it to claim that an institution always, or even usually, serves the same function. Nor that the function itself is socially necessary. These are questions for sociology in studying the nature of society.

The most important thrust of functional analysis is to give sociology a way of understanding connections between social phenomena that is different and separate from commonsense conceptions of cause and purpose held by participants in social life. 'We believe it a fruitful idea', writes Durkheim (1982b: 171), 'that social life must be explained, not by the conception of it formed by those who participate in it, but by the profound causes which escape their consciousness' and 'that these causes must be sought mainly in the way in which individuals associating together are formed in groups.' Durkheim's statement makes clear that social explanation in general is linked to an understanding of the dynamics of group life. The key to analysing social phenomena is in observing the way individuals are associated – in other words, by studying the organisation of society.

This concern with function initially led Durkheim to explain the nature of law, like much else, in terms of 'profound causes which escape consciousness'. The evolution of law as a social phenomenon throughout history was to be understood not in terms of changes in the beliefs reflected in it but in terms of structural changes in the nature of society (Durkheim, 1984), changes not attributable to the conscious acts of individuals. Understanding would thus be a matter for the sociologist as scientist, analysing functional relationships between social phenomena, not for the non-sociologist participant in social life or for philosophers speculating on the nature of belief or understanding.

But Durkheim's emphasis changes in his later work. He recognises ideas and beliefs as having causal force in themselves.[2] Ultimately he portrays society as actually consisting of patterns of shared beliefs or understandings.[3] With this change, it seems necessary to recognise that causes of social phenomena no longer 'escape consciousness' but are, in some sense, represented in all minds, even if imperfectly understood by them. Durkheim's later sociology seeks to take on board the interconnections between popular understandings and beliefs and social change (Alexander, 1982: 296). But all his work holds to the insistence that social phenomena are to be understood in relation to the general structure of society, the totality that embraces them and gives them meaning and significance. To understand law sociologically, for example, is to understand how it expresses the character of society in special, distinctive and variable ways.

Positivism

The position of functional analysis in Durkheim's work is paralleled by that of positivism in it. Positivism in this context entails two things: a particular view of the nature of social phenomena (as 'objective' data awaiting discovery) and a particular view of the means of gaining knowledge of them (by detached, value-neutral scientific observation). Sociological positivism treats social phenomena as facts to be recorded by the social scientific observer. These phenomena, Durkheim insists early in his career, are to be treated as *social facts* observable by the sociologist. As far as possible, the methods of studying them should be

'social facts'

2. 'If representations [ideas, beliefs, sentiments] . . . have the power to react directly upon each other and to combine according to their own laws, they are then realities which, while maintaining an intimate relation with their substratum, are to a certain extent independent of it' (Durkheim, 1953b: 23). See Lukes (1973: ch. 10).
3. See p. 54, below.

analogous to those of the natural sciences; that is, methods of detached, objective and systematic observation. Social facts should be treated as if they were 'things' (1982a: 60). They constitute positive data, much like the chemical processes or instances of the workings of physical laws that a natural scientist might study.

What, then, is distinctive about these facts? The phenomenon of suicide provides an example. A suicide act is highly personal. Perhaps its causes might be illuminated by psychology. Certainly it is a matter of specific personal motivations, an individual fact. But the suicide rate – the number of suicides as a proportion of a population – refers to a *social* fact. Despite the immense variety of individual motivations, generalisations can be made about changes in suicide rates or their constancy over time, and about their variation between different countries. Explanations can be offered about stability or variation in suicide rates. These are explanations of suicide as a *social phenomenon* (Durkheim, 1952). Again, the underlying idea is of 'profound causes which escape consciousness', rooted in social conditions. Of course, these causes are not independent of individual lives; they are located and expressed in innumerable diverse ways in the latter. But they can be studied independently of any particular person's circumstances. Because they are related to society in general, to the conditions of collective life, they cannot be reduced to the study of individual motivations. A social fact, therefore, refers to some aspect of collective experience that informs but is not fully encompassed by any individual life.

Social facts, in Durkheim's understanding, *constrain* individuals, in so far as individual life can neither escape nor ignore them (1982a: 51). Individuals are, in this way, constrained by such social institutions as property, work and family structure, and by cultural, political, religious and other traditions. All of these are social facts. Even if we reject these institutions or traditions, they influence us. Our lives are shaped by social facts, experienced, in this specific sense, as 'external' to the individual.

Law is, for Durkheim, a social fact. Viewed positivistically, legal ideas and practices amount to social data. Law can be understood as an observable social phenomenon. Such a view immediately sets up a profound tension with elements of the lawyer's typical view of law: 'a legal rule is what it is,' Durkheim writes in setting out his early positivist outlook, 'and there are no two ways of perceiving it' (1982a: 82). This seems initially a highly unpromising way to approach law. It appears to deny what all lawyers recognise: that law is, at least in part, a matter of interpretation. But it has the virtue of emphasising that, despite all arguments, uncertainties, discretionary judgements and forms of linguistic manipulation and construction that are familiar in professional legal experience, legal ideas and practices exert constraint on individuals. They are significant social phenomena, part of the structure of the social world. However they are shaped and used in discourse, they are typically experienced as important objects of factual knowledge about the social world, as social forces that limit and control (Carbonnier, 1994: 102). Equally important, treating law as a social fact entails that law and everything about it (including all matters relating to its interpretation) are historically specific. Law exists not as some timeless idea but as rules and related practices *in specific times and places*. But law as social fact is law observed in its effects, not interpreted for its meanings. Durkheim's approach highlights some aspects of legal experience while sidelining others.

If social facts are observable, it seems clear that some are more observable than others. Social cohesion – the bonding together of individuals and groups in patterns of stable social relationships with others in a society – is a most important social fact. The nature and extent of this cohesion could vary greatly from one society to another. But such a highly abstract social phenomenon is difficult to observe. Perhaps relatively observable social facts may indicate the existence of more abstract ones. In his earliest work Durkheim assumes that law, as a social fact, can be relatively easily observed in the form of legal codes, institutions and practices. And he argues that observed variations in law can serve to indicate variation in more abstract social facts. In particular, certain aspects of legal change provide a measure of changes in the character of social cohesion – or, as he calls it, social solidarity – in particular societies at particular periods in history (Durkheim, 1984).

The 'index thesis' – the claim that law can be studied as an index or measure of social solidarity – was presented in Durkheim's lecture course on 'Social Solidarity' at Bordeaux in 1887.[4] It features prominently in his first book *The Division of Labour in Society* in 1893 but does not reappear in his later work. The early implication that legal doctrine merely mirrors the moral condition of society is replaced in his later writings with a more subtle view of the intertwining of legal, moral and political aspects of society. Nevertheless, the claim that law should be studied objectively as a matter of social fact remains. Thus, the concept of a sociological study of law is eminently realistic within the Durkheimian project. So too is the idea of a sociological science of morality, treating moral ideas not as philosophically deduced but as data from historical experience, as moral convictions actually current in particular societies at particular times.

What does it mean to say that social facts are external to, and constrain, the individual? These facts are 'lived out' in individual lives.

4. Lukes (1973: 139); Arnaud (1981: 113–14). Durkheim used the index thesis the following year in his lectures on the sociology of the family. See Durkheim (1978c: 214–18).

The institutions of the nuclear family or of monogamous marriage as social facts exist in so far as individuals live in nuclear families or enter into and sustain monogamous marriages. Individuals are not just constrained by social facts but also influence and create them. Citizens (and officials) are not merely constrained by law as an external force operating on them. They influence it – some people more than others. But Durkheim's positivist view of social facts as external constraining 'things' seems to treat individuals as not implicated except as 'carriers' or recipients of these facts. It biases his sociology towards a view of social phenomena as more solid, constraining and unchanging than perhaps they are experienced as being.

His later thinking shows some modification of the strict positivist methods codified in his early work. In his final book, on the nature of religion (Durkheim 1915), for example, he writes of the social character of religion as an organised structure of practices and beliefs uniting individuals in a common perception of their identity in their social world. But he recognises also that for the religious believer, religion is something else which science cannot express, a structure of meaning existing in the believer's subjective universe. What appears from one standpoint as an observable social phenomenon is, from another, the unique subjective experience of an individual. And the former cannot be understood in isolation from the latter: 'he who does not bring to the study of religion a kind of religious sentiment cannot speak about it! He is like a blind man trying to talk about colour' (Durkheim, 1975b: 184).

The position of the Durkheimian sociologist as an observer of social facts cannot, it seems, be one of total detachment. For example, Durkheim argues that a focus of collective belief in some form – such as the great religions have provided – is sociologically necessary; it performs a seemingly indispensable social function. Without it society lacks something important to its well-being.[5] Some substitute for declining religious faith is therefore required. The sociologist cannot remain neutral in pointing out the moral necessity that sociological inquiry indicates.

Late in his career, in 1911, Durkheim noted:

The principal social phenomena, religion, morality, law, economics and aesthetics, are nothing more than systems of values and hence of ideals. Sociology moves from the beginning in the field of ideals . . . It does not set out to construct ideals, but . . . accepts them as given facts, as objects of study, and it tries to analyse and explain them. (Durkheim 1953c: 96)

5. See pp. 52–3, below.

In other words, it takes ideals as it finds them. But it tries to explain how they come about, how they are shaped, flourish or decline as a result of social conditions; how, indeed, as social facts they fit socio-logically into the wider pattern of social facts comprising society. By doing this Durkheimian sociology validates some ideals as 'normal' or 'natural' in given social conditions, and others as aberrant. Thus, it purports to provide, up to a point, a scientific means of making moral judgements. It harnesses social science to philosophy or ethics and facil-itates social criticism (see Cladis, 1992: ch. 8). Perhaps we should not be surprised, then, that Durkheim wrote in a letter to Georges Davy in 1911: 'Having started out from philosophy, I am tending to return to it, or rather I have naturally been led back to it by the nature of the questions which I found on my way' (quoted in Lukes, 1973: 406).

The philosophical vocation of sociology

Durkheim's claim to be returning to philosophy can, however, be misleading. In fact he consistently saw sociology's vocation, in part, as to transform philosophical inquiries, to pursue them in new ways and so renew them (1982a: 237). Not only Durkheim, but many of his closest followers were qualified in philosophy. In his early writings he fiercely attacks philosophy's pretentions, but the purpose of the attack is to create a space for sociology. 'By what privilege is the philosopher to be permitted to speculate about society, without entering into commerce with the detail of social facts?' he asks (quoted in Lukes, 1973: 405). His claim is that philosophy requires sociology. On the other hand sociology 'has no need to take sides between the grand hypotheses which divide the metaphysicians' (Durkheim, 1982a: 159). It bypasses disputes that are too abstract to address the complexity of social conditions, or which cannot be illuminated by empirical inquiry.[6] Sociology developed from philosophy to give social speculation a necessary empirical grounding, but 'is independent of all philosophy' (1982a: 159), posing its own questions in its own way. It demands that moral issues be posed and addressed in the light of systematic study of experience since we are 'in no way justified in seeing in the personal aspirations that a thinker feels . . . an adequate expression of moral reality' (1984: 6).

What bearing might these ideas have on the aims of a sociology of law? Sociology, as Durkheim conceives it, sets out to study law as a matter of social fact. It examines actual patterns of legal doctrine and

6. As will appear, however, Durkheim's own practice in studying the earliest sources of legal ideas does not always conform satisfactorily to these protocols. See espe-cially the account of the origins of property considered in Chapter 9, below.

the nature of legal practices as they exist in particular societies at particular times. Generalisations about law are to be based on systematic social observation. In this way they can be claimed to be scientific. Durkheimian study of law is positivistic, treating law as a datum of social life, to be recorded by the sociologist and systematically related to other observed social phenomena. To philosophise about law, to rationalise legal ideas or practices into abstract systems that are inventions of jurists, is, presumably, subject to the criticisms applied to philosophy in general. Unless analysis is based firmly in the study of social fact, 'by what privilege' does the jurist claim to understand law as a social phenomenon?

Nevertheless, as noted above, law is, for Durkheim, an expression of ideals. It has moral meaning. It is a repository of aspirations, something to philosophise about. To study moral conditions sociologically cannot be a morally neutral matter. By revealing the 'detail of social facts' – for example, the customs, institutions, moral expectations and legal rules existing in particular societies at particular historical moments – sociology points to the constraints that empirical reality imposes as a practical matter on philosophical speculation. It indicates the limits within which it makes practical sense to speculate morally or legally, to engage in legal philosophy, to press for change or to seek to conserve what presently exists. For Durkheim, 'sociology was ... the means, unique and certain, of reconstructing morality' (Bourgin quoted in Lukes, 1973: 320).

Certainly, sociology does not merely *describe* legal conditions. It seeks to explain theoretically how these conditions have come about, to see them as the consequence of social forces working in particular historical settings. It seeks scientific 'laws' of social development which will inform and guide this explanation. In *The Division of Labour*, Durkheim claimed that these laws were to be found by studying the distribution and growth of populations and changes in the intensity and extent of interaction in them.[7] This would explain much about the changing structure of societies and hence about the moral, legal and other institutions present in them. But in his later work this emphasis seemed to disappear and social development was explained primarily in terms of changing patterns of belief and understanding in societies (Durkheim, 1953b).

These matters will be considered in subsequent chapters. For the moment it is enough to emphasise that the vocation of Durkheimian legal study is to provide new ways of understanding law as a moral phenomenon. Hence the project of sociology, for Durkheim, includes the effort to evaluate law as a structure of ideas and understand its

7. See p. 83, below.

moral meaning. The line between philosophical and sociological inquiry, emphasised in his early work, is less clear in the overall scope of his writings. But he insists throughout his work that philosophical speculation about moral (including legal) matters must be grounded in comparative study of moral facts. Moral and legal phenomena must be studied as they are encountered in specific social environments.

2

A moral mission

Durkheim and his closest followers assumed law's fundamental socio-logical importance. One of them proclaims: 'As for sociology, it is obvious that it cannot do without the study of laws and customs, and that it must inscribe on the mansion that it seeks to build: "No-one may enter here who is not a jurist"' (Bouglé, 1935: 96). A more critical commentator, Georges Gurvitch, notes that 'from a certain view-point, Durkheim's entire sociology, especially in its beginnings, has a certain "juralizing" tendency,' and he criticises the 'rather exaggerated importance for the study of social reality attributed by Durkheim to jural symbols' (Gurvitch, 1947: 26). A recent writer even suggests that, for the Durkheimians, sociology of law was, in a sense, all of sociology (Vogt, 1983: 181; and see Bouglé, 1935: 98). This claim may seem strange given the wide range of subjects that they studied, but there is some support for it in Durkheim's own remarks. Instead of considering sociology generally, he wrote in 1900, 'we have always confined our-selves methodically to a clearly defined order of facts: apart from neces-sary excursions into fields adjacent to those we were exploring, we have been concerned only with legal and moral rules, studied in terms of their genesis . . . or their functioning' (1900b: 126; cf. 1973a: 15).

To understand Durkheim's distinctive outlook on legal ideas it is necessary to consider why he privileges law as a set of social facts for sociological study. Such an inquiry helps to clarify the fundamental purpose of his study of law. Certainly this study is not just a matter of intellectual curiosity. It is a means of addressing problems that are soci-ologically basic – pressing issues for social regulation.

The malady of the infinite

Regulation, indeed, is the key. Strictly speaking, it is not law, as lawyers think of it, that is central to Durkheim's sociology but regulation, and the need for it (Durkheim, 1961: 50–1). Time and again in his writ-ings and especially in his mature reflections on morality he makes a fundamental claim about the human condition. Human beings are continually threatened by their own desires. Unless individuals control their passions they become slaves to them. Most importantly, desire is insatiable if unchecked. There is no limit to what humans want if they freely follow their impulses. But the unlimited pursuit of desire brings misery – 'the malady of the infinite' (*mal de l'infini*) as Durkheim calls it (1925: 37; cf. 1961: 43; 1984: 183–6) – because desire without limit can never be fulfilled. It only becomes ever more intense (1961: 39–40).

This problem is not exactly one of human nature. Durkheim rejects the idea of an unchanging human nature (1984: 334–5; 1982a: 236–7; 1961: 51). The infinity of desire is culturally rather than naturally produced. For many population categories in many societies, natural conditions put practical limits on the range of objects of human desires. The 'malady of the infinite' becomes important as individuals are enabled seriously to envisage wants beyond those that nature (especially biological need) imposes as an everyday matter (cf. Giddens, 1971: 278). Desire becomes intellectualised, as Durkheim puts it, and in this way potentially unlimited in what it can attach to. Culture frees the imagination to envisage the possibility of fulfilling wants and needs hitherto unrecognised (Durkheim, 1984: 186ff).

Durkheim's sociological concern, therefore, is not with the psychology of desire – which he seems to treat as given, but with the variable social conditions to which desire can relate. His general argument is that the range of things wanted – that is, the scope of desire (though presumably not necessarily its intensity) – increases with civilisation and the growth of culture.

We should think therefore of human nature, not as the timeless expression of natural dispositions, but as changing modes of adjustment to the need to control desire. Desire must be constrained and channelled. Regulation is not something necessarily external to the individual but a component of human beings. Its absence or insufficiency Durkheim refers to as *anomie*: that is, literally, a lack of law or norms. 'If we believe that discipline is useful, necessary for the individual, it is because it seems to us demanded by nature itself ... Man's nature cannot be itself unless it is disciplined' (1925: 44; cf. 1961: 50–1). Human nature is not curbed but *fulfilled* through discipline, and it is continually evolving. As a result of civilisation, it becomes richer and the range of human activity expands. The 'boundaries of our intellectual, moral and emotional horizons ... constantly move back ... The normal limit is in a state of constant becoming' (1925: 45; cf. 1961: 51). Thus controls on desire are, themselves, not static but shifting as the conditions of life change. Regulation becomes a more complex matter as life becomes fuller and richer.

Basic to everything are the internalised restraints of self-discipline. While they are restrictions, preventing the unlimited pursuit of desire, they are also, for most individuals, welcome. They remove the intolerable anguish of the malady of the infinite – an 'inextinguishable thirst' that 'is constantly renewed torture' (1952: 247). They make it possible to live a life in which everyday existence can be satisfying, in which goals can be put in appropriate relation with means. They are social rules that have become a part of the individual's outlook, valued components of identity. Hence, it is a most important Durkheimian insight that social constraints can (and should) appear as objects of value, foci of attachment in themselves, in the eyes of those subject to them.

Regulation is central, therefore, to Durkheim's thinking as the necessary means of limiting desire. The most fundamental regulation in this sense is actually a component of shifting, evolving human nature. It is internalised, not imposed externally on the individual but a part of the individual's character. The line between 'external' constraint by legal coercion and moral pressure and 'internal' (self-imposed) constraint from ethical conviction is ultimately unclear. Durkheim initially stressed the element of external constraint in morality and law, but in his later writing he came to emphasise equally the idea of the individual's willing attachment to the whole range of social sources of moral authority from which ethical precepts are derived.[1]

Thus, the control of unlimited desire, central to the analysis of morality and law in Durkheimian sociology, is a complex phenomenon. The social facts of law and morality provide external constraint on the individual. But they may also be objects of attachment or commitment – and thus, in certain respects, internalised within the individual – in so far as they provide orientation for life. In this way they are an essential part of the means of removing the impossible burden of infinite wishes and replacing them with guides that lead the individual along paths of 'modest' self-fulfilment: the fulfilment of the self-controlled person in a well-ordered world.

The close relationship between external constraint and internalised commitments suggests that in considering legal processes a model of mere coercive power being exercised over the citizen by distant state institutions is not adequate. A more plausible model, up to a point, is that of law as educational process. For Durkheim (1961), education instils the forms of self-discipline society needs, both generally and in relation to specialised roles and fields. It relies on inspiring attachment and enthusiasm, on the one hand, and constraining deviance and indiscipline, on the other. An analogy with law cannot be pushed far, because the citizen is certainly not to be seen as a pupil whose social character is being formed in interaction with a benevolent, paternalistic legal authority. The moral authority which Durkheim, in his writings on the

---

1. See pp. 52–3, below.

sociology of education, requires of the school (1961: 165–6, 242ff.) is built on an acute sense of responsibility and care for the aspirations of the young. But it is not unrelated to aspects of an ideal relationship between citizens and lawmakers. This relationship is one in which law *earns the citizen's respect and commitment* by providing a secure moral environment in which aspirations can be defined, shaped and pursued, at the same time as it demands the fulfilment of duty.[2]

The constantly reiterated theme in Durkheim's writing of the dialectic between desire and restraint makes it clear why his sociology focuses so insistently on the importance of moral and legal rules. They control the threats posed by the unlimited pursuit of desires. 'The totality of moral rules really forms around each person a kind of imaginary wall, at the foot of which the flood of human passions simply dies without being able to go further' (1925: 36; cf. 1961: 42). Because passions are contained it becomes possible to satisfy them. But if the wall of regulation is breached, 'these previously restrained human forces pour tumultuously through the open breach; once loosed they find no limits at which to stop' (1925: 37; cf. 1961: 42).

Above all, Durkheim's view of the significance of regulation as a necessary expression of human nature implies that the sociological study of law is inseparable from a sociology of moral life. It is not that sociology of law is a special sub-branch of Durkheimian sociology, still less that the sociologist must become a jurist. It is rather that law should be seen – by sociologists and jurists alike – as the most visible, formalised element in a process of control that is part of the very fabric of social life, indeed a process that actually constitutes society. Law is not an unfortunate necessity. It is part of the regulation that gives direction to individual lives, and makes possible the most elementary forms of personal fulfilment, channelling the passions and making desires meaningful because capable of satisfaction.

Aspects of biography

It is almost irresistible to ask where Durkheim's specific focus comes from. Why does he adopt this particular basis for the study of law, this intense concern with regulation and its relation to the moral fulfilment of the individual? Durkheim's viewpoint on law and, above all, his focus on a continuum of regulation running from internalised individual self-discipline to publicly pronounced legal norms is highly distinctive. Keys to his outlook have sometimes been sought in his personal background and, while there is no necessity to try to explain the ideas in

2. See pp. 169–70, below.

terms of the man, some personal matters are thought-provoking. They shed light on his world of ideas.

According to Durkheim's main biographer, since childhood 'he retained an exacting sense of duty and a serious, indeed austere, view of life; he could never experience pleasure without a sense of remorse' (Lukes, 1973: 40). He seems to have come from a family closely bounded by rules and expectations of duty. Georges Davy describes Durkheim's childhood home as one 'where austerity rather than opulence reigned, where the observance of the law was precept and example, nothing coming in the way of duty' (quoted in Lacroix, 1981: 134). According to some accounts Durkheim was 'forbidding and serious' but Davy, who knew him well, describes him as warm and concerned in his relations with others (see Lukes, 1973: 367–8). He was a charismatic teacher and a considerate, caring and supportive colleague. Yet there is no doubt that he exercised a very powerful intellectual and moral authority and his writings make clear his asceticism: 'leisure is always dangerous,' he notes in an aside; it is important to keep busy, with useful pursuits (1961: 274). The ideas of duty and discipline, regulation and self-control, so fundamental to his thinking, seem embedded in his personality.

Beyond such simple connections, the relationship between Durkheim's biography and his thought remains a matter of deeply controversial speculation, not least when psychoanalytic concepts have been employed (e.g. Lacroix, 1981). Ultimately, there is a 'lack of adequate and firm evidence' (Pickering, 1984: 14, 518; and see Pickering, 1994: 32–3) about many of the influences shaping his ideas. Indeed, many aspects of Durkheim's biography, especially relating to his private life, remain unclear (Mestrovic, 1988: ch. 2).

Only one matter seems worth noting here, because it has often been linked with a fundamental change in his intellectual outlook which he himself emphasised and which will be referred to in later chapters as important to his views on law. Durkheim rejected Judaism as a religious faith at some time in his youth, probably while studying at the École Normale. He had grown up in 'a close-knit, orthodox and traditional Jewish family' with long rabbinical traditions and it seems that the break was a very painful one (Lukes, 1973: 39, 44). Nothing definite is known about the circumstances. In 1896, however, Durkheim's father, the rabbi Moïse Durkheim, died. Bernard Lacroix (1981) and others have speculated about the effect of this on the son's significant change of outlook as regards religion around this time.

Having earlier rejected religion, Émile Durkheim certainly did not come to embrace it after his father's death. He always viewed it as a social scientist, not as a believer. But he wrote later that around 1895 his studies had forced him to re-evaluate fundamentally the role of religion as a social phenomenon. 'It was in that year that, for the first time, I found a means of tackling sociologically the study of religion. It was a revelation to me,' he recalled (1982a: 259; and see Pickering, 1984: 48–9; Lacroix, 1981: 130–3). From the mid-1890s religion assumed a central, entirely dominating position in his thought. He saw it, for example, as the fundamental social phenomenon from which law and morality had evolved (Durkheim, 1982b: 173), the original, embryonic focus of all social commitment and regulatory force. Perhaps most importantly, religion appears in Durkheim's later writings as simultaneously a disciplining, constraining power over the individual and a powerful focus of attachment and commitment (Durkheim, 1915). In this way perhaps it provides a model of roles that law and morality as social forces might, in different ways, play.

Lacroix (1981: 137–43) notes the mysterious nervous illnesses that afflicted Durkheim in later years. And there are clues in Durkheim's own writings to a kind of continuing melancholy and regret about the loss of religious faith. 'Once established beliefs have been carried away ... they cannot be artificially reestablished; only reflection can guide us in life, after this' (1952: 169). Religion, he writes, protects people against the desire for self-destruction in so far as it provides a society in which they can live. It gives a sense of bonding and integration, something to believe in that is traditional, universal and obligatory (1952: 170). One might say it provides a safe harbour for desires, not necessarily mental peace but a kind of resolution of longings or regrets.

Ultimately speculation about reasons for Durkheim's changed outlook on religion remains inconclusive. The lecture course in which he first expressed his new views actually predated his father's death. However, after 1896, religion figured more and more prominently in Durkheim's explanations of the origins of social phenomena. It became a key he had been seeking. But if biographical inquiry suggests factors that may have coloured Durkheim's thought it does not further explain the ideas themselves. A better aid to understanding Durkheim's outlook on law can be gained by considering some of the social and political conditions that surrounded its development.

The political context

In 1870–1, France suffered defeat in the Franco-Prussian War and subsequent political chaos. The struggle over the revolutionary Paris Commune at that time showed the reality of unrestrained class conflict. Memories of these times from his boyhood remained with Durkheim. Davy writes that 'he felt himself called to something other than mere teaching; he must teach a doctrine, have disciples and not just students, play a role in the social reconstruction of a France wounded in defeat' (Davy, 1919: 183). A new philosophy of education in universities and schools was thought by leading politicians to be essential to the regeneration of France in the last decades of the nineteenth century. The politician Jules Ferry wrote in 1883 that the 'scientific spirit, gradually descending from higher education into the two other levels of education, is really the only barrier against the spirit of utopia and error which, left to itself and not regulated and enlightened by science, readily becomes disorder and anarchy' (quoted in Weisz, 1983: 90).

Durkheim supported many of the reformist aspirations of the Third Republic, the regime that arose after the defeats and chaos of 1870–1. Among the conditions that progressive politicians attacked was the Church's hold over education and society, its 'tenacious will to defend a social order menaced by the progress of socialism' and its reactionary, fearful, unimaginative social teachings which merely 'exalted religion, family, country, conscientious labour carried out humbly in submission to the boss, and resigned acceptance' (Arnaud, 1975: 77, 78).

Equally threatening to many reformers as well as conservatives was revolutionary socialism, associated with the pursuit of utopian aims through violence. The French legal scholar André-Jean Arnaud writes that the period from 1880 was marked by an obsession with socialism. Between 1880 and 1920 'the spectre of socialism' haunted the nation. Anarchist terrorism at the end of the century was linked with this threat (Arnaud, 1975: 75, 76, 78). But Third Republic legal reformers often favoured socialist aims of universal civil and political rights and of economic and industrial justice, pursued by democratic means. To be in favour of the Republican administration and its reformist outlook 'meant that one was necessarily a democrat, a political liberal, and probably if not a socialist at least concerned with major reforms of the social and economic order, all of which Durkheim was.'[3]

Socialism, in so far as seen as the enemy, was radical, potentially violent and socially disruptive revolutionary activity and agitation. Thus, 'the rise of academic social science in France was closely related to the ideological needs of the moderate republic; the new disciplines were conceived as a weapon of combat against socialism' (Weisz, 1983: 115). In the official view, rational social analysis could defuse irrational social agitation. Durkheim was drawn to socialism's aspirations for the betterment of the propertyless. But, in his view, socialism was not a science of society. Especially in its Marxist variants, it formed its programmes not around scientific understanding of society but generalised slogans and ideologies. Thus these programmes often carried

---

3. Bellah (1973: xvi). But, as will appear, none of these labels precisely captures the complexity of Durkheim's outlook.

enormous risks of unknown adverse social consequences. To this extent they appeared reckless.[4]

This is the outlook, not only of a cautious reformer in tune with prevailing politics, but also of the stern ascetic and the moral theorist of regulation of desire described earlier. For Durkheim, socialism often seeks too much, too soon. And it seems to assume that every desire for social betterment can be fulfilled if pursued unwaveringly. But the 'natural' dialectic of desire and control should teach otherwise. Social justice is possible only within constraints. The pursuit of utopias is bound to produce misery. Utopia, perhaps, is desire without limit. The morally responsible task is to work out scientifically the possibilities that actually existing social facts offer. A first stage is to understand these facts and their constraining power. A second is to recognise and pursue the forms of justice and morality that they make possible.

A distinctive attitude to politics emerges from the ideas just considered. The scheme of thought is always broad: concerned not so much with particular outcomes as with the way that political matters should be approached. Practical politics should be the effort to act publicly on the knowledge that scientific understanding of society can offer. If it is not informed by such an understanding, one can infer that for Durkheim it is sociologically uninteresting, at worst no more than the clash of personal or group ambitions and interests producing transient, often ignorant outcomes. Certainly, he had 'a deep aversion for the intrigue-ridden everyday political life of the Third Republic' (Müller, 1993: 106). As a student he 'always remained on the summits and only debated principles. The political arena was always odious to him.' Later in life he told a friend that he regretted that politics had become 'a thing so small and mediocre' (Davy quoted in Lukes, 1973: 47).

Nowadays, politics tends to be put at the centre of public life. But Durkheim puts morality and law in this position. Politics becomes meaningful for Durkheim only when it is concerned with the negotiation and co-ordination of (sometimes conflicting) moral principles and their translation into regulatory action.[5] This is why a sociology of law and morals essentially takes the place of political sociology in his thinking. But morality is not to be taken in a narrow sense. It embraces, for example, not only the morality of domestic and sexual relations, but especially that of economic and industrial life, and of citizenship.

Historical context clarifies the range of moral problems that underlie Durkheim's legal thought. In 1882 a Primary Education Law provided free, compulsory non-religious education for all children in France between the ages of six and thirteen, and attempted to weaken the

4. See pp. 186–8, below.
5. See Chapters 10 and 11, below.

Church's hold on education. A key question then became what should take the place of religious precepts as a basis of civic morality. In Durkheim's view, the main replacement had to be a secular faith in the importance of each individual human being as a moral entity entitled to dignity and respect. While he generally shied away from practical political involvements and associated himself with no particular political programmes or parties, the major exception to this aloofness from practical politics was an occasion on which he sought to emphasise this secular morality of the worth of the individual.

In the famous Dreyfus affair, which began in 1894, the French military and political authorities ultimately tried to scapegoat an innocent army officer in order to hide a scandal reaching to the heart of the French state. In the bitter controversies that arose, Durkheim (1969b) argued passionately that a morality requiring the preservation of traditional beliefs about the state and nation at all costs (such as the official punishment of a man whose innocence was deliberately obscured for reasons of state) was outdated and in modern circumstances iniquitous. In modern society such an archaic morality must give way to one demanding that each individual be guaranteed personal security and human dignity, and treated officially with integrity and respect.[6] His stance in the Dreyfus affair illustrates his more general conviction that morality reaches into all public and private relationships and colours the entire structure of society.

Economy and society

Developments in the economy and in industry raised the most urgent moral issues. In Durkheim's era big business expanded at the expense of small entrepreneurs and mass production was transformed by technical innovations. 'The conditions of distribution of services and resource exploitation entailed the concentration of business in urban areas. So associations and unions of workers proliferated, a reality that the jurists could not but come into contact with, being naturally based in the cities, especially if they were university academics' (Arnaud, 1975: 76). Questions of the legal regulation of rapidly changing economic and industrial life seemed urgent.

After the suppression of trade unions following the Paris Commune in 1871, the working-class movement recovered from around 1880 and major strike waves continued up to the First World War (Arnaud, 1975: 75). In 1884 workers gained the legal right to form trade unions, but informally this had been permitted earlier (Arnaud, 1975: 84). One of

6. See especially Chapter 7, below.

the reporters of the 1884 law to the French Senate noted at the time: 'The number of employers lessens every day, whilst that of employees grows in proportion remorselessly. It cannot be denied that this change has increased the antagonism between capital and labour, in a way that could become dangerous for the prosperity of our industries.' In these conditions people would naturally try to band together to protect their interests. 'If large-scale industry is the definitive form in which production must be organised, how can we progressively reduce the antagonism between capital and labour so as to substitute solidarity, except through the practice of association?' (quoted in Arnaud, 1975: 84, 85).

This statement evokes themes at the heart of Durkheim's sociology: association in groups is necessary to bond individuals within society; solidarity is the aim – the moral value to be nurtured; class conflict, like all fundamental social conflict, is a pathology caused by morally inadequate or insensitive regulation. Another contemporary commentator on the 1884 law noted: 'The working class is divided into two categories: the one, the more numerous undoubtedly, is made up of reasonable, hardworking, honest workers . . . the other, of revolutionary socialists . . . for whom the occupational associations are only a means of organising a revolutionary army . . .' (quoted in Arnaud, 1975: 85). The great division, or choice of direction, thus seemed to be between solidarity and radical socialism; social cohesion or social conflict. Thus, solidarity was a leading idea in France in the late nineteenth century, usually invoked to justify welfare reform that would not disturb the fundamentals of the social or economic order.

In Durkheim's *The Division of Labour in Society* a concern with social cohesion, or solidarity, is explicit and central. But his claims are quite different from the standard political arguments of the time. He offers a general sociological thesis: that social solidarity, understood as moral integration, is the natural state of any society. It is a social fact, even though often obscured by other social facts that reflect conflict in society. Actually, no society can exist unless it is ultimately more cohesive than conflict-ridden: unless, that is, it is defined primarily by the moral bonds that link its members rather than the forces that divide them. The problem in analysing social solidarity and its conditions of existence is to recognise that solidarity does not have the same nature in all societies. It may arise in different ways and take different forms.

In essence there are two pure types of social solidarity, wholly different in nature but combined in various ways in all known societies. *Mechanical solidarity* exists where members of a society share the same beliefs, values and ways of interpreting their social world (Durkheim, 1984: 60–1). They think in similar ways, share similar experiences, live similar lives. They are united by these shared beliefs and understandings. Mechanical solidarity is prevalent where the division of social

Social Solidarity

labour – the degree of specialisation and differentiation of social roles and functions – is relatively undeveloped. Thus it is a dominant feature of primitive societies or ancient agrarian societies with relatively uncomplicated economic structures and relatively simple forms of social organisation and interaction.

In complex modern societies, however, the scope for such shared beliefs and understandings declines. Life is varied and the roles and social positions that people occupy become increasingly specialised or distinct. Thus, *organic solidarity* exists where people may have widely differing beliefs, values and experiences but are, nevertheless, interdependent (Durkheim, 1984: 68ff.). They rely on each other. More generally, different groups – identified by their distinct social roles – require each other's social contribution. Individuals or groups fulfil roles necessary to the well-being of other individuals or groups. In this scenario society may be differentiated by moral understandings or by life experiences (a lawyer may have different commitments from a labourer or a priest; a city clerk lives a different life from a rural farmer). But society is ultimately united by functional interdependence. Like the different organs of the body, each of them necessary to its optimum working, different components of society fulfil different functions that may be appropriate to its ongoing existence as a social organism. The parts are necessary to the complex vitality of the whole. The division of social labour actually promotes solidarity.

When Durkheim wrote about the conditions of what he understood as modern society, he saw them as demanding and creating increasingly complex interdependence. The dominant form of solidarity in complex modern societies is thus organic. It arises through the effective integration of different social groups, reflecting different life experiences and values. But following the biological analogy noted in Chapter 1, and treating society as an organism, Durkheim emphasises not the integration of groups or individuals as such but of *functions*. Thus, just as the hand is defined as an organ in relation to the body by its function, so parts of society are functionally differentiated and need to be integrated in the total organism – society.

Politically, the most important integration to be achieved in late nineteenth-century France was that of capital and labour. The need was to defuse the class struggle.[7] But sociologically it would be simplistic to think only in these terms. The functions making up the complex network of society's activity are not merely reducible to the role of capital on the one hand and labour on the other. In production and distribution functions, management and labour are inseparable aspects. Direction and implementation depend on each other. They must

7. See Chapter 12, below.

interact, blend into each other, even exchange places and become impossible to identify separately. The essential questions are how to *organise* functionally differentiated industries or other areas of activity.

Curing society's malady

When he wrote *The Division of Labour*, Durkheim did not really consider these questions of organisation, though they figure importantly in his later thought.[8] In his 1893 book he is concerned primarily to show that the complexity of modern industrial society does not have to lead to fragmentation, conflict and class enmity, as Comte and Marx, in different ways, had suggested (Durkheim, 1984: bk 3, ch. 1). Nor does it create a situation in which social life has no significance except as the pursuit by isolated individuals of their private purposes. In this latter view society is merely the arena in which individuals negotiate with each other, concerned only to promote their own interests within the framework of a minimal state having no function except to keep order. Such a vision, associated in Durkheim's time particularly with the social theorist Herbert Spencer, represents a no less false diagnosis of the condition of modern society, in Durkheim's view, than does the conflict diagnosis (1984: bk 1, ch. 7).

He seeks to show that both visions fail to capture society's essence as a moral phenomenon. A contract, for example, is not just an agreement between the parties. It presupposes a framework of regulation. It relies on moral expectations that are socially (legally) guaranteed (1984: 158). Behind individual action is a set of moral meanings that make the action worthwhile, reliable and intelligible to others. Thus social solidarity is an ideal, but it is also a social fact. The fact makes possible the ideal, but the ideal resides in the social fact. What is and what ought to be are sociologically inseparable. The Durkheimian moral mission is to demonstrate the moral bonds that define social life. Established patterns of duty need to be understood so that efforts towards social improvement are made with sufficient awareness of the moral realities that provide limiting frameworks for all social action.

The theme of the control of desires, with which this chapter began, can be seen as underlying Durkheim's most important writings on all areas of law and morality. It implicitly informs his condemnation of radical socialism's 'unscientific' naivety and recklessness. The same theme of control of desires is explicit in much of his discussion of law and morality in family life.[9] And it is present, by implication, in much

8. See pp. 176–80, below.
9. See pp. 144–7, below.

that he says about the regulation of economic and industrial relations. The unfettered greed of ruthless employers is often matched by reckless industrial disruption, the latter unleashed by workers unable or unwilling to take account of ultimate economic and social consequences of their acts.[10]

The dialectic of control and desire teaches that harmonious, fulfilling conditions of social life are not achieved by the collective pursuit of interests; that is, by the organised effort to satisfy personal or group desires. They are achieved when people willingly compromise and restrain their particular interests because of a larger concern for some impersonal common well-being. Thus, in the industrial or economic spheres, trade unions or employers' associations cannot be, for Durkheim, the privileged agents of social cohesion: other kinds of intermediate groups, existing between the individual and the state and representing social functions within society as a whole, rather than personal or even group interests, are necessary.[11] The regulation of individual and collective life to encourage this subordination of desires poses formidable problems. The aim is certainly not to deny individual ambition or aspiration: quite the contrary. It is to make that ambition or aspiration meaningful and personally worthwhile because it can be understood as having a recognised place in a secure moral universe. In this way the 'malady of the infinite' – and the endless dissatisfaction, social disorder and pointless struggle which it inspires in political, social and economic life – might be cured. The moral mission of Durkheim's sociology, and its ambitions for law, are best understood in these terms.

10. See, for example, Durkheim (1984: xxxii) and pp. 182–4, below.
11. See pp. 177–9, below.

3

A legal environment

One other important context of Durkheim's legal theory needs to be sketched. What of lawyers' legal scholarship itself, the environment of juristic writing and teaching of law in relation to which the Durkheimian project locates itself? How are the intellectual ambitions of Durkheim's sociological inquiries about law intended to relate to the established worlds of lawyers' legal thought and practice?

Law as index

In *The Division of Labour,* which contains his earliest sustained writing on law, Durkheim makes sociology's scholarly project deeply dependent on legal knowledge. It really does seem that 'no-one may enter here who is not a jurist' (cf. Bouglé, 1935: 96) because a thesis of the book is that sociology gains its most fundamental knowledge about the nature of societies directly from law. Durkheim proposes that, by studying legal rules from a certain standpoint, one can learn about the kinds of solidarity present in a society (1984: 24–8). And nothing is more important to Durkheimian sociology than to understand the nature and conditions of social solidarity. The key is to examine the consequences provided for by law when social norms are breached.

Sometimes legal sanctions are penal. The main object of the sanction is to punish, to condemn the wrongdoer, to mark the deviant as a criminal; perhaps also to exact retribution or deter future deviance. Durkheim calls this kind of regulation penal or *repressive law*. Its typical sanctions are physical punishment of the body of the offender, or increasingly, in modern times, imprisonment or the imposition of fines. It makes demands on the offender's 'fortune, honour, life or liberty, depriving him of something he enjoys' (Durkheim, 1893a: 33; cf. 1984: 29). Criminal law is the most obvious kind of repressive law. But repressive law embraces all rules whose function is penal.

On the other hand, legal sanctions sometimes have a significantly different character. They are restitutive. The object is not to impose suffering on an offender but to ensure that someone who has transgressed compensates for the wrong, and thereby, as far as possible, puts matters right, restores the status quo (1984: 29). Thus, the typical sanction of co-operative or *restitutive law* is damages or other compensation or redress. The task of restitutive law is to restore an upset balance in social relations and so facilitate social interaction. Contract law is the most typical kind of restitutive law but Durkheim also mentions in this category 'civil law, commercial law, procedural law, administrative and constitutional law, excluding any penal rules found therein' (1893a: 34; cf. 1984: 29).

In *The Division of Labour* a straightforward connection is postulated between, on the one hand, these two very broadly differentiated types of legal regulation – repressive and restitutive – and, on the other, the two types of solidarity – mechanical and organic – discussed in Chapter 2.[1] Repressive law reflects or indicates the presence of mechanical solidarity. Restitutive law similarly reflects organic solidarity. Law is thus useful to sociology in a very direct, simple way. It is a marker of something more sociologically significant than itself. In *The Division of Labour* much is written about law, since it is used throughout as an indicator of the different patterns of solidarity existing in various societies. In simple, primitive or ancient societies, Durkheim argues, repressive law and mechanical solidarity predominate. In modern, complex, industrialised societies, a correspondingly predominant place is held by restitutive law and organic solidarity. The particular mix of repressive and restitutive law exactly mirrors the particular mix of kinds of solidarity in any given society.

Law is thus portrayed as essential to sociology, a vital key to sociological knowledge. But, at the same time, it is reduced to a mere tool of explanation. The great wealth of knowledge that comparative legal history offers – and which Durkheim uses liberally in his book – is just a convenient device for understanding the changing patterns of social solidarity. There is little to suggest that law is of interest in itself, and little effort is made by Durkheim to analyse it in all its variety. Indeed, as will be argued later, the concepts of repressive and restitutive law were probably never intended to be the basis of a sophisticated classification and analysis of law.[2]

This impression of much attention given to law but ultimate disinterest in it is the one we should be left with if *The Division of Labour* were Durkheim's sole contribution to legal analysis. If this were the case it would be easy to dismiss key elements of his sociology of law as simplistic. Consider, for example, some of his statements as to how the 'visible symbol' (Durkheim, 1984: 24) that law provides is to be

1. See pp. 27–8, above.
2. See pp. 70–1, 85–6, below.

used to understand social life. He declares that the number of social relationships in a given society 'is necessarily proportional to that of the legal rules that determine them' (1984: 25). This seems to mean that the intensity of social interaction can be measured by the number of legal rules.

Why this is so is never explained. Durkheim merely claims that law is the organisation of social life 'in its most stable and precise form' (1984: 25) and legal activity necessarily increases as social life expands its scope. 'Thus we may be sure to find reflected in the law all the essential varieties of social solidarity' (1984: 25). 'Since law reproduces the main forms of social solidarity, we have only to classify the different types of law in order to be able to investigate which types of social solidarity correspond to them' (1984: 28). How is the relative significance of different kinds of solidarity to be judged? Durkheim answers: by measuring law. To see how far, for example, organic solidarity has developed in a particular society 'it will be enough to compare the total number of legal rules which give it expression with the total volume of law' (1984: 28).

'Somewhat fantastically' (Hart, 1967: 253), Durkheim thinks that it is possible to add up the number of rules providing for restitutive sanctions and of those imposing repressive sanctions and by making a quantitative comparison arrive at useful knowledge of social conditions. He seems unaware of problems of the individuation of laws – of what constitutes a distinct law (e.g. Raz, 1980: ch. 4), or, indeed, of the simple point that it may be quite arbitrary how many distinct provisions in relation to any particular topic a legal code contains. Legal provisions may be more or less detailed depending on the intentions or skill of the law creator, the extent to which common understandings governing circumstances in which the law is to apply can be assumed, and prevailing attitudes to interpretation of law. He fails to note that repressive and restitutive sanctions may often be mixed[3] and that their relation to particular rules may be indirect and complex. In short, the index thesis, as he explains it, seems to show the worst aspects of the positivist orientations of his sociology. Yet Durkheim is certainly not the only sociologist to argue that law treated as an objective datum might lend itself to a kind of measurement as a social fact (see, for example, Black, 1976).

Fortunately, in practice, he takes this no further than assessing broadly the balance of different kinds of law in particular legal codes, or in certain historical legal systems – for example, ancient Athenian, Roman, Judaic, Frankish (Salic) or Indian law. But the failure to see law through lawyers' eyes, in terms of the host of practical problems

3. See further pp. 70–1, below.

of interpretation and application that make it hard to treat law as an unproblematic datum, conveys the impression of a distanced, unengaged view of law. Law appears as a sociological object with which the sociologist has no involvement and, indeed, no more concern than a natural scientist might have with some inanimate object observed in the laboratory.

Reaching out to lawyers

In reality, the view of law conveyed by Durkheim's writings as a whole is different from this. The index thesis caricatures law, presenting it in a way that obscures Durkheim's overall view of its importance. In fact, as seen in Chapter 2, law and other forms of regulation are, for him, foci of powerful moral engagement. Sociologically, law is more than just an index of something else. But this only really becomes clear in his writings after *The Division of Labour*.

A better guide to his outlook comes from a statement by his collaborator Georges Davy:

> Law appears [in sociological perspective] . . . no longer as an abstract entity or artificial creation, set firm as soon as it is created, but as a living idea, a social phenomenon whose constant evolution is promoted by the progress of all civilisations of the same type . . . The spirit [*l'âme*] of law has its history. So it is necessary to ask of history by what tentative steps it has come to shape this spirit. But this history follows its course . . . It is in the supple clay of our everyday jurisprudence and more generally of comparative jurisprudence that the ideal is roughly cast that tomorrow will be set in the marble of legal enactment.[4]

Law as 'a living idea' is crystallised in social processes, embedded in them. And these processes must be understood historically and comparatively. If law is an index of these processes in some sense, it is because it is part of them, contributing to them, alive in them.

Many of Durkheim's collaborators were 'insiders' in the world of jurists, not just observers of law from a distance. Indeed the 'inside–outside' distinction is meaningless in relation to much of their work. Apart from Paul Huvelin and Emmanuel Lévy, who were law professors, Hubert Bourgin, Maurice Halbwachs, Jean Ray and François Simiand held doctorates in law (Vogt, 1983: 177–8). Ray wrote on the

---

4. Quoted in Arnaud (1981: 114). On Durkheim's concern with law's 'spirit' see also Alexander (1982: 274–5); and Durkheim (1957: 28–9).

French Civil Code, Huvelin on Roman law and the early history of commercial law, and Lévy on the acquisition and transfer of property rights, among many other legal themes. Davy, Marcel Mauss, Louis Gernet and Georges Bourgin also had legal qualifications. Gernet wrote on law and its antecedents in Ancient Greece, Davy and Mauss on the social evolution of contractual relations. The work of some of these scholars is discussed in later chapters.

In the *Année sociologique* under Durkheim's editorship two major sections were devoted to legal matters. The section on 'Legal and Moral Sociology', subtitled 'the study of legal and moral rules considered in their genesis', was concerned with the history of law and its social development. The section on 'Criminal Sociology and Moral Statistics', subtitled 'the study of legal and moral rules considered in their functioning', included research on legal institutions. The scope of both sections was comparative in the broadest sense, including material from many different societies and historical periods. All fields of law were in principle included, but family law, property and inheritance law, criminal law and contract law were strong foci. Much of the material consisted of analytical book reviews.

Durkheim's own attitude to law and his assessment of its moral significance is to be gathered not only from *The Division of Labour* but especially from a later series of lectures published posthumously as *Professional Ethics and Civic Morals* (Durkheim, 1957), a further lecture series on *Moral Education* (Durkheim, 1961) and other works that fill in the larger context of thought in which he places law. Some of his writings show him attempting to work out a practical *modus vivendi* between legal scholarship and sociology. In his first public lecture at Bordeaux he welcomed law students to his audience, stating that they needed to know how law is formed under the pressure of social needs and how it becomes established and develops. Lawyers, he remarks, should know how the great legal institutions – property, contract and the family – have come into being, what their causes are, and how they vary and will probably change (Durkheim, 1978b: 68–9; Lukes, 1973: 102).

In the transcript of a 1907 discussion he argues that legal education must be made more vital. Everyone agrees, he says, that law is taught in too formal a manner. The student must be shown

 that law is not a collection of abstract and empty formulae but a living reality, or rather a system of realities; that is, social realities. Young people should be shown how legal institutions relate to social conditions, vary with these conditions, are interrelated with other political and economic institutions and moral ideas; how they relate to the very structure of societies. (1975a: I, 243–4)

If sociology were more advanced, it would have to provide this teaching. It would show how a given legal institution had evolved and 'accustom the student to see in law something other than conceptual games' (*jeux de concepts*) (1975a: I, 244). But he admits that sociology is insufficiently developed at present. The task must therefore fall to history as a provisional substitute for sociology (cf. 1961: 275). The 'only way to give an appropriate legal education to the young is to give them a sense of legal evolution; well planned historical teaching can do this' (1975a: I, 244).

To most readers today, Durkheim's suggestions will hardly seem a recipe for vital legal education. Even in 1907 they were not radical,[5] though they might have been if sociology had been able to provide law students with more than a descriptive account of the evolution of legal institutions. But Durkheim does not even advocate a broad comparative history of law. 'What is needed,' he asserts, 'is to choose a people whose legal development has had a remarkable extent and fullness, and to make this the centre of the teaching. This people exists: the Romans' (1975a: I, 244). Thus, Roman law, not legal sociology, is the recommendation for enlightenment.

One way to interpret this pedagogic conservatism is through Durkheim's ideas on the specialisation of disciplines. Jurists, as noted earlier, are welcome contributors to the enterprise of Durkheimian sociology if they engage in serious sociological inquiry about law – the effort to understand law as social fact. But it would be absurd to think of law students being taught to become sociologists. Law, Durkheim recognises, is not just a sociological concern, but a practice in its own right. Perhaps the immediate obligation of lawyers is to see their specific sphere – law – in terms of its evolutionary dynamics, to see it as in a continuous process of change, like all other aspects of society. A long view of legal history, focusing specifically on the process of development of one's own legal system is thus necessary for the lawyer. But to be required to engage in broader studies of society, as part of legal education, would be to go against the principle of necessary specialisation: the guiding principle, in Durkheim's view, of modern society and 'a moral rule for human conduct' (1984: 3). In general – one imagines him saying – law students are to become lawyers, not social scientists; one must keep to one's specialism.

---

5. In the same discussion Charles Gide advocated a complete liberalisation of the law curriculum, giving students a free choice of courses and professors freedom in determining the content of examinations. See Durkheim (1975a: I, 245).

Legal scholarship and social change

Another interpretation is simply that Durkheim's views are a reaction to existing conditions of academic life. Sociology had to find its place in a university world of social studies already dominated by the law faculties. W. P. Vogt (1983: 188) remarks that 'one finds an unaccustomed gentleness and a conciliatory tone on the part of most Durkheimians ... when they discussed the works of other scholars studying legal phenomena.' Often these scholars were invited to join a common enterprise. Durkheimian sociology treated progressive legal scholarship as moving in the right directions and needing encouragement (Vogt, 1983: 197) rather than radical critique or wholesale replacement. By the later years of the nineteenth century the more imaginative forms of legal scholarship were becoming receptive to social or historical inquiry. Sociologists saw themselves as able to provide guidance. The impetus for scholarly change came from within law itself. Legal developments were rapid in the period between about 1880 and 1920, especially in insurance, tort, social welfare, administrative and commercial law (Arnaud, 1975: 20). Legal scholarship had to come to terms with social changes expressed in and propelling new law. Social science subjects and teachers were brought into law faculties, partly to meet the need to teach students of administration, partly because the law schools wanted to control these new fields of inquiry (Weisz, 1983: 95–6).

Sociology's relations with legal philosophy were less friendly. Gaston Richard, an early collaborator of Durkheim who wrote on legal matters but later distanced himself from Durkheimian sociology, notes: 'From the first day of its existence sociology came into conflict with philosophy of law.' In Richard's view 'no transaction, no conciliation whatever is possible between the old philosophy of law and sociology as applied to law' (quoted in Vogt, 1983: 190). This 'old' legal philosophy had an interest in protecting its speculations from the need for continual revision and testing in the light of empirical inquiries. Typically, it asserted some universal ideal content in law, shown by uniform concepts of law and morals in all human societies (Vogt, 1983: 191). On this view, law had a mode of understanding or a sense of value special to it, irrespective of time and place. By contrast, the Durkheimian Georges Davy retorts: 'it is enough ... to believe in the reality of the collective consciousness [the pattern of actual beliefs, understandings and values common to most people in a particular society at a particular time] in order to account objectively for the ideal content of law.'[6] Thus, for a Durkheimian sociologist, not only law, but the ideals that inform and

---

6. Davy (1920: 382). On Durkheim's concept of the collective consciousness see pp. 53–4, below.

surround it, are social facts. They are to be understood *as they actually exist in a particular society*, not as a legal philosopher may rationalise them from abstract premises.

In fact, Durkheimian legal sociology does not dismiss out of hand the idea that law may have some universal features grounded in the experience of all societies. What is important is that those who put forward such a claim should present evidence that makes the claim plausible and useful. Thus, ethnographic inquiry serves Durkheimian sociology of law as a means of tracing legal ideas and institutions to their locations in earlier times and more distant places. Sociology seeks to identify what, if any, features of law may be considered common to all societies, and how these features vary and evolve in different social contexts (Vogt, 1983: 193). Paul Fauconnet argues in his sociological study of responsibility that variations in the nature of responsibility as understood in different societies are explicable, like all moral phenomena, in terms of social causes.

> But if variations in morality are social and have social causes, how could what is unchanging in morality not also be social and have its cause in the common constitution of all society? However diverse civilisations may be, there is still something that is civilisation. Sociology studies this immutable element in the same spirit as it does the variations appearing in the course of history. (Fauconnet, 1928: 20)

The universal is not to be treated as a matter of human nature or immutable reason, but as the empirically observable features present in all or most known forms of social life.

In late nineteenth-century France as elsewhere, legal philosophy no doubt often served the professional needs of lawyers for a rationalisation, justification and constructive 'internal' critique of their practice (cf. Cotterrell, 1989). Sociology had no such special commitment to reinforce, even through criticism, the integrity of the lawyer's world of practice. It invited jurists who wished to speculate seriously about the nature of law to join in a common quest to understand society, irrespective of disciplinary allegiance. It asked for a leap of faith: faith that this effort of social science would eventually lead to better, less narrowly conceived practice in such disciplines as law.

If legal philosophy asserted that it could guide law and clarify its ideals whereas sociology could only describe and explain, rebuttals were readily forthcoming from within Durkheimian sociology. Gaston Richard asserts that science gives 'the most precise knowledge of the possible' and so equips us to attain it if we wish (quoted in Vogt, 1983: 194). Emmanuel Lévy, one of the most politically engaged of

Durkheim's collaborators, continually argues that a sociological analysis of law reveals the directions that legal development is already taking. For those favouring these directions (in Lévy's view, towards a more socialistic renegotiation of the relations of capital and labour) and seeking to advance them, sociological inquiry provides reassurance – a clarity of vision in confused times (Lévy, 1909; 1926). But it also indicates the *relative* significance of particular legal developments. One might see this inquiry, through Lévy's eyes, as providing a map of the social terrain of contemporary law on which strategically significant battles could be planned.[7]

Despite Gaston Richard's remarks about legal philosophy, aimed especially at varieties of natural law theory in French legal thought, legal and social changes inspired movements in legal theory that were important in the context of Durkheimian concerns. Arnaud (1975: 22) refers to the period of legal development in France between 1880 and 1920 as characterised by a 'struggle against dogmatism'. The Durkheimian Célestin Bouglé, analysing legal science's encounters with sociology, refers to jurists' sense of a crisis in legal scholarship inspired by 'a revolt of facts against the law'. The risk, he writes, is of law, a product of history, being overtaken by history. In the face of social change, 'the precious arsenal of hallowed laws reveals its gaps' (Bouglé, 1935: 101). In the decades around the turn of the century, changing social and economic conditions and attitudes forced a revision of general legal principles: perhaps a specially painful process in a legal system whose codes were traditionally supposed to give legal principle a kind of timeless validity. Orthodox legal thinking risked losing touch with new patterns of social relations, for example in the workplace and between the sexes.[8] As always these pressures first affected specific doctrines, practices and procedures and only later began to be registered in new general theories and changed overall views of law.

Sociology in legal philosophy

Among the new general theories developed by 'jurists confronting society' (cf. Arnaud, 1975) two deserve mention for their contrasting relation to Durkheimian sociology. The institutionalism of Maurice Hauriou firmly rejected Durkheimian ideas, but Léon Duguit's influential work showed an enthusiastic, though partial, reaching out towards them.

Duguit was a Bordeaux law professor between 1886 and his death in 1928. Thus, for fifteen years he and Durkheim were colleagues in

7. See further pp. 188–93, below.
8. See pp. 184–5, below.

the same university. He is often called a disciple of Durkheim and sometimes referred to himself in such terms (Lukes, 1973: 103) but he did
not contribute to Durkheim's scientific project. Instead he adopted
certain Durkheimian ideas for use in practical legal debate. His writings assert a positivist approach to law as a social phenomenon, such
as Durkheim had recommended. He also insists, consistently with
Durkheim's view in *The Division of Labour*, that law must be understood as an expression or framework of social solidarity. But he follows
Durkheim only to a limited extent in the latter respect while going
beyond him in the former.

The positivist emphasis on social fact leads Duguit to reject all subjective aspects of law, such as the notion of rights, and to attempt an
analysis in entirely objective terms. For Duguit, law, treated as a social
fact, is 'objective law', different from law as the lawyer typically understands it (Duguit, 1921). Objective law is not a philosophical idea or
a creation of legal reasoning but a set of norms derived directly from
the conditions of life of a given society. Law is the product of other
social facts in the society in which it exists. Legal science should be
concerned to discover, rationally elaborate and develop law in this sense.
Objective law has obligatory force, given to it by its social character.
By contrast, what lawyers call positive law – the law 'posited' or laid
down by official authorities of the state such as legislatures or courts –
does not automatically have this binding force, unless it serves to express
objective law.

As will appear, Durkheim, despite a similar emphasis on law as social
fact, is more concerned than Duguit with subjective aspects of law,
expressed, for example, in terms of rights.[9] In addition, Durkheim's
view of law eventually attaches great significance to its links with
changing collective sentiments and values, and to the interpenetration
of law and moral commitments.[10] Duguit finds little place for such
connections. For him, material social conditions, rather than beliefs
or understandings, explain the demands that law makes, which are
expressed as objective law (Duguit, 1921: 826–7). Indeed, he refuses
to accept that beliefs or understandings can be *social* phenomena; his
conception of society is entirely individualistic. Only individuals have
beliefs or values. Duguit denies that collective beliefs or ideas can explain
or justify the content of law as a social fact (Hayward, 1960: 191; Pisier-
Kouchner, 1972: 12–13).

As regards the link between law and social solidarity, Durkheim seeks
to *explain* solidarity, identifying it through its legal expressions. But
Duguit merely takes solidarity as a given, using it to indicate the modern

9. See pp. 115–18, below.
10. See Chapter 4, below.

tasks of law. He has no serious interest in analysing the conditions of existence of social solidarity or its processes of change, which are Durkheim's foci in *The Division of Labour*. To assert that law's task is to express solidarity, however, is very important for Duguit. It allows him to deny the unlimited sovereignty of the state as lawmaker (Duguit, 1919) because the objective needs of solidarity and not the will of the state are what must determine law. Indeed, his theory replaces the idea of sovereignty with that of public service (Duguit, 1919: ch. 2; Pisier-Kouchner, 1972). So it facilitates the analysis of legal controls on government which was Duguit's central concern as a constitutional and administrative lawyer. It treats law as justified only in so far as it has social utility as an instrument to promote the integration of society. It denies that law has an inherent authority deriving from specific processes of political enactment or judicial decision. State authority is justified only by the need to promote social solidarity, a need recognised in widespread sentiments of sociality and justice.

Despite working with Durkheim's ideas only in a limited way, Duguit demonstrates some of the potential of Durkheimian approaches to legal scholarship. Charles Eisenmann (1968: 308) writes that Duguit's theories 'not only gained wide acceptance among legal scholars for methods of juridical analysis, but he also won adherents among the politically oriented for his realistic approach to the state and for his assertion that the power of those who govern is to be considered simply a social function . . .' Duguit's influence waned partly because jurists refused to limit their critique of law and state action and their advocacy of legal ideals within bounds given by sociology. They did not want to be confined to the positions that a controversial effort to theorise social conditions might reveal. And, like Duguit himself, most had no wish to become primarily concerned with social theorising, as such.

In the year that Durkheim's *Division of Labour* was first published, Maurice Hauriou, a law professor at Toulouse University, fiercely criticised what he saw as sociologists' efforts to control other disciplines. He claimed that sociology consisted of little more than dangerous speculation. It would be accepted by jurists only when it became a true science. For the present, he told sociologists, 'we do not want to let ourselves be directed by you; we intend to remain independent in philosophical matters' (quoted in Weisz, 1983: 97). Hauriou became a subtle, original and influential legal philosopher, and his mature ideas are sociologically oriented in certain respects. But he rails against sociological thinking that encourages the transformation of society, sociological thinking that its advocates 'wish to teach to large audiences and to insert into programmes of study'; it leads to 'social reforms, if not insurrections or criminal acts'; one should rather seek results 'that are not contrary to old moral and religious traditions' (quoted in Weisz, 1983: 98).

Sociology's failure, he claims, is that it treats questions of social structure as paramount and so feeds socialism. The proper focus should be
on individual psychology since progress will come through 'the improvement of the individual', not the reorganisation of society (quoted *ibid.*).

Hauriou's later legal philosophy shows real sociological insight
(Hauriou, 1970). But as his early radical conservatism suggests, his
ideas proceed in an almost entirely opposite direction to Duguit's.
Duguit sees law in terms of objective social conditions that give rise to
norms (he never really solves the problem of how social facts create
normative obligation). By contrast, Hauriou starts from the subjective
experience of individuals relating to each other. Social life is to be understood in terms of the subjective elements of individual action and belief
linked in collective enterprise. These elements provide drive, initiative,
energy. Objective elements – structure, control and organisation – are
also important. But, for Hauriou, law cannot be adequately grasped
in Duguit's purely objective view of it, which Hauriou (1970: 97) traces
directly to Durkheim. Since objective law is, according to Duguit,
produced by social conditions, how can it be, at the same time, a creative
force *producing* social conditions? Yet Duguit wants to see law as
creative. In fact, Hauriou asserts, the social milieu provides inertia, not
creative force. The subjective purposes that individuals pursue are the
real creative forces in society. Law is a dynamic force of individual
human action continually crystallising into stabilising rules and institutions. It is both subjective and objective: on the one hand, creative
energy producing innovation and movement; on the other, stable,
controlling structures that fix social life in predictable patterns.

The concept of the *institution* allows these two aspects of law to
coexist in the same framework. 'An institution is an idea of a work or
enterprise that is realised and endures juridically in a social milieu'
(Hauriou, 1970: 99). Institutions include constituted bodies or organisations, for example states, associations or trade unions. But they also
include established legal rules (1970: 100). In one aspect they have
objective existence – they are, in Durkheim's sense, social facts. But in
another aspect they are forces and products of change. They embody
energy and creativity: 'Institutions are born, live and die juridically'
(1970: 100).

Hauriou's thought is important here for its thorough rejection of
Duguit's engagement with Durkheimian ideas. It emphasises the inad-
equacy of considering law only as an 'external' social fact in the way
that Durkheim portrays it in *The Division of Labour*. More generally,
Hauriou harnesses into a sophisticated legal theory the kinds of familiar
reactions to Durkheimian sociology that lesser jurists registered only
unsystematically. First and foremost is a doubt that sociology is justified in replacing the individual with the social as the focus of analysis.

Second is a worry about the consequences of discounting the importance of subjective ideals and intentions and individual responsibility in favour of an emphasis on impersonal social forces. Third is a fear that sociology will ignore tradition and established values and encourage aspirations to overthrow existing social institutions – including much that makes up lawyers' intellectual capital and moral allegiances (Arnaud, 1975: 122–3). As will appear, these characterisations of sociology misrepresent Durkheim's mature positions in various ways. But such characterisations fuelled the hostility of some law professors to Durkheimian sociology.

Legal influences in sociology

Unsurprisingly, given its place in a synthesising sociological science, Durkheim's legal sociology makes much use of legal scholars' work. Apart from the continuous conversation with legal scholarship through the book reviews in the *Année sociologique* more specific influences can be noted.

Some commentators see Durkheim's encounter during his studies in Germany with the work of the jurist Rudolf von Jhering as significant (Pearce, 1989: 103–9; Vogt, 1983: 186). But Jhering's focus on conflicting wills or interests as the basis of law actually has little in common with Durkheim's consistent view of it as shaped by morality rather than interest. Durkheim acknowledges (1978b: 61; 1887: 286–97) the importance of Jhering and the German ethnological jurist A. H. Post in helping to make legal study a science, in other words orienting it towards systematic social inquiries. But there is little evidence of Jhering's influence on Durkheim's outlook. He devotes attention, however, to ethnographic work such as Post's which reports legal customs, ideas and practices from many different societies. Legal ethnography offers history rather than social science, Durkheim notes, and Post describes rather than explains the evolution of law and morals. But he is 'the only German moralist who has loved and studied the details [of laws and morals] for themselves' (1887: 339) rather than to prove a pre-existing philosophical theory.[11]

Since, indeed, Durkheimian sociology assumed that it alone could explain law theoretically as a social phenomenon, the best material from legal scholarship for its purposes was often descriptive (rather than explanatory) and comparative in a broad, imaginative way. Unsystematic, even undisciplined comparative legal scholarship could

---

11. On the relationship between Durkheim's work and that of the influential legal historian Henry Maine see pp. 94–5, below.

be useful, as long as it employed juristic skills to show connections or contrasts between legal ideas in different times and places. We have noted earlier that Durkheimian sociology is concerned both with functional analysis of law as an aspect of society and with explaining the social development of legal institutions and doctrines. Studies of ancient legal systems or primitive law could contribute powerfully to the latter, while comparative studies of recent or contemporary foreign law could provide inspiration for analysis of functions of law in modern societies. Broadly, the two main sections of the *Année sociologique* devoted to law were divided between these orientations. Durkheim himself in *The Division of Labour* uses much material from comparative legal history in elaborating his theses about social solidarity. Later, studies of the origins of legal ideas and practices became an important focus, in their own right, for Durkheimian scholarship. Particularly through the influence of Marcel Mauss' (1896; 1979) writings on early law and religion and on Inuit societies, the great value of ethnographic data in studying the origins and functions of law became accepted wisdom in Durkheimian circles (Vogt, 1983: 192; Lukes and Scull, 1983: 2).

In general, it can be said that Durkheim's sociology of law, while existing in some tension with juristic scholarship, parallels some of the latter's characteristics. To assume that there are steady patterns of evolution of legal ideas, or long continuities in law (e.g. Watson, 1985) is a familiar temptation for legal scholars to the extent that they consider law in relative isolation from its specific social contexts. This assumption is mirrored in some evolutionary approaches to legal sociology. Thus, Durkheim's writings frequently generalise over long periods of legal history or across many societies. Often they show an excessive reverence for law as stable, continuous in development, and consistent in its value orientations. Indeed, sometimes Durkheim writes as though law is an unbroken moral thread running through all of history.[12]

 Equally, he is rarely led to consider the practical complexities that surround the application of legal ideas to specific contexts. Like the jurists of the French universities in his time, Durkheim considers law, above all, as a structure of ideas with their own integrity. As in much legal scholarship, so in Durkheim's sociology, the practical politics of making, interpreting and enforcing law is kept at a distance,[13] firmly subordinated to questions about the substance of legal doctrine, seen in terms of its moral significance. For all the tensions with legal scholars noted earlier, Durkheim's outlook on law has many similarities with the more idealised views of some of his juristic contemporaries. It would

12. See Chapter 6, below.
13. See Chapter 11, below.

be surprising if matters were otherwise. As the following chapters will seek to show, Durkheim's legal sociology comes not to bury the law that jurists serve but to praise it – or rather, to put it in a perspective that reveals its potential moral worth and what has to be done in order to realise that worth to the full.

Part 2

Law in culture

4

Law, morality, belief

Like most creative thinkers, Durkheim does not present his theories
fully formed in his earliest writings so that, thereafter, they stay
constant. There are different emphases in his ideas about law at various
stages in his career. And it is important to decide whether what
occurs is an elaboration of his early views or a correction of them. In
exploring his legal thought in the following chapters the question
of changes in Durkheim's theoretical outlook will be ever-present.
Gradually their significance will have to be assessed. But this must
be the outcome of an analysis of his thinking on a range of topics
in the following chapters. Matters are complicated by the fact that
except in one very important case – his changed view from the mid-
1890s of the sociological importance of religion[1] – Durkheim never
admits to having significantly revised his theoretical viewpoints
(Alexander, 1982: 255).

The best entry into his legal theory is through his conception of
the relationship between law and morality. This relationship underlies
all his legal thought and his idea of law is worked out by reference to
a view of the nature of morality, evolved in his work over time. Closely
linked to his analyses of law and morality are questions about belief.
Durkheim stresses law's sometimes problematic connections with
beliefs and understandings widely held by members of society. The
focus of this and the following two chapters is on these connections.
The present chapter discusses his basic conception of law as he establishes it in relation to morality.

A focus of belief

Law, as Durkheim portrays it, is linked to morality and religion. Law's
technical details cannot necessarily be explained by reference to these
other phenomena. But its authority, its special nature as something to
be respected, must be understood as part of a broader understanding

1. See pp. 22–3, above.

of the essence of moral phenomena (Durkheim, 1978a: 80; Durkheim and Fauconnet, 1982: 191).

Durkheim's mature view of law depends in certain respects on his view of religion. But religion is understood in a distinct, sociological way, as fulfilling a social *function*. It is a source of meaning for individual lives, something individuals can relate to as greater than themselves, giving direction, confidence and a source of authority, a grand scheme to which the seemingly insignificant details of life can be related, an ultimate source of values and understandings (Durkheim, 1915: 190, 225–6; 1957: 160). It is a means of making sense of the fact that the life of the group (society) endures while its individual members are born and die (1915: 268–9) The link between law and religion is not through law expressing religious ideas – in modern societies it clearly does not generally do so. The point is that law and religion have certain similarities as social phenomena. They are both foci of duty and commitment. They impose obligations on those subject to them, who accept their authority. And ultimately law, like religion, is not merely a matter of duty or obligation. The ultimate logic of Durkheim's position, as will appear, is that, up to a point, law must also be, like religion, a focus of willing allegiance, something to be believed in and involved with.[2]

Such an approach to law needs much analysis. But it can be said immediately that it need not neglect issues of power and coercion, the idea of law as a site of struggle and conflict. If we press the analogy with religion further than Durkheim himself does, it can be noted that religion, like law, may coerce those subject to its authority and be used as a weapon (cf. Erikson, 1966). Religious communities are often wracked by power struggles. A religious faith is one thing; the priests or lay believers who use it to exert power over other individuals may be quite another matter. A church (like a society under law) can be considered a community. But every church has its leaders, its doctrinal disputes, its power struggles, its enemies and its methods of social control over those within and beyond its membership. People may be forced – sometimes through physical violence – to believe, or to behave as though they do. Certainly Durkheim has little interest in these matters of power and coercion. But a sociological comparison of law and religion could highlight them. Law, like religion, is a site and an instrument of power and conflict. Nevertheless, it may also be a focus of commitment, attachment and solidarity. It is a source of duty and responsibility, but also of identity – of moral meaning as well as discipline in individual lives. This is the universe of thought about law that Durkheim's work inhabits.

2. See pp. 193–6, below.

Vogt (1993: 71) writes of the 'trinity' that law, morality and religion form in Durkheim's work. These constitute 'society itself, living and active, for a society is characterised by its law, morality and religion' (Durkheim and Fauconnet, 1982: 191). How do they relate? Vogt interprets Durkheim as claiming that in early societies morality is imbued with religion and expressed in religious principles, while in modern societies morality is mainly expressed through law (Vogt, 1993: 72, 93). But this oversimplifies. Law, for Durkheim, is intertwined with morality and religion in early or ancient societies (Durkheim, 1982b: 173). Yet, as his index thesis assumes,[3] law is an important expression of morality and belief even in these societies. For Durkheim, law is no less important in them than in modern societies. But its character and, in particular, its relation with religion is different. In ancient or early societies much of law actually expresses religious precepts. Law is mainly repressive. Its role is to express and affirm the shared beliefs and understandings that characterise the society. And these beliefs and understandings are essentially religious.

In modern society the situation is much more complex. It is no longer possible to think of religion as providing an all-embracing structure of beliefs dominating society. But, for Durkheim, society still requires a moral foundation. The question is where that foundation is to be found. Perhaps it derives directly from the nature of modern society itself as a complex structure of interdependence. This is essentially Durkheim's thesis in *The Division of Labour*. Perhaps, as his later work suggests, it is rooted in value systems that modern society inspires and which, in some sense, take the place of religion or take on quasi-religious overtones. But, as Vogt suggests, Durkheim's view is that, whatever the ultimate moral foundations of modern society, law's function is to express, protect and guarantee that foundation.

Durkheimian sociology's concern is with religion in general as a social phenomenon, not with any particular set of beliefs or doctrines. A religion is 'a unified system of beliefs and practices relative to sacred things, that is to say, things set apart and forbidden – beliefs and practices which unite into a single moral community, called a Church, all those who adhere to them' (Durkheim, 1915: 47). In principle, *any* such beliefs and practices could satisfy religion's social function. A belief in God, gods or spirits is not required. The essence is 'abstract powers, anonymous forces' which can be attached to rituals, procedures and ceremonies, to words said and actions done in particular settings (1912: 285; cf. 1915: 200). Even where religion is personified in specific deities, impersonal forces and powers are what is fundamental.

3. See pp. 31–4, above.

This is what gives religion its universal aspect. Wherever and whenever it exists it is a 'spiritual discipline' and 'a means enabling men to face the world with greater confidence' (1915: 190; and see 1975b: 182). After the change in his views in the mid-1890s Durkheim developed a twofold position on religion. On the one hand, religious ideas and practices are the *source* of everything social. 'In principle everything is religious.' Thus, religion gave rise to law (1982b: 173). On the other hand, there is something *permanent* in the social phenomenon that religion represents (1915: 427). Its social function is necessary in all societies. Somehow this function must be met, even where belief in established religions has disappeared.

In impressing on individuals a sense of the sacredness of something outside themselves, religion encapsulates a sense of life lived not by the individual in isolation but in common with all other people, and by past and future generations. It locates individual life in a larger pattern, and thereby gives meaning and direction to it (1915: 225). As noted above, for Durkheim, religious belief is always belief in abstract forces of some kind. And, as has been seen, the abstract force that, for him, gives meaning to the individual life is a discipline willingly adhered to, believed in as a matter of commitment, internalised in the individual's way of thinking and acting.[4] Thus, it seems that religious belief, in Durkheim's very specific sense, can be partly translated into *a belief in regulation* – including, no doubt, a belief in law – as necessary, welcome, natural and obligatory (cf. Hamnett, 1975: 114). As cultural possibilities grow with the complexity of society, so the need for regulation grows.

He never goes so far as to suggest that law replaces religion in modern society.[5] What kinds of beliefs can fulfil the social function of established but declining religions in Western societies remains a difficult question.[6] Nevertheless, religion provides an object of attachment. For Durkheim this object can only be social – found in the experience of collective life (1915: 10, 47). And we have seen that law and morality are, for him, the pre-eminent expressions of this collective life – of society itself.

Durkheim's reassessment of the significance of religion has rightly been claimed as important for the development of his view of law (Alexander, 1982: 274ff.). In *The Division of Labour*, before the reassessment, he had portrayed law in modern society as mainly the expression of organic solidarity. As restitutive law, it represented functional co-ordination in society and thus *distanced* itself from law's religious

4. See Chapter 2, above.
5. One of his followers, the jurist Emmanuel Lévy, is less cautious, declaring that reliance on rights and legal redress 'is a religion – a practical substitute for religion – in relation to which the critical spirit is ill at ease' (Lévy, 1933: 14).
6. See pp. 195–6, below.

origins: God, Durkheim laconically notes, has progressively withdrawn from human relationships leaving the world to men and their quarrels (1984: 119). But the post-1895 writings *re-emphasise* the spiritual bases of law, close to or analogous with those of religion: 'Law is meaningless if it is detached from religion, which has given it its main distinguishing marks, and of which it is partially only a derivation' (Durkheim and Fauconnet, 1982: 205). Religion now means, for Durkheim, not the declining traditional religions but some shared focus of belief and attachment that is necessary to every society (1915: 427). The law–religion nexus poses, thereafter, unresolved issues. In what ways does law relate to such an object of attachment? How far is law a 'spiritual' and not merely coercive phenomenon? And how is the idea of law as something to be believed in, as well as to be obeyed, reconcilable with the idea of law as an instrument of government – a coercive mechanism for co-ordinating complex societies? In Durkheim's thinking after the mid-1890s law is not just a modern phenomenon that has freed itself from the archaic world of religion. It seems that it requires (and maybe provides) a grounding of belief (Alexander, 1982: 215; Lenoir, 1994: 30).

Morality, religion and law

How does morality relate to religion? Religion provides a manner of making sense of the world, a universe of interpretation, or at least the fundamental underpinnings of one (Durkheim, 1915: 425). Thus it can provide the beliefs that inform and justify moral conviction. In *The Division of Labour*, when Durkheim refers to repressive law as reflecting shared beliefs, he sees these beliefs as derived in most societies throughout history from the all-embracing world-views that the traditional religions shaped. The general structure of shared beliefs and understandings existing in a particular society he calls the 'collective consciousness' (*conscience collective*), or common consciousness. This is the 'totality of beliefs and sentiments common to the average members of a society' (1984: 38–9). The collective consciousness is extensive – that is, the range of shared beliefs and sentiments is great – in societies dominated by mechanical solidarity and repressive law. Thus, in early or simple societies, law and morality are both largely expressions of collective beliefs or sentiments rooted in religious sources.

In *The Division of Labour*, Durkheim argues that the scope of the collective consciousness becomes smaller as the division of labour progresses. It does not disappear in complex modern societies but is much reduced in importance (1984: 39). Thus, Durkheim's concern with modern societies, where beliefs, understandings and moral outlooks

are diverse, pulls him away from the idea of the collective consciousness and hence from any idea that the major part of modern law and
morality can be significantly grounded in shared beliefs. Rather he tries
to find their basis in the requirements of interdependence in modern
society. However, his later writings show a change of outlook. They
return to the emphasis on collective beliefs and ideas and see these as
important in modern no less than earlier societies. Indeed, Durkheim's
later work claims that society as a complex phenomenon is actually
made up of understandings, interpretations and perceptions – for
which he often uses the general term 'representations' (*représentations*)
(Durkheim, 1953b). In 'social life, everything consists of representations, ideas and sentiments' (1982a: 247). All the established social
institutions – for example, marriage, the family, money, property – exist
only in so far as they are generally recognised or collectively understood. They live in the shared perceptions of citizens. So he refers
to 'collective representations' to mean specific elements of common
understanding or belief that constitute particular social institutions
and practices.

The concepts of collective consciousness or collective representations
make it possible to refer to widely held beliefs, sentiments or understandings as social facts. Religion figures in Durkheim's later work as
a focus for addressing the problem of how people become attached to
ideals and general understandings of the world and their place in it,
and live these ideas out as part of their very being. Morality is concerned
with how individuals relate obligations to situations (Joas, 1993: 241).
The source of these obligations may be shared beliefs, religious or quasi-
religious in nature (that is, beliefs occupying the functional place
of religion in society), or it may be more directly located in the objective requirements of social solidarity. In the later phases of Durkheim's
work he emphasises the link between modern morality and belief. In
his early work, morality is seen as a matter of duty and rules. However,
as religion becomes from the mid-1890s an important focus in his
writing, questions of attachment and belief gradually become imposed
on his view of morality too (Durkheim, 1961). A secular morality must
somehow acquire some of the vitality, the quality of being enthusiasti-
cally lived out with a sense of personal commitment, that attaches to
religious ideas in the consciousness of the true believer. This makes
morality more than just a set of rules or prohibitions.

In Durkheim's later work, morality seems to link law, which epito-
mises the most pressing demands of social duty, with the kind of
generalised belief that religion represents. In the first edition of *The
Division of Labour* he had suggested that, to be a living thing, 'an effective discipline of wills' rather than 'a dead letter, an abstraction', morality
must be expressed in law. Law, taking on moral meaning, can, in turn,

provide criteria (such as property, ownership, lawful authority) with which morality operates (1893b: 277). Thus, thought of in terms of duty, morality faces towards law, and is most effective when embodied in law. This does not mean law must be the authoritarian enforcer of moral prejudices. Rather law expresses the essential core of the moral code needed for society's cohesion in particular historical conditions. When, however, as in Durkheim's later writings, morality is thought of as more than duty, as something giving meaning to life (as in his lectures on *Moral Education*, discussed below), the link with religion seems more prominent in discussion than the link with law. Morality then has something of the social function of religion – focusing individuals' social identity, attaching them to something greater than themselves.

Sociology as a key to morality

Durkheim is clear as to what morality is not. It is not utilitarian calculation – working out how to satisfy wants (1984: 418, 421; 1969b; and see Cladis, 1992: 15–16). Moral institutions are certainly useful to society. They serve a social function (1907: 570). But acting morally is not a matter of calculating how to further interests. Moral action is certainly not the pursuit of personal benefit, even the personal benefit of the majority of individuals in a society. Morality 'necessarily implies some spirit of sacrifice and abnegation' (1984: xli), a matter of foregoing one's interests up to a point rather than pursuing them.

Neither is morality a matter of acting for the good of particular others, chosen on the basis of personal preference. Durkheim argues that actions cannot be moral if, in deliberately choosing to benefit some people, we arbitrarily exclude others (1961: 58–9). How are the favoured to be selected from the rest of humanity? Selection is hard to justify unless social conditions themselves provide objective reasons for distinctions drawn. In other words, society determines the nature and scope of moral duties. Thus, morality can only be thought of as duties owed to *society at large*, to the common good (which, however, often requires acting to benefit particular others in particular circumstances).[7] To act morally is to act in the way society requires to promote and maintain social solidarity.

Morality is also not a matter of deduction from some master principle. It consists, Durkheim claims, in innumerable specific precepts (1961: 24–6). What exist are 'the individual and the particular' of which 'the general is only a schematic expression' (1893b: 267–8; and see

7. Presumably for Durkheim the felt need to acknowledge and, if possible, repay personal kindness received is related to the need to recognise interdependence as a moral condition.

1961: 25). Thus general ideas of property rights or of parental responsibility for children are rationalisations from many particular rules 'that
directly, and without intermediary, impose themselves on the will at
each moment' (1893b: 268). Acting morally is not a matter of examining higher principles to judge how they apply to a case. We decide
directly what the particular case requires. There are 'definite and specific
ways of acting imposed on us' and these moral demands are 'like moulds
in which we have to make our actions run' (1893b: 269).

Durkheim's argument here is less than clear. He surely does not
mean to suggest that it is impossible to rationalise moral responses;
nor presumably would he deny that it is natural to seek to do so. The
point seems to be that morality is to be understood empirically and that
it reflects the unsystematic nature of experience. We can rationalise it
only in so far as we can theorise about the empirical character of particular societies. Sociology properly observes the complexity and richness
of moral life. Philosophy fails when it tries to rationalise this complexity
and richness into timeless, abstract systems. No philosophical laws
govern 'so vast and varied a world' (1893b: 269). No blueprint controls
moral life. Morality can be rationally modified or developed. But this
cannot be done according to some comprehensive a priori scheme:
'morality does not have to be constructed from fundamentals ... we
only have to supervise its workings' (1979: 32).

If, however, there is so much complexity and moral diversity how is
it possible to know what is morally right? The answer given in *The
Division of Labour* is that social experience, interpreted by sociology,
reveals the moral principles required in a particular society. The nature
of social relations in that society and their conditions of existence determine appropriate morality. By understanding the nature and conditions
of social solidarity in a society we can understand that society's morality
(1984: 331) – the morality that will be normal in it (accepted as appropriate by average members of the society) and optimal for it (appropriate
to the structure of the society). This does not mean that people necessarily act on this morality. But, for solidarity to exist, the morality
appropriate to it must be operative to a significant extent. Most importantly, the *essence* of this morality must be *officially* operative. It must
be publicly in place and officially pronounced as good. This is why
morality as a social fact, revealed by sociological inquiry, finds substantial expression in law. Durkheim sees law as the most important
expression of morality as a social fact.

Where do these ideas lead? Morality, on this view, is a matter for
historians and sociologists to clarify, rather than for philosophers to
deduce. It is not, for example, the elaboration of Kant's categorical
imperative or Bentham's principle of utility: 'These are the generalisations of philosophers, the hypotheses of theoreticians' (1961: 25–6).

Morality has no philosophical unity. It certainly cannot find unity in some abstract idea of (human) nature (1984: 335). Morality's unity exists only in so far as empirical social conditions themselves constitute a unity in a certain setting (1961: 111). In so far as a society can be thought of as a totality made up of parts, it is possible to think of morality in that society as a unity – a single, complex social fact.

However, just as society is always changing and developing, so morality, as an aggregate of moral experience, is always reforming itself in new ways. Justice Holmes' famous words about the 'life of the law' might be applied to morality: the life of morals 'has not been logic but experience' (cf. Holmes, 1881: 1). Thus, 'experience alone can decide if they are suitable' to the time and place (Durkheim, 1893b: 271). It is for sociology to observe morals as social facts and to interpret moral experience to show how it relates to social development. Sociology, for Durkheim, is the key to a positive science of morality. It threatens to displace philosophy in so far as the latter fails to conduct and interpret the empirical social inquiries without which the meaning of moral prescriptions cannot be understood.

Thus, Durkheim asserts that law is rooted in a morality that sociology can identify. But is it really to be believed that law inevitably expresses the morality society needs, as its guarantee of social solidarity? Are law's moral stances always best for the society it regulates? Ultimately Durkheim's answer is 'yes' and 'no'. The basic moral tenets reflected in law must be those that constitute moral 'common sense' for that society. Any other value system in law is pointless and perhaps ultimately impossible. When he considers autocracies imposing legal rules that oppose a fundamental popular moral sense he has no doubt that such regimes cannot last and can only contribute to eventual social breakdown (Lukes, 1973: 547–8, 552; Durkheim, 1957: 87). Besides, national legal systems have to relate to transnational expectations and pressures for international solidarity. The ultimate sanction for ignoring these – as in the case of Germany in the First World War, in Durkheim's view (Lukes, 1973: 552) – may well be military defeat.

On the other hand, legal regulation can often be insensitive, ignorant or unjustifiably coercive. It can exacerbate social tensions, inflame class conflicts, contribute to commercial or industrial failures, or produce moral disruption. Law can regulate too much, too little, or in the wrong ways. It is ultimately an independent governmental force, not just the agent of morality. And politics can obstruct morally appropriate regulation. Durkheim discusses these possibilities in *The Division of Labour* (1984: book 3) and we shall return to them later.[8] But anyone who sees conflict as natural to social life will not be satisfied with Durkheim's

8. See Chapter 12, below.

accounts. He portrays all such regulatory conditions as 'abnormal forms'. Ultimately, for him, law normally and necessarily expresses the *fundamentals* of society's moral framework. It cannot do less than this if it is to retain its character as more than mere political compromise – 'a thing so small and mediocre' (cf. Lukes, 1973: 47). And it cannot do much more because 'we cannot aspire to a morality other than that which is related to the state of our society' (Durkheim, 1953d: 61). But, understanding morality in this way, we can demand with all the force of informed social criticism, legal regulation that takes proper account of it (1953d: 38).

The nature of moral rules

Every rule, of whatever kind, commands us, writes Durkheim. It contains 'something that resists us, is beyond us, imposes itself on us and constrains us'; it is independent and dominating, 'resistant to the will' (1925: 25, 26; cf. 1961: 28, 29), so is not just an internal state of mind, like a sentiment or habit. Rules combine the idea of regularity with that of authority, authority being 'that influence which is imposed on us by any moral power that we acknowledge as superior' (1925: 25; cf. 1961: 29).

Rules of hygiene in preparing one's own food, for example, are supported by the authority of science. But conformity to these rules is not just due to this authority but for utilitarian reasons: harm is likely to follow if the rules are not followed (1953d: 42–3; 1961: 30). A doctor's order is obeyed not just because of the scientific authority that supports it but because the patient wants to be cured (1961: 30). Ultimately, Durkheim argues, such purely technical rules are not obligatory. They are followed because they indicate a causal link with consequences that the rule follower desires (Lukes, 1973: 412–13). Morality, too, 'consists of a system of rules of action that predetermine conduct. They state how one must act in a given situation; and to behave properly is to obey conscientiously' (Durkheim, 1961: 24). The essence of morality is, thus, obedience to rule. But Durkheim insists that moral rules are to be followed purely because of their moral authority, not to achieve some desired purpose.

Legal rules, as will appear, are, for Durkheim, a special category of moral rules. And moral rules in general, he argues (1893b: 274–5), have two distinctive qualities. First, they attract social intervention opposing known deviation from the rule. They thus have sanctions – for example, punishment for homicide or theft, public scorn for a breach of laws of honour, the demand for restitution when a contract is broken. Secondly, these sanctions regularly and predictably follow, either through the effects of public opinion or through legal procedures. Morality consists of *rules of sanctioned conduct* (1893b: 275). Sanction is 'the essential element of any moral rule at all' (1957: 2); it is the external symbol of obligation. It is what makes moral rules social facts – external constraints on the individual.

Durkheim defines a sanction as 'the consequence of an act that does not result from the content of that act, but from the violation by that act of a pre-established rule' (1953d: 43). Thus, sanctions distinguish moral (including legal) rules from other rules. In the case of disregard of a personal hygiene rule the unhygienic act causes the consequence (illness). But with moral rules, the breach of the rule itself attracts the sanction. Social sanctions must be manifested in some way: 'For the reproach to be efficacious it must be expressed outwardly . . .', for example by the shunning of an offender (1893b: 277). In Durkheim's early writings on morality, where the focus is almost entirely on duty, discussion is typically of negative sanctions (blame, punishment). Later, however, he notes that sanctions may be positive (praise, honour) too (1953d: 43–4).

Problems, which Durkheim does not seem to see, can be noted in this identification of moral rules. The distinction from hygiene rules is plausible if the breach of a hygiene rule prejudices only the person breaking it. But, when others are likely to be affected – either specific individuals or people generally (as where a food manufacturer, retailer or restaurant owner prepares or stores food unhygienically), moral issues clearly arise. This forces further reflection on Durkheim's effort to deny utilitarian bases of morality. Hygiene rules become the basis of moral (and frequently legal) rules when their breach threatens harm to others beyond the person in breach. We might say that the hygiene rule is adopted as the substantive content of a moral or legal rule when it is considered important to society at large. It becomes a moral rule fulfilling Durkheim's criteria. But its content still embodies the utilitarian calculation that made the hygiene rule purely technical for Durkheim. Thus, he is wrong to try firmly to separate utilitarian calculation from morality. But he is perhaps right to see the essence of 'the moral' in duties imposed by society for its general well-being rather than in a calculation of benefits in private negotiations between individuals or groups or in the pursuit of private interpersonal relations.

More general difficulties in Durkheim's definition of moral duty also remain unaddressed. Who must attach sanctions to a breach of a rule if that rule is to be considered a moral one? What proportion, or what sections, of a population? How must public opinion manifest itself? Can rules of etiquette or politeness be distinguished from moral rules? And what of rules of grammar? Their breach might produce scorn or disdain. Are they then moral rules? The social reaction might be that the offender needs educating. But that could apply to a breach of any moral rule, especially when a child commits it.

Legal rules as a category of moral rules

Durkheim's identification of moral rules is far from rigorous. But perhaps it is sufficient for his purposes. His category of moral rules ranges from the fundamental to the seemingly trivial. The word *mœurs*, which he often uses, refers to manners and customs as well as morals. Perhaps for his purposes there is no need to distinguish sociologically the various categories of social rules mentioned above. All, in one way or another, are constraining social facts. All have sociological significance as sanctioned rules of conduct. This conclusion would explain why, when he does wish to identify clearly a category of moral rules that he sees as socially most significant and imperative – given that they attract special social processes for their sanctioning – he has no hesitation in identifying them as *law*. Law and morality are 'too intimately related to be radically separated'; they are 'inseparable and arise from one and the same science' (1893b: 276, 277). So morality in the broadest sense – as mores or *mœurs* – can be thought of as a vast spectrum. It ranges from the most insignificant expectations about social interaction to the most insistent and enduring, the most fiercely defended, the most publicly sanctioned.

As we should expect, legal rules, for Durkheim, differ from other moral rules only in degree. While most jurists are anxious to mark out a distinct realm of law apart from morality, Durkheim's sociological purposes are quite different. Law is a particular way in which the sanctioning of moral rules may be carried out. Legal sanctions are not distinguished by their intrinsic character. They are, indeed, sometimes 'purely moral', as where they entail 'deprivation of certain rights, such as infamy among the Romans, dishonour among the Greeks, civic degradation, etc.' (1893b: 277–8). Nor are they necessarily harsher than moral sanctions. Durkheim sees penal rules as 'notable for their clarity and precision, whilst purely moral rules are generally somewhat fluid in character' (1984: 38) but he attaches little weight to this generalisation.

The real difference is in the way sanctions are administered. Moral sanctions are *diffuse* – 'administered . . . by everybody without distinction'. By contrast, legal sanctions are *organised* – 'applied only through the medium of a definite body' (1984: 29; 1893b: 278). Law has 'specially authorised representatives' charged with the task of enforcement (1978b: 63). Its rules 'are instituted by definite organs and under a definite form and . . . the whole system which the law uses to realise its precepts is regulated and organised . . .' (1900c: 320, 321). These criteria, Durkheim notes, do not distinguish legal rules from many religious precepts. In general, however, the manner of deciding responsibility and applying punishments is what distinguishes legal from moral rules. Vogt claims that Fauconnet provides one of the most explicit Durkheimian definitions of law. He interprets Fauconnet as holding that, while judgments of moral responsibility are diffused through collective opinion, an attribution of legal responsibility requires 'the intervention of a specifically designated intermediary person or institution that makes the judgment after a process of deliberation and applies the sanction according to rules of procedure' (Vogt, 1983: 183; cf. Fauconnet, 1928: 12–18).

In fact, however, for Durkheim, rules of procedure are not necessary for law to exist. Elaborate organisation or identification of sanctions is not required. Often, indeed, laws do not specify particular sanctions. Determining the sanction may be left until the enforcement stage (Durkheim, 1984: 51). In ancient Rome the assembly of the people decided on punishment. 'So it is not the regulation of punishment . . . Nor is it the institution of a criminal procedure' that marks the emergence of law. In history, 'for a long time this was lacking'. 'The only organisation met with everywhere' where legal sanctioning exists is 'the establishment of a court of law' (*un tribunal*) (1984: 52; 1893a: 63). This could be composed of the people as a whole, as in ancient Rome or Athens or among primitive Germanic tribes (1984: 36), or it might comprise an elite of judges. Certainly, it might not follow regular procedures. Through it, however, 'the offence, instead of being judged by each person, is submitted for consideration to a constituted body' and 'the collective reaction is expressed through the intermediary of a defined organ.' Thus sanctioning 'ceases to be diffuse; it is organised' (1893a: 64; cf. 1984: 52). In law, society judges, but in an organised way. Law thus requires *some* institutionalised means for publicly declaring or affirming norms.

Law beyond morality?

Law is thus, for Durkheim, an aspect of morality but it has special features differentiating it in degree if not in kind from other moral rules. If organisation is the key it is clear that this does not need to be political organisation in any usual sense. A community might organise itself purely for the purpose of legal sanctioning, not for government generally. Nevertheless, the factor of organisation clearly points towards law's development as a *political instrument*. A communal organisation of the administration of justice can evolve into an organisation of elders or special judges or priests. And the sanctioning of deviance can become an aspect of wider responsibilities of government or social control. In such a way law becomes part of government. The path is set for law to separate from the rest of the universe of moral rules and fulfil special technical governmental needs. An elite of judges can become, or become part of, an elite that rules. Deciding responsibility can merge with creating responsibility, imposing rules, issuing commands.

In *The Division of Labour* Durkheim notes that restitutive law – the law required by social complexity for expressing organic solidarity – requires much more extensive organisation than repressive or penal law (1984: 70). Law's relations with morality would seem to become more complex as society develops with the intensification of the division of labour. Law is no longer mainly an expression of the collective consciousness. It must somehow negotiate the diverse beliefs and under-standings of diverse groups. What is now required, we may suggest, is not just the authoritative expression of shared values and sentiments but the *creative art of government,* to be practised by leaders who need to be wise and skilled in negotiating differences and controlling conflict. Thus, for sociology of law, it becomes necessary to analyse the nature of political power and of the state as the source of law. It also becomes necessary ultimately to analyse the kinds of beliefs that underpin govern-ment authority itself.

These projections of law's historical development seem to take it away from morality. But could it be that morality itself becomes a more complex matter, no longer to be thought of merely in terms of rules and duty – controls and constraints – but as a means of creatively facil-itating and organising social life? Morality would then appear as not just a repressive phenomenon, holding the individual in place, but a means of stimulating activity, drawing people together, constructing solidarity and fostering relationships in conditions of social complexity. Especially in his later lectures on *Moral Education* (Durkheim, 1961), Durkheim writes about morality in general in these different terms, going well beyond his original emphases on the nature of moral rules as controls over the individual. He never systematically discusses law in ways that connect it explicitly with his final conception of morality. But there is no reason to suppose that in developing this conception he means to exclude law from the place – as a distinct but inseparable part of morality – consistently given to it in his writings.

In the *Moral Education* lectures, morality is no longer identified just with obedience to sanctioned rules. Certainly, regularity and authority, discipline and duty are still fundamental elements (1961: 31). But, whereas these elements make the individual passive, merely subject to the 'external' constraint of moral rules, Durkheim adds two other components of morality that make the individual an active participant in moral life. The first is *attachment* to social groups (1961: chs 4–6).

Morality involves individuals attributing value to something beyond themselves in society. By drawing individuals outside themselves 'into the nourishing milieu of society' morality develops the personality (1961: 73). To immerse oneself in society's concerns is to enrich one's life. So morality is more than duty. It is also active involvement with others. The idea of moral attachment emphasises that morality is nurtured by involvement with social groups. Attachment to a business community, a local community, a church or a nation may all create moral consequences – and these may vary significantly depending on the nature of the group.

The other component of morality beyond discipline and attachment is *autonomy* (1961: chs 7–8). Autonomy is the freedom of the individual to assess moral rules. It is necessary not merely to know moral rules but also to know what they mean socially, what they are for. Reasons for conduct beyond mere acceptance of authority are required. Teaching morality ought, therefore, not to be preaching or indoctrinating, but explaining (1961: 120). Autonomy consists in rationally understanding the natural order of things, including society, and the rules appropriate to it (1961: 116). This is, as Robert Bellah (1973: xxxix–xl) notes, the specifically modern component of morality, the one that gives sociology its special responsibility to guide moral understanding. Moral discipline makes social order and regularity possible, and moral attachment provides in individual motivations the essential pre-requisite of social solidarity. But moral autonomy gives the possibility of systematically and critically reflecting on moral matters, examining them empirically, considering the moral conditions of the present in the light of historical experience and plotting the future.

Morality in this sense, it might be suggested, does not lose touch with the complex demands placed on modern law. Law is the most important means of planning the future, no less than regulating the present. It not only imposes duties – moral discipline – but can also facilitate social solidarity. Its task is somehow to frame and organise the complex social networks of attachment. And law, as a moral phenomenon, needs to be understood rationally. Moral autonomy requires that law be understood scientifically – that is, sociologically.

This, I suggest, is the view of law implicit in Durkheim's later view of morality. Law is not often discussed in connection with this view. Nevertheless, given its inseparability from morality in Durkheim's thought, a Durkheimian conception of law must reflect these understandings of morality. It will be noted that his conception of morality eventually takes on qualities that he came to see in religion as a social phenomenon – in particular the combination of duty and discipline on the one hand, and commitment and attachment on the other. But the stress on autonomy as an element in morality must colour any use of

Law's task

religion as a model for modern morality. If there is to be belief in law and commitment to morality, the element of moral autonomy indicates that this belief and commitment will be founded on a secular reason. If jurists are priests, they have to be priests of reason charged with the task of scientifically grounding legal faith, armed with the knowledge that sociology offers.

5

Crime and punishment

Criminal law – or, more broadly, penal law, the law aimed at punishing wrongdoers – has a special place in Durkheim's legal sociology. He always understood penal law as serving law's most elementary social function – that of expressing shared beliefs – and it is, according to his analysis, the oldest form of law. His account of the nature of crime parallels and complements his analyses of penal law and punishment. The question to be considered in this chapter is how far Durkheim's writings on crime and punishment help to clarify and develop the ideas about relationships between law, morality and belief that were introduced in Chapter 4.

Crime and collective sentiments

'The only feature common to all crimes', writes Durkheim, 'is that . . . they comprise acts universally condemned by the members of each society . . .' Crime 'disturbs those feelings that in any one type of society are to be found in every healthy consciousness' (1984: 33–4). An act is criminal because it offends the collective consciousness (1984: 40) and so is condemned as a breach of penal or repressive law. Crimes have in common that universally 'they strike the moral consciousness of nations in the same way and universally produce the same consequence' (1984: 31).

These statements from *The Division of Labour* are puzzling in many respects. Although crime is said to produce a 'universal' reaction, Durkheim properly notes that what counts as crime varies greatly from one society to another (1984: 32). And it is treated differently in different societies. Thus crime is specific to each society, but universal in its fundamental character. If it varies with time and place, what is fundamental and therefore universal about it? Again, when Durkheim writes that crime is 'universally disapproved of' in any given society, he must be aware that some crimes are condemned more than others, and by some people more than others. And not everyone agrees as to whether certain acts are, or should be, crimes. Finally, it must be asked, what is a 'healthy consciousness'?

The 'healthy' or the 'normal' is, for most purposes of analysis in Durkheim's early writings, simply what is average (1982a: ch. 3). The collective consciousness informs the normal moral outlook expressed in repressive law and it was seen in Chapter 4 that the collective consciousness in a particular society is defined as the range of beliefs and sentiments common to average members of that society.[1] But the concepts of social 'health' and 'normality' are problematic. Surely there is something wrong with the idea that only the beliefs and sentiments of the average can be healthy? The essence of the difficulty here is that while Durkheim is very ready to recognise moral diversity and difference of attitudes, sentiments and beliefs in considering the conditions of organic solidarity and restitutive law, he will not do so in considering repressive law and punishment. Crime is what the collective consciousness condemns. Repressive law expresses the collective consciousness. Therefore, this law defines crime. But there can be only one collective consciousness, according to Durkheim's conception, in any particular society. Repressive law expresses shared beliefs. Therefore, by definition, in any society, this law, like the beliefs it reflects, is assumed to be universal.

Thus, the idea of crime and punishment is tied to the concept of a uniform, all-embracing collective consciousness. Restitutive law in *The Division of Labour* represents social complexity and differentiation – it points towards the rich moral diversity of modern societies, and the need to balance and negotiate different outlooks, sentiments and values. But repressive law and the whole of Durkheim's thought about crime and punishment revolve around the idea of social *homogeneity*. Thus, the ordinary criminal is not someone who has 'alternative' ideas or attitudes as compared with other people. Criminals are set apart from society by their actions and attitudes, condemned as outside the embrace of social uniformity. Despite the tendency in Durkheim's later work for the concept of collective consciousness to be replaced with that of collective representations – implying less monolithic or universal structures of shared belief or understanding – this does not seem to affect his view of the nature of crime and punishment. Indeed, his writing on crime – though not his most important writing on punishment – comes mainly from the early phases of his career.

We 'should not say that an act offends the common consciousness because it is criminal, but that it is criminal because it offends that consciousness. We do not condemn it because it is a crime, but it is a crime because we condemn it' (Durkheim, 1984: 40). All that crimes have in common, therefore, for Durkheim, is that they are socially condemned as contrary to the beliefs and sentiments of average

1. See p. 53, above.

members of the society. Crime is directly linked with punishment, but punishment is not the result of crime. Durkheim puts matters the other way around. Crime is that which is socially punished. What is punished is what transgresses social beliefs and sentiments.

Not all offences against shared beliefs are treated as crimes. As was seen in Chapter 4, for Durkheim, law is to be understood as a part of morality sanctioned in special ways because of its special importance. Legal duties are distinguished from moral ones only in degree – by the fact that the sanctioning of lawbreaking is organised rather than diffuse.[2] The collective consciousness may, in early or ancient societies, cover a vast scope. Everything that runs counter to it may meet disapproval, and perhaps social sanctioning. But affronts to the collective consciousness will only be treated as a matter of *law* – that is, as crimes – where the sentiments offended have 'a certain average intensity. Not only are they engraven on all consciences but they are strongly engraven' (1893a: 43; cf. 1984: 37). Crime is a classification reserved for attacks on 'the heart and centre of the common consciousness' (1984: 69), the part of it where sentiments are most *intense*. In addition, Durkheim claims, the sentiments attacked must also be *precise* (1984: 38). This is clearly an application of his general, subsidiary means of differentiating law from morality: moral rules are often fluid, while legal ones are precise.[3] Thus, 'strong, well-defined states' of the collective consciousness 'are at the root of penal law' (1984: 39, 106).

The requirement of 'intensity' distinguishing crimes from other offences against shared beliefs and sentiments is obviously different from the criterion of 'organisation' distinguishing law from morality in general. Whereas the latter criterion appears to lend itself to empirical observation, the former seems less accessible to sociological study. The difficulty for Durkheim here is that the criterion of 'organisation' itself becomes vague in so far as he wishes to identify very early forms of repressive law and punishment.

Thus, it was noted in Chapter 4 that ultimately the simplest identifier of legal organisation is the existence of a court to condemn the offender and determine punishment.[4] But, for Durkheim, this could be just a gathering of everyone in a certain community, or presumably of some of them. No special procedures are necessary for this to be recognised as a court. So the mark of organisation remains unclear. Durkheim's criterion of law reduces to the idea that somehow 'society' is the empirically recognisable author of condemnation and punishment – not individuals in their personal capacity. Thus, the criterion of 'intensity' asserts his claim that punishment – as a public process – affirms,

2. See pp. 60–1, above.
3. See p. 60, above.
4. See p. 60, above.

against a wrongdoer, the special beliefs and values that give an ultimate, irreducible meaning to the idea of society. This does not make
easy the task of distinguishing crime from other wrongs, or legal duties
from moral duties. But it expresses Durkheim's insistence that condemnation and punishment gain their legal quality from the fact that they
are actions of society in general, and never actions of individuals representing only themselves.

The problem of regulatory offences

Crime, therefore, is not defined in terms of the harms it causes.
Durkheim writes:

> There are a whole host of acts which have been, and still are, regarded
> as criminal, without in themselves being harmful to society. The act
> of touching an object that is taboo, or an animal or man who is impure
> or consecrated, of letting the sacred fire die out, of eating certain
> kinds of meat, of not offering the traditional sacrifice on one's parents'
> grave, of not pronouncing the precise ritual formula, or of not
> celebrating certain feasts, etc. – how have these ever constituted a
> danger to society? Yet we know the prominent position occupied in
> the repressive law of a large number of peoples by such a regulation
> of ritual, etiquette, ceremonial and religious practices. (1984: 32)

Crime, for Durkheim, is a matter of offence to sentiments or beliefs.
Thus, the reaction to crime – punishment – is not a rational social
defence against harm done or threatened. It is a *passionate reaction*, a
matter of feelings.

He certainly does not wish, however, to convey the idea that fickle
attitudes inspire punishment, or that attributing criminality depends
on shifting public opinion. The sentiments concerned 'are in no way
mere halting, superficial caprices of the will, but emotions and dispositions strongly rooted within us' (1984: 37). This actually makes
criminal law more permanent and stable than most other forms of law.
It changes slowly because the most fundamental moral sentiments that
determine the law are well established and evolve only gradually. Penal
law is thus 'the one sector of positive law least amenable to change'
(1984: 37).

The force of this claim can be seen when fundamental criminal
offences such as murder or theft are considered. Prohibitions central
to criminal law stay recognisably the same in many societies over
time. But when we move away from this moral 'core' of the law,
problems are more obvious. The law concerned to punish rather than

to compensate seems much less stable and unchanging than he suggests. For example, nowadays much penal law consists of what is called 'regulatory law'. This includes penal health and safety laws, environmental and anti-pollution laws, trading standards and consumer protection regulations. Its purpose is to protect general health and welfare. Leon Sheleff argues that it is hard to know how regulatory law fits into Durkheim's picture of the development of repressive law, although Sheleff seems to see it as a kind of repressive law in Durkheim's sense (Sheleff, 1997: ch. 9). But, in fact, although regulatory law uses penal sanctions it seems unlike Durkheim's repressive law. It is not obviously the stable expression of intense beliefs and sentiments common to average members of society. It is a technical and variable kind of regulation. It seems concerned to balance competing commercial and consumer interests. It does not necessarily express generally shared cultural values so much as policy determined by government and framed according to administrative imperatives.

Durkheim has little concern with regulatory law and, in so far as it existed in his era, it was certainly less extensive than in many legal systems today. But he does recognise the existence of offences unlike ordinary crimes. He notes that offences of fishing or hunting in the close season or having an overloaded vehicle on the highway do not strongly engage public sentiments. And his explanation of the reason why these offences are punished more severely than public sentiment often demands is important even if very briefly developed. 'It is undoubtedly the case', he claims, 'that once some governmental authority is instituted it possesses enough power of itself to attach penal sanctions on its own initiative to certain rules of conduct. By its own action it has the ability to create certain crimes or to attach greater seriousness to the criminal character of certain others' (1984: 41). How does governmental authority – the state – acquire this power? It is because, in taking on the general task of punishing wrongdoers on behalf of society, the state expresses the collective consciousness and is assumed to be its defender. 'It thus becomes the symbol of that consciousness, in everybody's eyes its living expression' (1984: 42). Here, then, Durkheim suggests a moral basis of governmental authority. Government, up to a point and under certain conditions, is treated as being generally authorised to act by the collective consciousness. The consequence is that the state can create rules which it enforces penally even where these rules are not supported by strong public sentiment. The state does not merely act as the mouthpiece of the collective consciousness.

Although Durkheim insists that crime is a single category always to be explained in the same way (1984: 41–2) it is clear that he has in mind at least two different categories of offences: first, crimes that directly affront strong public sentiments and, second, offences created by the state and punished merely because they break the state's rules. In the first category there is a direct link between crime and popular sentiments and beliefs. In the second, there is no such necessary link. Popular sentiment does not necessarily support the content of the law. It supports the state's authority to govern, which is a very important but quite different matter. This distinction seems to mirror legal opinion. Common law historically distinguished between *mala in se*, actions wrongful in themselves, and *mala prohibita*, actions wrong because they are specifically prohibited (Gross, 1979: 122–4). The underpinning of law's authority as regards the former is strong moral sentiment diffused throughout society at large. In the latter case the source of legal authority lies in the state's general legislative legitimacy.[5] Durkheim is able to recognise this distinction but his theory of crime and punishment can say little that is useful about the nature of regulatory offences because it cannot explain their content at all. They are merely what the state, for one reason or another, creates. And punishment of them has none of the meaning that attaches to punishment in Durkheim's general theory. It is not a passionate reaction, an affirmation of society's shared beliefs or a strengthening of common convictions. Ultimately, we are forced to accept that Durkheim has no place for regulatory law in his general understanding of repressive law and its workings.

Indeed, Paul Fauconnet, in his Durkheimian study of the nature of responsibility (Fauconnet, 1928), suggests that Durkheim's simple distinction between repressive and restitutive sanctions needs supplementing. Responsibility, for Fauconnet, is the quality attributed to those persons chosen morally or legally to be subjects of a sanction, in Durkheim's sense. In order to analyse the many forms of responsibility recognised in different societies at various times in history, Fauconnet argues, it is important to identify, beside Durkheim's repressive and restitutive sanctions, a third class of 'mixed sanctions' combining elements of punishment and restitution (1928: 13–14). There is no reason why Durkheim's original categorisation of repressive and restitutive law – introduced specifically for the purposes of his discussion of forms of solidarity in *The Division of Labour* – should not be supplemented.

Regulatory law might well be considered to create a form of responsibility identified by mixed sanctions in Fauconnet's sense. The form of the law is penal and it is used to vindicate values that are general in society (for example, the values of public health and a safe environment). But it is also law that reflects problems created by the modern intensification of social interaction (Sheleff, 1997: 179). Often it seeks

---

5. For Durkheim's theory of the basis of this legitimacy, elaborated after publication of *The Division of Labour*, see Chapters 10 and 11, below.

to normalise social or economic relations and to facilitate reliable transactions. It mediates between the entrepreneur and the consumer. And, as is well known, the practices by which regulatory law is applied are often those of negotiation, compromise and balancing, no less than of penal enforcement (Cotterrell, 1992: ch. 8). Regulatory law has strong *restitutive* aspects.

Thus, the proliferation of regulatory offences does not necessarily undermine Durkheim's claim about the fundamental character of repressive law. It merely forces us to recognise that the categories of repressive and restitutive law are not exclusive, for the purposes of analysis of law. They present a polarity that matches the polarity of mechanical and organic solidarity but is not necessarily appropriate to represent the whole range of law with which sociology might concern itself.

 ## Punishment, morality and utility

These questions about regulatory law are important because they reveal Durkheim's discussion of punishment as limited and incomplete (cf. Garland, 1990: 46). He underemphasises important uses of penal sanctions because his concern is to link penal law with shared beliefs and understandings. He wants to connect this law not with political debate and policy but directly with culture – that is, in this context, with understandings, evaluations and judgements arising and reinforced in the everyday experience of collective life. Although, in modern societies, the state and its agencies punish crime, Durkheim portrays the state in a subsidiary role in this context. It is the agent of culture or, more specifically, of the collective consciousness.

Denial of State role [margin annotation]

This emphasis is no doubt the result of the bipolarity of repressive and restitutive law that is central to the theses of *The Division of Labour*. Restitutive law reflects moral differences and complexities of social organisation that government must mediate and organise. So this kind of regulation demands governmental creativity. But penal law, by and large, falls into another category. As the form of law that arises earliest in the development of societies, it can exist with minimal organisation. What defines it and gives it authority is not governmental organisation but cultural homogeneity. It gains its immense moral force from the intense shared beliefs expressed directly through it. It is the agent not of political power but of popular moral sentiment.

Much that is important about penal law is swept aside by this emphasis. This can be seen by referring again to Durkheim's attempt to distinguish technical rules from moral rules, considered in Chapter 4. It was noted there that he claims that utilitarian considerations are essential to technical rules and encourage obedience to them, but that these considerations do not apply to compliance with moral duties.[6] Morality is not a matter of calculating personal advantage. But Durkheim does not seem to see that, for example, hygiene rules or rules about driving a vehicle safely become morally sanctioned when their breach threatens harm to other people. Such rules are incorporated into moral rules to prevent social harm. Thus, even though a rule of moral conduct is obeyed for itself – because the rule is good – its content may derive from utilitarian calculations about harm. The line between utility and morality cannot be drawn in the way Durkheim wishes. The argument applies to law, which for Durkheim is only a special part of morality. Thus, much of regulatory law actually consists of hygiene rules or other technical rules turned into moral rules and – because of the social seriousness of breaking them – legally sanctioned. At their base are utilitarian considerations.

Morality can still have the characteristics Durkheim sees as important to it even if utilitarian considerations often inform moral rules. He never makes clear why he wants to distinguish morality and utility so firmly. But the reason is surely that utilitarian calculations threaten to replace solidarity entirely with personal interest at the heart of moral rules. Utilitarian calculations are supposedly rational judgements of interest which individuals and groups can make for themselves, but which governments might make for them. Utilitarianism makes the calculation of balance of interests paramount. But if utility underlies morality it makes law also a matter of this balancing. Durkheim, however, wants to see law as transcending questions of interests (that would reduce it to politics) and focusing on moral requirements of solidarity, integration and co-operation. Utility is a matter of compromises between particular claims (cf. Cladis, 1992: 15). But law should, in Durkheim's view, express the *common requirements of social well-being*. This role is what gives law its moral authority. Sometimes this role involves expressing shared beliefs or sentiments. Sometimes (and increasingly in modern societies) it entails forging common requirements out of the experiences of different functional groups and framing them as restitutive law. But this is different from merely compromising interests.

We shall see in later chapters that Durkheim's attempt to marginalise the balancing of interests as a function of law is central to much of his legal theory. But he tends to take the exclusion of interests from law far further than his moralistic theory really requires. Surely all that is necessary is to insist that compromising interests is not a *sufficient* role for law. To possess moral authority, law must have a different role. It must express and promote collective, unifying values. But as a subsidiary or derivative matter it undoubtedly makes possible the compromising of private claims and interests.

6. See pp. 58–9, above.

Punishment and the nature of the state

For Durkheim, penal law is stable and enduring because it is firmly grounded in the most fundamental shared beliefs and sentiments of the society in which it exists. But surely punishment practices (quite apart from those associated with regulatory offences) can vary greatly for reasons that have little to do with the slow evolution of the collective consciousness. They may reflect political expediency or partisan prejudices. Crimes caused or suffered by members of one part of a population may be judged differently from those caused or suffered by members of another. Often variations relate to the fact that society consists of different social classes, or different ethnic, religious or other groups. Sometimes criminal prosecutions and judicial decisions do not just depend on abstract definitions of criminal offences, but on who, in fact, commits these offences and against whom (see, for example, Black, 1976). Official views and policies on such matters may vary with time and place, even in the same society. Sometimes, the definitions of offences themselves are modified by reference to different kinds of offender and victim. Durkheim does not seem to consider any of these factors, or even recognise their salience.

In one respect only, he considers the relationship between types of political regime and patterns of punishment. His paper 'Two laws of penal evolution' (Durkheim, 1973b), published eight years after *The Division of Labour*, modifies the ideas about punishment set out in his earlier work, but also builds on them. As regards the possibility of deliberate, politically introduced changes in penal law and practice, he offers in this essay a new, general hypothesis: the intensity of punishment is greater (other things being equal) the more absolute the government in a society becomes – in other words, the more that government lacks legal restraints on its powers. Thus, punishment and the operation of repressive law are not just determined by stable, long enduring and slowly evolving moral sentiments diffused throughout society, as his earlier writing claimed. They can also be determined by the nature of state power. The more absolute the regime, the more severe the punishments employed (Durkheim, 1973b: 22).

To explain this correlation he extends his earlier direct linking of punishment with the collective consciousness. In *The Division of Labour* he had noted that crimes against the state are often punished more severely than public opinion demands (1984: 41). The explanation for this was that the state becomes the 'symbol' and 'living expression' (1984: 42) of society's collective beliefs. Attacks on the state are thus treated as attacks on the collective consciousness itself rather than on any particular aspect of it. So they are specially serious. The state's role as the agent of essential cultural values is itself protected by punishment.

This idea of the state as moral agent is extended in 'Two laws of penal evolution'. When the state becomes absolute, Durkheim argues, its moral power as symbol and living expression of society's beliefs is intensified and overlaid with a kind of religiosity. He writes:

> The constitution of an absolute power necessarily has the effect of raising the one who wields it above the rest of humanity, making of him something superhuman . . . In fact, wherever the government takes this form, the one who controls it appears to the people as a divinity . . . [They] see in the power which is invested in him an emanation of divine power. From that moment, this religiosity cannot fail to have its usual effects on punishment. On the one hand, offences directed against a being so palpably superior to all its offenders will not be considered as ordinary crimes, but as sacrilegious acts and, by virtue of this, will be violently repressed. (1973b: 45)

On the other hand, since all law in such a society is attributed to the sovereign power, major violations will always be seen as attacks on this power and punished as such. Absolutism thus, by its nature, infuses intense sentiment into the collective consciousness. The nature of the state makes a difference, Durkheim seems to be arguing, because the state as the medium by which collective sentiment is focused and expressed in punishment can inflame this sentiment, like a magnifying glass that concentrates the sun's rays to create fire. To this extent, the nature of the state itself is a concern of penal theory.

Functions of crime and punishment

Durkheim's analysis of the politics of punishment does not go beyond this. He considers no other political factors that might disrupt slow, evolutionary change in penal law and its operation.[7] The nature of penal law is defined in relation to shared beliefs and understandings – to cultural rather than political conditions. Durkheim sees that the state as an instrument of the collective consciousness gains a degree of independent authority to punish. But he has nothing to say about the ways in which this authority might be used, or its scope. So he offers few resources for analysing political repression sociologically. The authority that interests him is moral authority. Where this authority depends on collective sentiment he sees the state as having little influence over it. The situation is different as regards restitutive law, which

---

7. Durkheim's published lectures on the theory of the state, considered in Chapters 10 and 11 below, entirely ignore the question of punishment.

is not tied to cultural conditions in the same way. Restitutive law reflects the complexity of social structure and, as will be seen later, there is no reason why it cannot serve as a governmental instrument actively shaping social relations.[8]

Thus Durkheim's view of the nature of crime and punishment has serious limitations. Treated as a partial perspective on relationships between law and culture, it is valuable in encouraging questions as to how collective convictions are expressed through penal law and practices. But some of his most famous claims seem merely sensational. For example, he argues that crime and the shared sentiments of the collective conciousness are actually symbiotic. According to Durkheim, it would be impossible to have a society without crime because the intense sentiments that crime offends would fade unless they were strengthened through punishment of offenders. 'Thus there would result a relaxation of the bonds of social solidarity' (1984: 63). The existence of crime 'draws honest consciousnesses together, concentrating them' (1984: 58). Thus society, up to a point, actually *needs* crime to strengthen its moral unity through the condemnation of those considered to have offended this unity. This argument is, to say the least, unproven (Hart, 1967) – can these sentiments not be sustained by other means? But it allows Durkheim to claim that crime 'is a factor in public health, an integrative element in any healthy society' (1982a: 98). This remarkable statement should not, however, be taken at face value. It is not criminal acts but the condemnations and punishments following them (and defining them as crime) that are, for him, integrative elements.

Nevertheless, he does suggest that occasionally criminal acts in themselves have value. If all behaviour conformed to dominant social sentiments, society would be unbearably repressive. The existence of crime shows, up to a point, individuality in society (Durkheim, 1982a: 101); in other words, a degree of creative non-conformity which only in certain circumstances produces criminal acts. Also, in exceptional cases, crime can indicate behaviour which, while presently condemned as contrary to society's legal demands, is 'an anticipation of the morality to come' (1982a: 102). Thus, Socrates' prescient questioning of prevailing Athenian morality led to his condemnation. Durkheim stresses that moral criminals of this kind seek not merely to reject rules as inconvenient, but to put a new moral rule in place of the old (1961: 53). In his terms, they assert autonomy as one of morality's important components.[9]

He has little interest in criminal motivations as such (Vogt, 1993: 76). Psychology may study individual criminals but, for Durkheim, crime is to be understood sociologically. The claim that crime is, to a

8. See Chapter 7, below.
9. See pp. 63, above.

degree, necessary to society is one of the clearest illustrations of his early, rather militant functional outlook. Crime as a social fact has a functional relationship to society as a whole. A 'normal' amount of crime in any society promotes integration. This is because it is the focus of punishment which reaffirms collective sentiments. Crime also represents the extremes of a non-conformity essential in some degree for social development. If a society had no crime it would have to invent some, Durkheim declares. Even a society of saints would need its deviants: members who could be condemned for failing to meet the shared standards of the group (1982a: 100). However saintly everyone was, the group would decide that some were not saintly enough. In this way the collective consciousness could be reaffirmed by condemnation and punishment.

Durkheim's view that the condemnation and punishment of some is essential to the moral unity of the rest, so that it must be engineered by more stringent standards if necessary, is not merely unproven but dangerous. It suggests, groundlessly, that a community of shared beliefs can exist only through an aggressive solidarity based on hatred of outsiders, those not sharing or acting on the same beliefs. This kind of aggressive solidarity is certainly often a factor in unifying social groups. But there is no reason to assume its functional necessity.

He is on much stronger ground in recognising that where a society is united by common sentiments and values it must express these publicly in some way and that some will be expressed in law. Law vindicates these sentiments and values (1984: 63; 1961: 167) and punishes attacks on them in some way. But everything turns on how it does this. Both political and moral considerations would seem to be important in this context. Durkheim is also on strong ground in recognising the social value, indeed necessity, of a degree of non-conformity. The most productive idea that emerges from his account of the functions of crime and punishment is of a continuous negotiation between freedom and constraint in society: innovation in behaviour on the one hand, and control of deviance on the other. Penal law should be concerned with this process of negotiation. But the image of repressive law in *The Division of Labour* is mainly one of constraint.

Variations in punishment

The process of negotiation just referred to is highlighted in Durkheim's accounts of penal variation and evolution. In many ways these are the most important parts of his discussion of punishment because they make clear his view that criminal law and punishment practices change their character fundamentally throughout history. While criminal law serves a constant repressive function – protecting and expressing shared beliefs and sentiments – its content changes radically, because the collective consciousness that underpins it is itself radically altered in character. But to understand Durkheim's view of penal evolution it is necessary to put it in the context of his more general ideas about variation in punishment.

He notes in *The Division of Labour* (1984: 63, 68) that punishment is always proportionate to the crime committed. It may be a passionate reaction but it is also a calculated one, measuring the criminal's act against a standard. Punishment is inflicted not with the criminal's concerns in view but to vindicate the sentiments of the law-abiding (1984: 63). Nevertheless, in his later lectures on *Moral Education*, Durkheim discusses punishment in terms of its effect on the punished. This is a highly significant shift of emphasis. The essence of punishment, he writes, is the sense of blame it arouses (1961: 181). To punish is to express disapproval of the misdeed. This implies that punishment is a kind of *communication process*, 'a notation, a language' (1961: 176). Far from being mere social vengeance wreaked on the offender, it is the calculated creation of an understanding or definition of a social situation (the offence) through certain rituals. Speaking of the punishment of children in school, he suggests that the object is to give the child 'the most vivid impression possible of the feelings evoked by his behaviour' (1961: 182). Excessively harsh punishment is counterproductive. It distorts the message. It does not convey exactly to what extent normal sentiments have been disturbed by the wrong committed. In relation both to the offender and the law-abiding population punishment should seem meaningful (1961: 197; and see Garland, 1990: 45).

It is true that when Durkheim emphasises the importance of meaning to the offender his context is that of punishment in schools, as part of the process of education. But he usually makes no clear distinction between the nature of punishment in this context and in relation to society at large, and he often refers to both contexts together.[10] He refers to the school as a small society (see also Garland, 1990: 41ff.). Thus, there is some warrant for suggesting that the process of punishment involves a kind of negotiation of reality by both the punishing authority and the offender being punished. Punishment is an attribution of status – that of criminal or rule-breaker – to an individual (cf. Garfinkel, 1956). And it is important to the affirmation of society's values and beliefs that this status be understood and accepted *by the offender* as well as by society at large.

Careful grading of the intensity of punishment in relation to the offence (Durkheim, 1984: 48, 52) is essential to this process. Since

10. See, for example, Durkheim (1961: 166–8, 197, 202–3).

blame – and, ideally, its acceptance by the offender – is central, suffering for its own sake is not required (1961: 176, 198–9). In any case, he suggests, punishment cannot make 'basically rebellious souls really suffer' (1961: 168) – presumably meaning that it cannot make them suffer regret. More generally, as the severity of punishment increases, its influence lessens (1961: 200). Punishment is whatever is required to assert convincingly the validity and power of the particular shared sentiments that the wrongdoer has offended in the particular context of the offence.

Punishment acts 'from the outside and on externals' so it 'cannot touch the moral life at its source' (1961: 161). Nevertheless, penal discipline of adult offenders ought to be 'a kind of educational rehabilitation' and punishment should, where possible, be 'useful to him who is punished' (1961: 197). By 'useful' Durkheim, of course, means morally useful in encouraging adjustment to society's moral code. This is entirely different from deterring the offender from future offences, or deterring others from similar conduct. The effectiveness of deterrence in either of these forms 'may rightly be questioned; in any case it is mediocre' (1984: 62–3). Deterrence involves inducing people merely to make a utilitarian calculation that their best interests lie in compliance. It does not address the moral significance of conduct. Again, for Durkheim, morality lies beyond utilitarian considerations.

These ideas summarise his ideals for punishment in modern conditions. But what of the values that punishment communicates and affirms? The picture of penal evolution Durkheim paints shows penal practice increasingly moving towards the forms indicated above, though he hints that there is still a long way to go (1973b: 47). The values and shared sentiments that punishment gradually comes to express make it both possible and necessary to treat the offender's situation and perceptions as relevant to the success or otherwise of the punishment process and to make the grading of punishments reflect not only society's shared sentiments (1984: 57) but also a kind of negotiation between these and the offender's self-perception and personality.

The evolution of punishment

At one level Durkheim insists that punishment's character has remained unchanged throughout history (1984: 48). It has always marked out the guilty person, 'holding him at a distance, ostracising him, making a void around him, and separating him from decent people' (1961: 175). But primitive societies, he suggests, punish in ways that modern societies tend to disfavour. They punish for the sake of punishing, 'causing the guilty person to suffer solely for the sake of suffering and without expecting any advantage to themselves from the suffering they inflict.' They do not aim to punish 'fairly or usefully' (1984: 44) and they often direct punishment at animals or inanimate things. Often the wrongdoer's kin are punished. In early societies it may not be important to connect a responsible individual with the wrong done. Punishment seems blind or clumsily directed, ending only when passions are spent (1984: 44).

In 'Two laws of penal evolution', alongside the claim about the relationship between absolutism and penal severity, Durkheim proposes two further hypotheses about the way punishment develops as societies develop. Both hypotheses relate to the kinds of punishments exacted. He argues, first, that the less developed the society is, the more severe punishments tend to be. Secondly, he claims that, as social development proceeds, deprivation of liberty, varying in time with the severity of the crime, tends to become the normal and sole means of penal control. Less developed societies use a wide variety of punishments, usually relatively severe. More developed societies favour imprisonment for a prescribed period as the normal means of punishing.

Many criticisms have been made of these hypotheses as summations of penal history. It is hard to see neat correlations between stages of social development and penal practices (see, for example, Spitzer, 1975, 1979; Lenman and Parker, 1980; Grabosky, 1978). But it is certainly true that in modern Western societies imprisonment has come to occupy a place of prominence in penal practice that it does not have in earlier times. It is also true that in these societies the general tendency has been to abolish, as morally unacceptable, the most barbaric and extreme physical punishments – for example, killing, mutilation and torture. Durkheim's explanation of these developments is important. In modern society the central, shared sentiment which criminal law and punishment vindicates and protects attaches supreme value to the individual life and individual dignity. This does not mean that in practice individual dignity is, indeed, protected. It means only that there is a widespread conviction and an official recognition that it should be. The central areas of criminal law have become those protecting the physical person (for example, offences of murder, manslaughter, rape and assault) and property (such as offences of theft, criminal damage or fraud). Most other offences no longer register significantly in public consciousness (Durkheim, 1957: 110). The vast collective consciousness of earlier times, imbued with traditional religious overtones, has been reduced to a small but important modern compass. The modern value that underlies penal law and punishment is *the value of human dignity and the protection of the security of persons and their property*.

We shall examine later Durkheim's important explanation of why this value, which demands respect for *all* individuals and punishes the most blatant denials of this respect, becomes so important in modern society.[11] It is enough to note here that he explains the two principles of penal evolution mentioned above in terms of it. If the individual is the focus of the criminal law's protection the intensity of punishment lessens because an 'offence of man against man cannot arouse the same indignation as an offence of man against God', as when criminal law was replete with traditional religious overtones in earlier societies (1973b: 42). More importantly, offenders are individuals too and the respect for human dignity must extend even to them. So punishment must take some account of the offender's welfare, putting limits to severity. Punishment of an offender's body would violently affront respect for his human dignity and seriously transgress the very value that is central to the law (1961: 183).[12] Hence the individual is no longer typically subjected to physical punishment. Punishment normally involves constraining the offender's freedom for a time. But it must not involve cruel or degrading treatment or conditions. Conversely, where the value of individuality weakens and becomes subordinated to a concern only for the group and its interests – as in war, family vendettas or political claims of state necessity – individual life and property again lose the respect that in other circumstances in modern conditions they normally attract (1957: 116–17).

Another reason, beyond those he himself gives but consistent with his theories, for the use of imprisonment as the favoured modern punishment for serious crime can be suggested. If in modern society the moral conditions of solidarity are those of interdependence, then removal from that situation of interdependence is morally the most severe punishment. If meaning is given to individual life by the responsibility of playing one's part, fulfilling one's functional role, then to be imprisoned is to be forcibly excluded from the world of moral meaning created by the division of labour. The moral message of imprisonment is that the prisoner is no longer a part of the structures of interdependence in society. Imprisonment must not undermine the prisoner's physical well-being. But it takes away moral well-being, and, no doubt in Durkheim's view, works best if it encourages the prisoner to reflect constructively on the causes and consequences of this situation.

Thus crime and punishment in Durkheim's view keep their essential character yet change fundamentally in content over time. The *broad* picture of change which he identifies in modern penal history seems plausible, and the idea that a supreme value of the worth of the individual emerges as the basis of modern penal practice is one important

11. See pp. 112–15, below.
12. For related reasons, Durkheim (1961: 182) opposes all use of corporal punishment in schools.

aspect of a wider and fundamental claim about contemporary values that underpins Durkheim's explanation of the nature of modern law. It will be examined in Part 3 of this book. As so often in Durkheim's writings the imaginative sweep of explanation is thought provoking and valuable. Perhaps it is especially valuable in his later writings where he tends to leave behind the early emphasis of *The Division of Labour* on crime and punishment as purely collective phenomena and emphasises the individual as both object of protection and focus of retribution through penal practices. But his image of a steady, uniform evolutionary penal development is problematic (Garland, 1990: 48ff.). History is more complex and contradictory than Durkheim implies. To understand how significant historical evidence may be in assessing his ideas it is necessary to evaluate his picture of legal evolution as a whole. This is the concern of the next chapter.

6

Legal evolution

This chapter is concerned with Durkheim's general ideas on the historical development of law. Interpreting his thought here requires much effort to escape from past misunderstandings. The thesis on legal evolution which is such a prominent feature of *The Division of Labour* is the most famous and perhaps most frequently misinterpreted aspect of his writings on law. Disproving it seems to have been one of social science's simplest tasks. But my argument is that much of this criticism has missed its mark and that the legal evolution thesis has often been judged by the wrong criteria. In fact, it is not intended to provide a comprehensive explanation of legal development. It has a different object. This chapter examines the purpose of the thesis, the kinds of criticism it has received, and the way it illustrates Durkheim's distinctive conception of the nature of law.

The legal evolution thesis

As has been seen, a direct link is proposed in *The Division of Labour* between forms of law (repressive and restitutive) and forms of solidarity (mechanical and organic). Durkheim claims that as societies become more complex and functionally differentiated, organic solidarity becomes the predominant form of solidarity, while mechanical solidarity declines in relative significance. Since law reflects these forms of solidarity, this evolutionary movement can be plotted by studying legal change. In the legal systems of simple and ancient societies, repressive law is found to predominate. In more complex societies, restitutive law prevails. Thus, a pattern of legal evolution is suggested. As societies become more complex, repressive law increasingly gives way to restitutive law.

The cause of this evolution, according to Durkheim, is the advancing division of labour. The process of specialization of social tasks and roles changes the conditions and nature of social solidarity. Greater social differentiation undermines the possibility for shared beliefs and sentiments to provide the basis of law and solidarity. Hence repressive law, expressing these beliefs and sentiments, declines in scope. But differentiation of roles also promotes interdependence. Specialists depend on other specialists. The parts of society cannot exist without the whole. Functional co-ordination and integration are the consequence of, and also condition for, the continuing progress of the division of labour. Hence restitutive law, concerned entirely with fostering and guaranteeing this integration and balancing relationships, grows.

The division of labour itself progresses because of 'certain variations of the social environment' (1984: 200). These relate to what Durkheim calls *social morphology* – the structure of society, the way its population is distributed and organised at a certain point in its development and in relation to its environment (1982a: 241–2). The division of labour advances when certain conditions of social morphology are met. The organisation of social life exclusively on the basis of kinship groups or clans must have given way to a looser patterning which makes possible more varied interaction. Increased social interaction results from population growth, greater geographical concentration of population and the development of towns, and improvement in communications and means of travel (1984: 201–4). Eventually ties to locality also weaken with social mobility (1984: 138–9). Thus, according to Durkheim's thesis, the evolution of law is not caused by changes in values or beliefs, political theories or legal experience. It is promoted by changes, over which individuals have little control, in the *organisational structure* of societies over long historical periods. The consequence is that the proportion of law devoted to punishment declines, while the proportion devoted to compensation, restitution and the repairing or balancing of social relationships increases.

Here, apparently, is a bold, testable claim about legal change over the centuries. Durkheim uses evidence from the law of Ancient Greece and Egypt, the Twelve Tables of early Roman law, the Biblical law of the Pentateuch, the Indian Laws of Manu and the Salic law of the Franks, among other sources. For each legal system referred to, he tries to assess the stage of social development of the relevant society and the proportion of repressive law in its legal codes. In societies judged as least socially developed he finds that law is dominated by religious prohibitions (for example, relating to sacrilege, ceremonies and rituals, or sexual relations) and penal sanctions. Thus, ancient Jewish law is almost wholly penal and replete with religious offences (1984: 35, 112). The Laws of Manu are strongly penal (1984: 94–5). The law of the Greek city states is less dominated by harsh punishment and less penal in its treatment of sexual morals than ancient Jewish law (1984: 109, 110). But laws governing dress, the shaving of beards, and the coiffure of women illustrate its penal detail (1984: 111), typical of early law.

Durkheim presents early Roman law and society as much more advanced. In the law of the Twelve Tables 'we find in embryonic form the main elements of our present body of law, whereas there is nothing in common, so to speak, between Hebraic law and our own'; the Roman law is 'completely secular' and 'presented from the beginning as an entirely human edifice intended to cover only human relationships' (1984: 95). Repressive and restitutive rules are, by this time, clearly distinguished from each other. Yet penal law is still very extensive. In Durkheim's view, the presently available sources of Roman law probably underestimate the extent of penal law, given that there was less need to elaborate it in so far as it was popularly understood, and perhaps less juristic interest in doing so (1984: 96; and see Daube, 1973). Durkheim's claims about underestimation here have been dismissed as 'idle speculation' (Sheleff, 1997: 118), but they emphasise his views about the nature of early law.

He says less in this context about more modern legal systems. He seems content to allow the reader to compare specific, if impressionistic, claims about ancient law with general, commonsense perceptions of more recent legal conditions. Thus, in modern law the panoply of religious offences associated with early law has disappeared. As noted in Chapter 5, Durkheim emphasises that criminal law has become largely restricted to the protection of the individual from harm – a concern substantially absent from much early penal law, since individual harm often led not to punishment but to some form of compensation. Alongside orthodox criminal law, which is thus much reduced in scope, contract and commercial law flourish in modern law. So does the law of compensation for civil wrongs (tort or delict). Constitutional and administrative law and a whole apparatus of other legal forms have developed to provide intricate regulatory structures for organising and co-ordinating social, political and economic relationships.

The triumph of restitutive law is also the triumph of highly organised over loosely organised law. It demands bureaucratic structures largely absent from early penal systems. Law becomes increasingly a governmental system concerned with expressing and co-ordinating the functional interdependence that typifies modern societies. It is no longer the expression of a uniform collective consciousness except as regards one limited but vitally important moral sphere – the protection of individual life and dignity. Law is thus portrayed in *The Division of Labour* as having severed its ties from religion to become the modern instrument of social and economic co-ordination.

Law as a sociological concept

In setting out the legal evolution thesis, Durkheim presents law as an index or measure. If the measure is inaccurate, his wider claims about social solidarity may be suspect. Hence criticism of the legal evolution thesis is encouraged by the sociological prominence Durkheim gives it. But jurists and legal sociologists have often taken it solely as a gener- alisation about legal history. Then the question becomes, simply, is Durkheim right to argue that law becomes less concerned with punish- ment? Do penal sanctions play a less significant role in law? At the end of the last chapter it was seen that, for penologists, other questions are added by the 'Two laws of penal evolution' essay. Does punish- ment become less harsh as societies become more developed? Is there a steady progress towards deprivation of liberty as the sole and normal penal sanction?

If the thesis is taken simply as a claim about legal history – that is, about the destiny of the penal element in law, it is easy to criticise. Leon Sheleff points to the growth of regulatory law, noted in the previous chapter, and the punitive use of tort law to show that penal sanctioning proliferates in contemporary societies (Sheleff, 1997: chs 7 and 9). He argues that, historically, penal law expands as states become powerful enough to take over the control of interpersonal conflict, previ- ously left to individuals or feuding groups. Indeed, he suggests that the actual process of legal evolution is the reverse of what Durkheim proposed: there is a historical movement from restitutive to repressive law (Sheleff, 1975: 19–20; 1997: 137).

It is vital to recognise, however, that Durkheim's thesis is *not intended as a survey of legal history*. To treat it in this way is to misunderstand the specific sociological purpose of the concepts of repressive and resti- tutive law. They gain their meaning *only* in relation to the concepts of mechanical and organic solidarity. They do not offer a comprehensive conceptualisation of the scope of law or its transformations. Careful attention to the meanings of Durkheim's terms is needed. The temp- tation is to assimilate them to categories more familiar to lawyers or sociologists, or to assume a definition of law that is not Durkheim's. Thus, it was suggested in Chapter 5 that regulatory law is effectively left outside the scope of the legal classifications in *The Division of Labour*. Indeed, there are general problems with testing the presence of repres- sive and restitutive law in legal history. Sociological concepts are not necessarily translatable into legal ones. The sociological concepts of repressive and restitutive law are not formulated for analysing law in terms of lawyers' ideas and arguments.

Thus, it is significant that Durkheim, who is usually careful to define his terms, makes almost no effort to relate repressive and restitutive law precisely to familiar legal categories. Introducing his concepts, he briefly associates repressive law with penal sanctions and restitutive law with contract, commercial, constitutional and administrative law. But he does not differentiate these legal fields rigorously or describe their varying functions in relation to restitutive law (see Durkheim, 1984: 29). In *The Division of Labour* he seems uninterested in lawyers' legal categories. He wants only to distinguish clearly, on the one hand, an idea of punishment as a passionate social reaction and, on the other, an idea of functional social co-ordination through regulation. In fact, lawyers recognise numerous kinds of penal rules and sanctions involving combinations of punishment, restitution, rectification, nullification, disqualification and compensation. But Durkheim's concern is only with society condemning the offender in a ritual of some kind. Again, while lawyers distinguish many kinds of regulation concerning arbitration, mediation, compromise, representation, participation, governance, mutual responsibility and organisation, Durkheim is concerned only with a general idea of society legally balancing different specialised functions within it.

This is why it is extremely difficult to confront Durkheim's thesis with evidence from legal history. His concepts specify *social conditions rather than legal ideas.* For example, it must be 'society' that condemns the offender if repressive law is to exist, so society must be organised in a way that makes this collective action possible. Private vengeance or feud is to be distinguished from society punishing. The latter requires a collective condemnation of the offender by or on behalf of *society as a whole.* But it is not always easy to see when procedures will be identifiable as those of society acting rather than individuals or specific groups.

Again, private arbitrations or local systems of mediation to resolve disputes have no necessary relationship with restitutive law. For this law to exist it must be possible for *society as a whole,* in some way, to balance the functions that make up the entirety of social life. Society, and not individuals negotiating with each other or calling on third-party mediators or arbitrators, is the author of restitutive law. Thus, this law presupposes the relatively high degree of social organisation and centralisation of regulatory power that makes society-wide co-ordination feasible. Again, the question is what indicates that a certain historical situation is to be interpreted as a matter of 'society' regulating through restitutive law rather than merely a matter of individuals or groups negotiating compensatory compromises.

Durkheim makes abundantly clear in his writings that society's involvement in sanctioning distinguishes law from arbitration or mediation on the one hand, and feud and vengeance on the other. The starting point for law is 'society's intervention in the settlement of conflicts' (Durkheim, 1983a: 150). Arbitration is possible when a shared conception of goals of mutual protection keeps in check the struggle between opposed individual interests. But it becomes a matter of law only when given a *general social guarantee.* This does not need to be a matter of enforcement by state agencies because law can exist before the state: law's ultimate authority is not political but lies in the 'very conscience of societies' (1983a: 149). For the emergence of the idea of a legal wrong – an offence – 'it is sufficient that there is a coherent society conscious of its unity' (1983a: 150).

This consciousness of unity surely implies the existence of a collective consciousness in Durkheim's sense. Hence it seems that a collective consciousness and repressive law must precede the social recognition of individual offence and so restitutive law, and that for Durkheim this is a *logical* necessity. This does not mean that laws dealing with harm to individuals cannot be found in ancient legal codes, nor that social life in early or simple societies is free of extensive reciprocal social relationships. It means that laws dealing with harm to individuals must be understood in the context of an evolving collective consciousness, and that reciprocal relationships should not be interpreted as necessarily fundamental to the legal constitution of society. The consequence of Durkheim's position is clear: 'It is wholly inaccurate to make society a kind of third party arbitrator between the other parties' (1984: 70). In essence, law does not reconcile conflicting individual interests, suggest compromises or seek the most advantageous outcome for the parties. It merely applies society's most important moral rules.[1] Of course, the effect of law is that private interests are mediated and compromised, but this is surely a by-product rather than central to law's nature.

Thus, Durkheim's argument about the very nature of restitutive law ensures that what he understands as repressive law must precede it in social development.

As regards the distinction between penal law and feud or vengeance, the arguments are similar. Durkheim's concepts are established in such a way as to make clear that law in its origins is not to be equated with private dispute resolution of any kind (for example between opposing kinship groups) but with the public vindication of collective values and beliefs of society as a whole. Punishment 'has its origins not in vengeance, but in the reaction of the group against its members' (1983b: 157). This is why it is so important to Durkheim to insist on the religious character of early penal law. Religious matters belong to society – the social group as a whole, not to individuals or particular kinship groups. 'Private vengeance is, therefore, far from being the prototype of punishment . . . it is only an incomplete punishment' (1984: 51). It is 'indeed society and not ourselves that we are avenging' through punishment; 'we all know that it is society that punishes' (1984: 48, 57).

The importance of this argument is that for Durkheim force cannot create law in the sense that he understands law. Violence merely leads to other violence. Law must have a moral foundation. It cannot find

---

1. Durkheim (1984: 70); and see pp. 71–2, above.

this in individual or group interests, such as those served by private vengeance or feud, but only in the collective beliefs or values of society as a whole. Vengeance has no conception of a social purpose and so is 'a prey to the blind forces that drive it on, and with nothing to curb its outbursts of rage.'[2] Thus, penal law can be seen as the social control of vengeance, or its formalisation as a social rather than an individual or group action (Duxbury, 1989). This seems to be a particular example of law's role as the regulator of otherwise insatiable desire. Basic to everything is an idea of law as the instrument of society, not of private interest.

It follows that Durkheim can hardly avoid seeing religious prohibitions as central to early penal law. 'The religious life is made up entirely of abnegation and altruism. Thus if criminal law was originally religious law, we may be sure that the interests it served were social' (1984: 49–50). He well recognises that harms to individuals are often dealt with in early and ancient legal systems by provision for compensation rather than by punishment. Protection of the security of the individual is likely to become a central concern of repressive law only when the individual becomes 'sacred' within society's value system as a whole, in other words when the collective consciousness has changed, as in modern societies, to focus on the dignity of the individual as a central value in the shared sentiments of people in general.

Durkheim notes some stages of this increasing appreciation of the individual in law. Thus, vendettas become punishments that are recognised by society as legitimate but left to individuals or groups to carry out. They are partly private and to that extent not legal processes at all (1984: 50) but they show law needing to regulate individual relations. And, in Roman law, 'private offences' are 'a kind of intermediate stage between real crime and the purely civil offence.' Society pronounces sentence but leaves it to the injured party to carry it out (1984: 50). In a sense, law cautiously eases itself into the position of being able to deal with matters that involve individual interests and relationships, as it first allies itself with then formalises and gradually supplants private processes and remedies. Durkheim makes little reference to the factors of political power necessary for this development. They simply do not interest him. As always, his concern is with the moral authority of law which he sees, in this case, as gradually developing to touch individual lives and protect them.[3]

2. Durkheim (1893a: 54; cf. 1984: 45). See also Gewirth (1988: 1046): 'Before law – without courts – there is revenge after revenge, a cycle of violence without end. This . . . is the inner contradiction of revenge: it does not stop. With law, there is the possibility of an ending, both in individual cases and in systemic struggles.'
3. Cf. R. J. Bonner, quoted in Duxbury (1989: 255): 'The idea that murder is a menace to society is modern. In [the Ancient Greece of] Homer it is regarded as the concern of the relatives alone and such partisans as they can assemble.'

Testing Durkheim

These aspects of Durkheim's understanding of law are crucial in evaluating his thesis. But they are often ignored and his ideas are taken out of context. Schwartz and Miller's (1964) comparative analysis of legal development in fifty-one societies has, for example, often been treated as refuting Durkheim (e.g. Clarke, 1976; Sheleff, 1997: 127), despite its authors' caution and the fact that it uses concepts entirely different from Durkheim's. Schwartz and Miller rank societies by relative complexity and try to assess how the development of legal institutions in any particular society corresponds with its degree of complexity. Instead of Durkheim's categories of repressive or restitutive law they use concepts of mediation, police and counsel. Mediation refers to 'regular use of non-kin third party intervention in dispute settlement'. Counsel exist where there is 'regular use of specialised non-kin advocates in the settlement of disputes'. Police refers to a 'specialised armed force used partially or wholly for norm enforcement' (Schwartz and Miller, 1964: 161). Examining the presence of mediation, police and counsel in each of the societies, the study shows that where counsel exist, mediation and police are also found. Where a society has police it almost invariably also has mediation but may not have counsel. Thus an evolutionary development paralleling the growth in complexity of societies and involving the successive appearance of mediation, police and counsel is strongly suggested by the data.[4]

Schwartz and Miller note that restitutive sanctions (damages and mediation) are found in societies lacking even rudimentary specialisation, while organised penal sanctioning accompanies a more developed division of labour. 'Thus Durkheim's hypothesis seems the reverse of the empirical situation in the range of societies studied here' (Schwartz and Miller, 1964: 166). But they note that he specifies more elaborate organisation for restitutive as compared with repressive law: 'In thus suggesting that restitutive law exists only with highly complex organisational forms, Durkheim virtually ensured that his thesis would be proven – that restitutive law would be found only in complex societies' (1964: 166).

As my discussion above may suggest, there is something in this last claim. But it is not entirely fair to Durkheim. As has been seen, he insists that law is regulation by or on behalf of society generally, not on behalf of private or localised group interests. If he had not seen law in this way, he could not have used it in *The Division of Labour* as an index of the character (more specifically the solidarity) of a society as a whole, a unified entity. The idea of law as an instrument of society

---

4. Wimberley (1973) suggests a fourth stage of legal evolution marked by the existence of courts and judges, and occurring between the stage of the emergence of mediation and that of the emergence of police.

as a unity determines the criterion of organisation. The extent of organisation is whatever is necessary for law to fulfil this function in different societies. There must be an adequate framework for judgements to be made, punishments inflicted, rules formulated and regulatory structures developed – on behalf of society at large. The public condemnation of an offender as an expression of shared understandings may need minimal organisation. But more than a minimum is needed for a society-wide working out of understandings and responsibilities governing relationships of functional interdependence.

As Upendra Baxi (1974) has pointed out, repressive law is not what Schwartz and Miller call police. In fact, in a later paper, Schwartz (1974) replaces the police concept with that of 'organised repressive sanctions' and shows that his and Miller's picture of legal evolution is not altered by the substitution. But the deeper difficulty in confronting Durkheim on his own terms surely remains. Repressive law can exist with minimal organisation as long as *something* in the sanctioning process makes clear its public, social character. Thus, its operation 'always tends to some extent to remain diffuse' because it reflects sentiments general throughout society (Durkheim, 1984: 36). The earliest repressive law requires neither police nor much in the way of organisation to identify its social character.

Baxi also notes that to disprove Durkheim it is not enough to show the existence of restitutive sanctioning in simple societies because Durkheim recognises that all societies are likely to contain elements of mechanical and organic solidarity, and so of repressive and restitutive law. But a stronger argument than Baxi's is that Durkheim's restitutive law is quite different from what Schwartz and Miller call mediation (Cotterrell, 1977: 247–8; and see Durkheim, 1984: 70). As noted earlier, Durkheim recognises the presence of mediation and arbitration in early societies, but does not necessarily see these as matters of law. Finally, Baxi notes that Durkheim's concern is less with details of organisation than with types of social control. But again, it might be added that Durkheim's essential, general concern in this respect is with the distinction between public (legal) and private controls, or between societal actions (legal processes) on the one hand, and purely private, individual or localised group actions on the other.

The root of the problem of testing Durkheim's thesis is thus the theoretical issue of the *definition of law*. His mark of law is organised sanctioning. But, as has been seen, this turns out to be a slippery criterion. Organisational requirements for Durkheimian law vary in different social contexts. And Durkheim's legal categories are not designed to correlate with juristic classifications of law. So they take no real account of the varieties of juristic forms in different societies and different periods of history. Durkheim does not provide a sociology of legal history because his use of legal materials is too impressionistic and generalised. And, far from trying to observe law empirically, he sets up his conception of law in a way that allows it to vary with social complexity. Durkheimian law in *The Division of Labour* is a 'moving target' for sociological observation. Despite his claims, it does not serve as a concrete social fact to measure solidarity.

Thus, it is necessary to ask what Durkheim really seeks to offer with the legal evolution thesis. The answer, I suggest, is that the thesis provides a philosophical device for discussing solidarity as an idea and, more generally, for conceptualising fundamental moral conditions of society. It is a means of depicting graphically Durkheim's ideas about the kinds of moral bonds that can provide social cohesion in different kinds of society. The purpose of the legal symbols of *The Division of Labour* is not to underpin a study of legal history. It is to develop the *philosophy of society* – the view of its essentially moral character (and of the way that moral character changes with social development) – that animates all Durkheim's later work. We might add, however, that his concern is surely also to propose a philosophy of law as an offshoot of this. According to this philosophy, law is to be considered the primary form in which society, as a unity, expresses its moral essence, that is the distinctive moral character that gives it some kind of integrity and cohesion. As will appear, Durkheim's concern after *The Division of Labour* is not so much to show that law's form changes (from repressive to restitutive) as a result of social evolution, but to explore how the moral ideas that make up its content have tended to change (towards an increasingly individualistic morality).

It has to be said that such a philosophy of law is not argued for but merely presupposed by Durkheim in *The Division of Labour*. His later legal theory explores its implications, to see what conclusions, for example about government, administration, adjudication and law enforcement, follow if law is thought of in this moralistic way. His claims about legal evolution are arranged in terms of this view of law. The legal evolution thesis is an initial presentation of a problem for legal theory to solve: what is the moral essence of complex societies that modern law expresses (and must express in order to retain its own moral force and be something more than 'mere' politics)? In one way or another, most of Durkheim's work after *The Division of Labour* addresses this problem.

Uses of history

If Durkheim is understood in this way, some empirical criticism of his thesis may be beside the point. To attack him on his own terrain it is not enough to claim, for example, that restitutive sanctions of some kind are present or even widespread in early societies, or that harm to individuals is not necessarily criminally punished in these societies, for he accepts these points. Nor is it enough to show that penal sanctions are important and widespread in modern societies, or that punishment can take different forms from those Durkheim indicates, for these phenomena may simply fall outside his conception of repressive law. Finally, it is insufficient to show that some forms of law are not taken into account in his thesis, for he does not suggest that the thesis embraces the whole of law.[5] To substantiate claims such as these helps to put his theories in perspective, but does not necessarily undermine them.

Some criticism cannot, however, be dismissed in this way because it confronts directly what I have called above Durkheim's philosophy of society – his understanding of society's moral nature. For example, the anthropologist Bronislaw Malinowski's (1926: 56) denial that Trobriand Islands society is dominated by penal law is part of a broader claim about the importance of relations of reciprocity – rather than, for example, shared belief or sentiments – as the foundation of the simplest forms of society.

From another viewpoint, claims that Durkheim's evolutionary picture marginalises political factors in shaping law and its operation have similar significance. They challenge the relevance of his general outlook on the moral nature of society. Thus, John Barnes notes that ethnographic evidence suggests that repressive law is not important in simple, stateless societies and that 'it is governmental action that is typically repressive' (Barnes, 1966: 168–9). Durkheim was perhaps misled, Barnes suggests, by his reliance on evidence from societies with written legal codes.

Much commentary is concerned with putting the role of government more clearly into the picture. Criticism of Durkheim's generalisations about penal history has been fierce (e.g. Grabosky, 1978; Garland, 1983) and often designed to highlight political determinants of variation in punishment practices (e.g. Spitzer, 1975, 1979). Indeed, Durkheim's arguments simply do not take serious account of these determinants (e.g. Lenman and Parker, 1980) and, it might be added, of political economy generally. The problem is in his limited conception of punishment as a reflection of cultural values and beliefs. Because of this focus, the only aspect of penal evolution that is clearly presented in the foreground of his historical picture is the emergence of a certain conception of the dignity of the individual as an overriding moral value. The legal concepts of *The Division of Labour* serve as devices for presenting the idea of solidarity as a moral phenomenon. In the same way, the changes

5. See also p. 136, below.

in punishment practices noted in 'Two laws of penal evolution' are treated almost entirely as indicators of the growth of the value of individual worth in modern society. In both cases, what is indicated is theoretically of great interest and significance. But the methods of indicating it are historical generalisations that can easily be criticised as partial. They select certain historical matters for emphasis while leaving out of account many others. Thus, it might well be said that Durkheim's approach is inadequate. But the criticisms do not necessarily destroy the logic of his approach once its limited compass is recognised.

My purpose is thus not to defend Durkheim's legal history. It is to suggest that historical generalisation is hardly ever his real concern (cf. Garland, 1990: 49). Where history is invoked it is as *a device for writing about moral ideas*. It is a way of linking very abstract concepts (solidarity as a moral phenomenon or individualism as a moral value) with aspects of historical experience. It is not an attempt to convey a comprehensive or even balanced historical picture. No doubt a comprehensive picture is impossible anyway. And balance, which is a matter of appropriate selection of facts, depends on the nature of the story being told. In Durkheim's case it is a story about moral abstractions that are important even if hard to capture through empirical generalisations.

How then should the legal evolution thesis be read? It certainly should not be treated as immune from historical criticism. Durkheim would have rejected any interpretation of his work that removed it from empirical evaluation. He makes historical claims which deserve to be taken seriously and evaluated accordingly. But historical criticism of Durkheim is difficult, first, because of the elaborate nature of his sociological concepts and their theoretical purposes. Secondly, it is difficult because his theses are ultimately not about history but about the moral nature of social phenomena and the conditions necessary for these phenomena to exist. Thirdly, because of this, his historical references are usually extremely general and therefore difficult to confront with specific historical evidence.[6]

Historical criticism of Durkheim is useful in so far as it makes plausible or implausible his theoretical claims about the moral character of society. It is also useful in so far as it facilitates judgements about the value of his theoretical understandings of the nature of legal phenomena. To show, for example, that his account of penal evolution leaves out of account certain political factors does not destroy the value of the claims he makes about the nature of punishment. But it puts them into a different perspective. It reveals them as a *limited* view of a complex historical phenomenon. To show that legal history is more

6. For Durkheim's views on the relationship between history and sociology see Durkheim (1982c), especially at p. 212: 'We are not talking about events, but the inner motives which may have determined those events.'

complex than it appears in Durkheim's portrayal is to make clear that his legal theory, in so far as it is couched in historical terms, is merely one of many that historical reflection can inspire. It focuses on limited, but not necessarily unimportant, phenomena. It is a partial perspective on the complexity of moral experience.

Religion and early law

Viewed in this light, some of the potentially most telling criticism of Durkheim is that which casts doubt on the religious character of early law. His insistence on this religious character is the means by which he sets up the idea of law as the instrument of society as a whole. Religious practices reach beyond private spheres: 'offences against the gods are offences against society' (Durkheim, 1984: 50). This emphasis, in turn, allows society to be conceptualised as a moral unity, not a mere coalition or compromise of interests; from its beginnings society has this character. And, finally, behind all of this is the idea that duty – enshrined in the idea of law – must be accompanied by a belief in something that makes the acceptance of duty worthwhile; the compromise of interests could never supply that belief. Thus, in ancient societies, much law is concerned with injuries to the public interest, often expressed in the form of religious prohibitions (Durkheim, 1984: 50). The disappearance of religious prohibitions from later legal systems (1984: 111–12) indicates, for Durkheim, a fundamental change not only in the nature of society's moral outlook but in the bases of its cohesion and unity.

It is not clear how far Durkheim was influenced by the jurist Henry Maine's famous claims about the religious nature of early law (Shils, 1991: 170–1; Cocks, 1988: 156–7). Certainly Durkheim's ideas are close to Maine's. Maine's 'religious theory' of law, suggesting that law, morality and religion are 'mingled up ... without any regard to differences in their essential character' in early society (Maine, 1861: 9), has been fiercely criticised. According to A. S. Diamond, the ancient legal codes 'contain no evidence to support a religious theory of the origin of law', and as regards unwritten tribal law 'here, too, there is no evidence to support the theory' (Diamond, 1935: 52, 53; and see Sheleff, 1997: 114ff.). The 'foundation of the religious theory was not an analysis of evidence, but the power of the emotional appeal of religion in the second half of the last century' (1935: 162). Law and religion, Diamond maintains, are clearly separated in ancient law (1935: 163–4). Nevertheless, he admits that 'there is a close relation in all ages [of early law] between the criminal law and religious or magico-religious thought' (Diamond, 1951: 226).

The anthropologist E. A. Hoebel argues, however, that Diamond and others misinterpret Maine. Maine did not claim that all law originated in religion but rather that religion and law are intertwined in early society (Hoebel, 1964: 258). This is close to Durkheim's view, though Durkheim does not claim that law and religion are merged. For him, the factor of organisation allows law's distinct social identity – however nebulous – to be established. Hoebel states: 'I believe a review of the evidence will show that primitive criminal law coincides with certain notions of sin with remarkable frequency, albeit not exclusively . . . The religious complex, being universal and of primary importance in the primitive world, of necessity acts upon law and is in turn affected by it' (1964: 259, 266). All in all, it cannot be said that law originates in religion but the link between early penal law and religion is close.

On the whole this seems consistent with Durkheim's position. Although he does speak of penal law as having religious origins (1982b: 173), this is not essential to his claims. What his theory relies on is the claim that law and religion are part of the same universe of common beliefs and sentiments – the collective consciousness – of early societies and that, because of this, law expresses the convictions and judgements of society as a whole (see Mauss, 1896; Gernet, 1951: 7–8).

The birth of individual rights

The canvas on which Durkheim's picture of legal evolution is painted is chronologically and geographically vast. This, in itself, suggests an impressionistic use of historical material to develop essentially abstract conceptions of the nature of law. The decline of law's religious aspects and the growth of its concern for individual rights, protections and relationships are portrayed as key features of a slow evolution many of whose details are lost in the mists of ancient history. But a difficult problem is left by the portrayal of law's early religious nature. How, it might be asked, do *individual* claims, transactions and relationships ever enter law's field of concerns if its character is formed in the way that Durkheim describes?

The Division of Labour suggests that the increasing complexity of society creates a competing source of morality, alongside, but separate from that of the collective consciousness. A morality of interdependence and reciprocity is brought about by the gradual specialisation of social roles. Durkheim sees such a morality as needed in a complex society. Given its importance this morality will be expressed in law. So restitutive law is the necessary expression of organic solidarity. But how does the increasing specialisation of social roles and functions create a new kind of law and morality? It may provide the need but by what means are these regulatory forms actually produced? Law and morality in conditions of mechanical solidarity are expressions of the collective consciousness. They derive directly from shared sentiments. But Durkheim insists that restitutive law – the law governing private transactions and relationships – is not a product of the collective consciousness (1984: 69). What brings it into existence?

The question of the way that restitutive law's techniques evolve is important. Durkheim does not answer it in *The Division of Labour*. Since his concern there is not to explain legal history but to use a study of law to reveal the nature of society, this might seem understandable. But it is no less understandable that a jurist wanting to develop a Durkheimian interpretation of early legal history would try to supplement Durkheim's analyses in this respect.

This is the primary importance of Paul Huvelin's imaginative work. Huvelin, a law professor at the University of Lyons specialising in Roman legal history, was a committed member of Durkheim's *Année sociologique* group. His writings try to show, consistently with Durkheim's legal evolution thesis, how private law evolved from the religious matrix of early law (Huvelin, 1900; 1907; Gurvitch, 1963: 133–41). To do this he sets out to explore the role of magic in early societies. Certainly magic is typically regarded as a very significant social force in them. As Diamond notes, it 'is largely employed, when other mundane methods fail, to give man confidence to meet the hazards of life' (1951: 53, 81). It is often distinguished sociologically from religion on the basis that magic seems to give individuals the ability to control supernatural powers while in religion this control is not considered to exist (Hoebel, 1964: 267; Gurvitch, 1942: 106). The religious believer humbly prays to ask for spiritual aid, but the magician seeks to command the spirit world. As Georges Gurvitch notes, magic force 'is elastic; it can be manipulated'; it is vital, immanent energy. Religion involves the idea of duty and subjection; magic can involve that of initiative and power. It harnesses the 'fear of risk and and the desire of success' (1942: 105, 106; 1963: 101).

Durkheim's focus on early law's relation to religion emphasises social duty rather than individual initiative. Magic, for him, lacks religion's social nature. It does not bind together its adherents in the way religion does. Magic and religion have common sources in social belief but are opposing forces, mutually hostile (Durkheim, 1915: 42–4). The magician can work alone with a clientele rather than a church. Durkheim's followers Henri Hubert and Marcel Mauss described magic rites not as elements uniting society but as sometimes illicit, and often secret and private, activities (Mauss, 1972). Thus, it would seem that, for Durkheim, magic – despite its relation to religion and its existence as social practices – could not have the importance for legal development that religion had. Religion represents society's unity to its members through their shared belief. Magic offers no such representation. Religion centres on the idea of the sacred but magic is a transference of aspects of religious thought and practice away from the field of sacred things. It is indirectly a product of the social forces that religion represents (Durkheim, 1915: 362). But belief in magic is utilitarian. Unlike religious rites, magic rites have no value in themselves. Their value is only in the effects they produce (1915: 301). Casting a spell is important only if it is thought that the spell will work.

Huvelin, however, sees in magical rites the mechanisms that precede and facilitate the emergence, in social evolution, of private legal relationships and claims. The contribution of magic in early or ancient societies is to give individuals or specific groups access to assumed forces they can harness to their private purposes. Magic gives the victim of theft a (social or psychological) weapon against the wrongdoer (Huvelin, 1907: 13). Private property gains its first social protection not with fully fledged restitutive sanctions but because magical practices and ideas are thought to bind individuals to things associated with them. Vengeance may be exacted on a thief caught in the act. But if the thief is not known, magic may be the only recourse: 'the magical rite takes the place of a vengeance that cannot be exacted' (Huvelin, 1907: 23). Sometimes it is focused on traces left by the thief. Similar practices may be used when a borrower or custodian acts in bad faith. Indeed, often no distinction is made between a thief and a defaulting debtor (1907: 13, 14). Huvelin suggests that these rites in their pure form have only a punitive purpose. The universal belief is that they can harm wrongdoers; they have social or psychological power. But they can be given a restitutive purpose by attaching conditions to them. If the harm can be put right a spell is made to take effect only if restitution is not made or until this is done (1907: 15). Huvelin gives many examples of such magical practices as, for example, in the solemn investigation of theft in Ancient Greek, Roman and Salic law. Often material and magical interventions are hard to separate (1907: 23). Their effects merge.

Some of his most interesting speculations are about the emergence of contractual bonds.[7] In early times, Huvelin notes (1907: 25), it is very difficult to accept agreement of wills as a source of obligations and to provide reliable sanctions for these obligations. Even if individual will is seen as significant at all, it is hard to see it as producing future effects, such as a future repayment or the carrying out of a promised performance. The debtor's own body may be the creditor's only security. Huvelin asks: how is it possible to bind the debtor apart from

---

7. See further Chapter 8, below.

relying on this physical security? His answer is that, in early times before the organised force of law is available to secure such an arrangement, magic fulfils this function. Eventually, the magical bond itself becomes a matter of agreement. The debtor subjects himself to the magical elements of the contract by agreement with the creditor (1907: 27). The use of oaths, symbolic rituals and writing – this last's supernatural powers well recognised in ancient times – played their parts in such early procedures (1907: 31–6).

Magic's relation to law subsequently evolves in two directions, in Huvelin's view. Sometimes, magic's illicit character leads to its prohibition under the threat of public (legal) penalties. In other cases the illicit character of magic weakens and it actually turns into legal technique (1907: 37). Thus law takes on oaths, precise verbal formulae and solemn procedures as part of the means by which individuals can invoke its authority. The sanctions that make these practices effective in transactions cease to be magical and become gradually those of law's coercive power. Thus, in Huvelin's picture of the emergence of private law, magic performs a vital role. It carries from religion a kind of social power which becomes available to strengthen private transactions and forms of redress. It gives them a social force beyond the private capacities of the parties involved. In this way it paves the way for the emergence of legal techniques for recognising and enforcing private claims and individual rights.

Huvelin's work is speculative. But it is scholarly and rich in historical example. It sketches a very general theory about the nature of the social forces – which Louis Gernet (1951) has called 'pre-law' – that historically precede and pave the way for the emergence of ideas of legal obligation. But it leaves some unanswered questions about the social nature of magic. On the one hand, according to Huvelin, magic becomes important to 'pre-law' by breaking away from the collective nature of religion to provide a resource that can be privately appropriated. On the other hand, magic gets its power from the fact that it reflects collective beliefs. It is a social force, not a purely individual one. Hence, the line between religion and magic (and between collective beliefs and individual interests) in early societies is not as easily drawn as he seems to imply (Gernet, 1951: 10–11).

Nevertheless, Huvelin's stress on the importance of relations between law and magic has been strongly echoed by some other writers (e.g. Gurvitch, 1963: ch. 9; Hoebel, 1964: ch. 10; Hägerström, 1953: ch. 6). Magic represents the irrational. Today we are inclined to reject any connections, however remote, between it and modern legal rationality. But it may be very important not to lose sight of a dependence of law on belief (cf. Fitzpatrick, 1992) – of which belief in magic is one early historical form. Durkheim himself, having portrayed legal

evolution as a process by which law leaves behind its religious associations, later re-emphasises, as we have already noted in Chapter 4, the
importance of belief as the foundation of regulatory authority. This is
a way of emphasising law's rootedness in culture. It might be said that
law needs faith as well as rationality. Indeed, the latter is built, in part,
on the former.

Part 3

Legal values and social complexity

7

Moral foundations of modern law

It is significant that Durkheim does not explicitly endorse Paul Huvelin's thesis of the sources of private law in magic, discussed in Chapter 6.[1] Durkheim had high respect for Huvelin's legal scholarship. And Huvelin saw himself as following Durkheim's approach to the analysis of legal development, trying to show in Durkheimian terms the seed from which modern individual rights grew. But, despite its ingenuity, his account of the social forces that made possible private law techniques and the legal recognition of individual claims is ultimately incompatible with some of Durkheim's key claims. Like Durkheim, Huvelin portrays magic as purely utilitarian. It is a useful device for promoting private interests. Yet crucially, as has been seen, Durkheim insists that law does not develop from the pursuit of private advantage. It is a matter of morality and solidarity, not of the compromise of interests. This is what makes it meaningful, authoritative, worthy of respect; not mere coercion, but rather coercion that serves values universally understood as socially important. Hence the problem of the moral basis of restitutive law – and, indeed, of much of modern law – must be solved. This is the concern of the present chapter.

Exploring this issue allows us to identify a problem that may explain why Durkheim ceased to use the terms 'repressive law' and 'restitutive law' in explanation after *The Division of Labour*. It was argued in Chapter 6 that these terms were devised specifically to serve the theses about solidarity that he sought to present in that book. I shall argue in this chapter that the framework of explanation there was unable to clarify adequately the moral basis of restitutive law, and more generally the individualistic character of modern law. As Durkheim's ideas about morality evolved and his view of the sociological importance of religion changed, he developed a different view of modern law, marginalising some of the ideas relied on heavily in *The Division of Labour*.

---

1. As regards Huvelin's thesis on the relations of law and magical formulae, Durkheim (1903: 464) merely remarks: 'This last idea, although hypothetical, is particularly interesting.'

Modern law: the early thesis

In *The Division of Labour* Durkheim suggests that rules emerge auto-matically from social conditions as societies become more complex. The division of labour produces different patterns of action corre-sponding to different functions. These patterns are repeated identi-cally in similar circumstances. So relationships between different functions become stable and regular. Ways of acting in connection with them become habits. These habits, 'as they grow in strength, are trans-formed into rules of conduct . . . In other words, there exists a certain allocation of rights and duties that is established by usage and that ends up by becoming obligatory' (1984: 302). Thus, in this explana-tion, beliefs or sentiments do not enter the picture. Restitutive law is not inspired by the collective consciousness. This law, which expresses and fulfils the requirements of specialisation and social differentiation, is produced directly by the division of labour itself in an automatic process. Restitutive law and the values informing it arise as a matter of functional necessity. Restitutive law's growth has nothing to do with shared sentiments of average members of society. Beliefs do not create restitutive law. The source of this law lies in changing social structure – the aspects of social morphology described earlier.[2]

This functional view of restitutive law therefore separates it completely from the collective consciousness. It exists in a different realm, 'more or less outside the collective consciousness' (1984: 70). It 'springs from the regions furthest from the heart of [this] conscious-ness and extends well beyond them. The more it becomes truly itself, the more it separates itself off' (1893a: 81; cf. 1984: 69). Sometimes Durkheim suggests that 'purely moral rules' (that is, those not enshrined in law) are closer to the collective consciousness than is restitutive law in general (1984: 69). Thus, this law, driven forward by organisational needs of modern society, seems a social rather than a cultural phenom-enon – inspired by evolving patterns of social relationships rather than by common attitudes or convictions.

A further consequence of Durkheim's view is that restitutive law contrasts totally with repressive law. They are wholly different in char-acter. Not only are their sanctioning methods different but so are their sources. Repressive law is rooted in beliefs and sentiments. Restitutive law is not. Thus, it is hard for Durkheim to identify any relationship between the two except that as one declines the other advances. It is not easy to see how the content of restitutive law could influence that of repressive law and vice versa. Repressive law changes its content as the collective consciousness changes. But when Durkheim describes the

2. See pp. 82–3, above.

collective conciousness as evolving to lose its religious aspects and to embrace instead the overriding value of the dignity of the individual he does not connect this evolution with the growth of restitutive law.

I shall refer to these ideas as Durkheim's early thesis about modern law. Its merit is that it identifies, in the advance of the division of labour, a clear sociological cause of restitutive law. But it has problems. The main one is the lack of any clear relation between the collective consciousness and the underlying values of restitutive law. As will appear, this creates problems for the analysis of both repressive and restitutive law.

As regards restitutive law the question remains: what is this law's moral basis? As has been seen, for Durkheim, all law is a special kind of morality, distinguishable by its organisational characteristics but qualitatively inseparable from a broader moral domain. But Durkheim's early thesis does not explain where the morality of restitutive law comes from. His explanation is only of changes in social structure that make this law functionally necessary. Huvelin's explanation of processes by which restitutive law takes shape does not help here. It is not an explanation in moral terms – as Durkheim understands morality. It involves the use of forces that do not unify society morally. Magic is a resource to further private interests, not morality. What is the society-wide morality that informs the society-wide application of restitutive law? How does such a morality come to exist, when the picture of modern society's complexity that Durkheim paints is one in which the division of labour creates different functional groups with *different beliefs, sentiments and values*? Restitutive law is presented as the guardian and expression of organic solidarity but it is hard to see where it derives any moral force that can unify modern societies. Different groups have different moral expectations arising from different collective experience. Durkheim seems to recognise the problem, pointing to restitutive law's weak moral force (1984: 82).

As regards repressive law, his early thesis emphasises the drastic reduction of its significance as a force for social cohesion as it evolves to its modern form. Its central value becomes the protection of the dignity of the individual. This value is certainly rooted in the collective consciousness, but the argument of *The Division of Labour* is that solidarity in modern societies is not guaranteed by the collective consciousness but by the effects of the division of labour. Hence Durkheim dismisses any idea that the value of individual dignity can be a morally unifying force. Although this value is based in shared sentiments and 'it impels everyone towards the same end, that end is not a social one. Thus ... [the value of individual dignity] holds a wholly exceptional position within the collective consciousness. It is indeed from society that it draws all this strength, but it is not to society that it binds us: it is to ourselves' (1984: 122). This value glorifies the individual as autonomous and inviolable, standing alone without interference by others. 'Thus,' he adds, driving the point home, 'it does not constitute a truly social link' (1984: 122). Indeed, 'what a small thing this [value] is, especially when one thinks of the ever-increasing scope of social life' (1893a: 396; cf. 1984: 333).

Thus, Durkheim's early thesis does not explain where modern law finds its moral basis. It is hard to analyse the content of this law in moral terms. Restitutive law is the heart of modern law but its relationship with morality is wholly unclear. Repressive law occupies a very subsidiary position in Durkheim's picture of modern society. Although it has a clear central value – the protection of the individual – that value appears to have no contribution to make to the moral cohesion of modern society. Durkheim never admits these problems for his analysis of law. But their cumulative effect is that the early thesis cannot show the relationship between law and morality in complex modern societies. Yet for him there must be such a relationship. Law is inconceivable without it.

Modern law: an alternative later thesis?

I suggest that these problems in the analysis of law in *The Division of Labour* explain why Durkheim ceased to treat law in his later work as an index of solidarity, or to refer to the distinction between restitutive and repressive law. The index thesis implies that solidarity as a social fact automatically creates the law it needs, while the repressive–restitutive distinction implies that this process as regards modern law is largely unconnected with beliefs and sentiments. The ideas of Durkheim's first book remain indispensable for his overall analysis of law. But to analyse modern law's moral foundations he needed to change his thinking. The role of ideas in directing legal development had to be recognised fully. The notion of the shrinking, relatively insignificant 'rump' of the collective consciousness had to be revised. Instead of shared beliefs and sentiments being treated as peripheral to modern society some such ideas had to be seen as fundamental. The idea that the value of individual dignity could not be a unifying social value had to be discarded in favour of a view that emphasised its importance for social cohesion. The lack of any significant relationship between penal law and law concerned with restitution and balancing relationships needed to be replaced with the idea that *all* modern law is underpinned by a distinctively modern value system. Finally, restitutive law had to be linked with the collective consciousness – or with what Durkheim increasingly came to refer to as collective representations, matters of common belief or understanding. All of these changes of outlook are reflected gradually in his work after the *The Division of Labour*.

A good illustration of the kind of undesirable conclusions that could be reached if these changes were not introduced is provided by Paul Fauconnet's (1928) Durkheimian analysis of the modern idea of responsibility. Fauconnet bases himself firmly on Durkheim's early thesis about the nature of modern law.[3] Thus, Fauconnet assumes that the individualistic values of responsibility in modern law cannot be considered to be a socially unifying moral force. They are a weakened form of collective consciousness which has ceased to have social relevance. They direct individuals to be free to pursue their own purposes and to respect those of others. But they do not produce or express social solidarity. He sees the modern collective consciousness as an attenuation of its earlier self. So he wholeheartedly adopts the negative view of it that characterises Durkheim's early thesis.

Thus, the gradual move from early religious and social determinants of punishment and responsibility towards a focus purely on the individual is not, for Fauconnet, a purification or perfection of ideas of responsibility but a weakening of them. 'Strictly personal responsibility is like the last positive value of a responsibility that is tending towards zero-point. From this viewpoint, the evolution of punishment seems a regression. What is taken to be perfect responsibility is responsibility weakened and reduced to vanishing point' (Fauconnet, 1928: 344). Thus, for Fauconnet, the social character and purpose of punishment and responsibility have disappeared. Responsibility focuses now solely on relationships between isolated individuals. It no longer cements social bonds or expresses values promoting social cohesion.

He seems to suggest that a way forward is to recognise collective responsibility for social conditions that create crime. 'The solidary responsibility of society in relation to crime is felt actively by our contemporaries. But this is a collective responsibility. . . . Responsibility will rejuvenate and maintain itself only by getting back in touch with its source' (1928: 344). The direction of argument is clear. Purely individualistic values are anti-social. Punishment and responsibility do not aid solidarity unless they express values that unite society. The values of individualism, including purely individual responsibility, do not help. Thus, for Fauconnet, contemporary forms of punishment are abnormal (because incompatible with the generally sensed conditions of solidarity) and unstable.

3. The preface to *La responsabilité* (Fauconnet, 1928) notes that Durkheim had suggested that Fauconnet should write on the subject of responsibility. He gave Fauconnet manuscripts of four lectures on this subject which he, Durkheim, had delivered at Bordeaux in 1894. It seems that these manuscripts no longer exist. See Lukes (1973: 256, 258).

He is no less critical of what he calls the 'spiritualisation' of responsibility (1928: ch. 9). This is the idea of responsibility as subjective: that is, dependent on the wrongdoer's state of mind, the *mens rea* or intention underlying the act. Sociology, in Fauconnet's view, teaches that responsibility is something determined by society, an objective social matter, a social fact, not a matter of the individual's state of mind. In early society this is explicit: responsibility is fixed in a purely social process. Society attributes responsibility for acts that offend the collective consciousness. The social act of punishing – not the offender's acts or intentions – determines what counts as crime. The spiritualisation of responsibility, however, makes the social determinants of responsibility appear as merely a residue in the individual conscience. And this process is 'an immense impoverishment, a perpetual abolition'. Subjective responsibility is 'only an atrophied form of responsibility' (Fauconnet, 1928: 350). It privatises responsibility, removing its social character and putting it into the recesses of an individual's mind.[4]

Fauconnet's line of thought thus appears to pit sociology against fundamental currents of modern social development. It seems to demand a kind of regression to earlier times. It treats the growth of individual responsibility – a central part of the individualistic value systems of modern societies – as an aberration.

Durkheim refuses to be trapped in these arguments. His outlook is entirely different in this respect from Fauconnet's. The individualistic system of values is, for him, natural and normal. How could it be otherwise when individualism is so characteristic of modern society? The problem for sociology is to explain why this is so. And for legal theory, the problem is to explain how the value of respect for the individual can serve as a moral foundation of modern law, in other words as a value that unites society and can thus be the basis of a modern legal system.

Durkheim offers no explicit later thesis of modern law alternative to that found in *The Division of Labour*. But he establishes the elements of a different view in his writings. It stresses the social role of sentiments and ideas (cf. Durkheim, 1953b). Thus we might label it an *ideational view* rather than (as with the early thesis) a functional one. It is reflected in his later view of punishment as a communication process between society and the offender rather than as merely a matter of social condemnation.[5] His changed outlook is expressed also in his

4. In fact, Fauconnet recognises that modern law's attributions of responsibility in practice involve a mixture of objective and subjective elements. Law does not, for example, punish mere intention without some related action (1928: 377–8). Equally, objective tests of intention are a means by which law tries to address the problem of defining states of mind.
5. See pp. 77–8, above.

developed view of morality, which emphasises the moral autonomy of the individual as well as ideas of duty and attachment.[6] Again, the alternative outlook appears in the claim that law and religion have something of the same nature (in modern societies no less than early ones), and in the complete absence of any reference in his later work to the contrast between restitutive and repressive law. Most importantly, as will appear, Durkheim changes entirely his view of individualism as a modern value. Instead of treating it as a residue in the collective consciousness without bearing on social cohesion, he comes to treat it as the key to social cohesion in modern society (see Cladis, 1992: ch. 2). It becomes the value to which all forms of modern law can be related. Its unfolding explains all aspects of this law.

The morality of restitutive law

Many commentators have discussed Durkheim's changing outlook after *The Division of Labour* although they have rarely related this change to his ideas on law. Robert Nisbet (1965: 37; 1966: 86) claims that Durkheim's work shows a 'reversal of argument', in so far as he never returned to the organic/mechanical dichotomy after *The Division of Labour*, nor to his early concern with the division of labour as a source of social cohesion. His focus switched to questions of collective belief, moral authority and community. Bernard Lacroix (1981: 127) traces the 'slow suicide' of Durkheim's 'original political purpose' of critically explaining the nature of modern society in terms of structural change: that is, in terms of social morphology. W. S. F. Pickering (1984: 283–4; 1975: 349) refers to many writers – including some close to Durkheim such as Gaston Richard, Georges Davy and Celestin Bouglé – who recognised his changed emphasis from around the turn of the century away from social morphology and towards study of the causal force of ideas.[7] As Pickering notes, however, it is hard to say when such a change occurred. It is neither sudden nor necessarily consistent. Some other commentators have been much less ready to accept that there is any significant change in Durkheim's outlook in his later work. Anthony Giddens (1972: 236), for example, argues that Nisbet is wrong and that Durkheim never rejected the distinctions that were central to his theses in *The Division of Labour*.

It is not necessary to enter into these controversies about Durkheim's sociology as a whole. But there can be no doubt about his change of view on the importance of individualism. As has been seen, in *The*

6. See pp. 63–4, above.
7. See pp. 10–11, above.

Division of Labour Durkheim (1984: 122) explicitly denies that the value of individual dignity and worth can be a source of social cohesion.[8] Thus, it cannot provide the moral foundation of modern law. But in his later writing he explicitly reverses this view. The consequences of his changed thinking are crucial for his outlook on law.

To see why it is crucial we should look at Durkheim's efforts in *The Division of Labour* to explain the morality of organic solidarity. He does this not in terms of the value of individual dignity and worth but in terms of a morality of specialisation. The moral injunction of modernity is: 'Equip yourself to fulfil usefully a specific function' (1984: 4). One should specialise just as far as is socially necessary (1984: 333–4). This morality 'asks us only to be gentle towards our fellow men and to be just, to perform our tasks efficiently, to work to ensure that everyone is called to the function he is best able to perform and receives just reward for his labours' (1893a: 404; cf. 1984: 338). But this is surely an odd kind of morality. It is less a moral code for the individual to live by than a code of management for society – a morality for administration, an injunction to ensure that all are in their proper places, working steadily, properly cared for. Such a morality of good social management is entirely different from the sort of morality that resides in the sentiments of the collective consciousness. Indeed, Durkheim notes that the special tasks that the morality of specialisation justifies are by their nature exempt from the effects of the collective consciousness (1984: 82).

What then, according to this reasoning, is the morality of restitutive law? First it should be noted that not all aspects of organic solidarity are expressed through law. Custom and usage are often its non-legal expression. The customs and usages surrounding restitutive law are much more numerous than those surrounding repressive law because 'they must be as diverse as the social functions themselves' (1984: 101). Like repressive law, however, restitutive law is embedded in a wider network of social rules. On the other hand, Durkheim suggests that change in restitutive law is much more readily accepted than in repressive law. Restitutive law has no deep roots in popular sentiment, expectations and understandings (1984: 69). Its moral basis remains hidden, therefore, from the perceptions of most individuals, except in a few areas such as those of recognisably immoral or fraudulent contracts or contracts entered under duress (1984: 69). Therefore, restitutive law is rooted in social life – part of a wider network of social rules. Yet it is not rooted in any moral understandings of individuals.

Durkheim does not hide this problematic conclusion. Restitutive law's moral force is said to derive not from popular sentiments but from the

8. See pp. 105–6, above.

specialisation of tasks. Contract law, for example, gains moral power because it is society's means of bringing together different roles or functions and co-ordinating them. It is the legal instrument of interdependence. It enables the consumer to buy from the retailer and the retailer from the producer. It enables one person to provide services to another for reward, and one organisation to co-operate with another in a co-ordinated way. But Durkheim notes that as specialisation proceeds there can be less and less general feeling attaching to specialised tasks. They directly concern only those involved in them. The rules governing these tasks 'cannot therefore possess that superior force and transcendent authority which, when it suffers harm, exacts expiation . . . All that we require is for the functions to work together in a regular fashion' (1984: 82). This suggests why modern restitutive law becomes technical rather than morally resonant. It becomes more and more detailed and further removed from moral intuitions.

This, in turn, seems to explain why procedural law is an important part of restitutive law (1984: 81). The way things are co-ordinated is as important as what is co-ordinated. Thus, law is increasingly concerned with process rather than substance: not so much with what the various social functions and tasks are as with how they are to be related to each other. Where law does define functions directly these are often administrative ones necessary to society's co-ordinating processes. Thus administrative law indicates and relates the 'ill-defined functions that are termed administrative' and which concern policy implementation. Constitutional law does the same for governmental functions of directing and organising social co-ordination (1984: 81).

Although these ideas are vague they point in realistic directions. Modern law is, according to this view, increasingly a law of management, organisation and co-ordination of social and economic life. This is no doubt why it 'sets up for itself ever more specialised bodies: consular courts, and industrial and administrative tribunals of every kind' (1984: 70). It is not so much a law that tells people what to do as one that provides the means of minimising friction as a result of the various things that are done. It sets and holds the balance across a vast, growing diversity of social activities. The thrust of Durkheim's thinking on restitutive law thus points away from the link between law and morality that we have seen to be fundamental to his general view of the nature of law. It points towards a conception of restitutive law as an instrument of government: a political rather than moral phenomenon.

But this direction would make restitutive law an *aberrant* form of law for Durkheim, just as Fauconnet's analysis portrays modern responsibility as aberrant. It would be a kind of law that has discarded law's fundamental character as a form of morality sanctioned in an organised way. Durkheim could not deny restitutive law's grounding in morality without denying the entire outlook of his sociology. It seems, therefore, that he is forced to locate this morality not in a foundation of popular sentiments and collective beliefs but in governmental beliefs and values. Thus, what could be called (the term is mine, not Durkheim's) the *governmental morality* of organic solidarity is the sole moral basis of restitutive law. The values of this law are those of good management of social complexity, of wise balancing of social roles and functions. And what counts as good and wise will be determined not by popular convictions but by science – by sociological understanding of the nature of the particular society and the demands which its complexity poses for legal regulation. Sociology's task is to reveal the necessary morality of modern government. This, however, is a conception of morality that accepts its divorce from the consciousness of ordinary citizens and entrusts it to politicians and administrators. From that point of view, it could appear as a fragile or at least artificial moral base for modern law.

The cult of the individual

In fact we shall see that this idea of a governmental morality or moral consciousness – related to citizens' experience but shaped by political deliberation – is not as fragile or artificial as it might at first appear. It will be considered in detail later.[9] But Durkheim's writings a few years after *The Division of Labour* made clear that he had revised his view of the impossibility of a popular morality to unify modern society and its law. Five years after insisting that respect of individual freedom and dignity could not be a genuine social bond, he was claiming that individualism 'is henceforth the only system of beliefs which can ensure the moral unity of the country' (1969b: 66). This was because it is a 'glorification, not of the self, but of the individual in general. Its motive force is not egoism but sympathy for all that is human, a wider pity for all sufferings, for all human miseries, a more ardent desire to combat and alleviate them, a greater thirst for justice' (1969b: 64). Similarly, in *Suicide* in 1897 he claims, in stark opposition to the view he had expressed in 1893, that: 'Far from detaching individuals from society and from every aim beyond themselves, [individualism] . . . unites them in one thought, makes them servants of one work' because it does not justify selfishness but proclaims the value of 'man in general, ideal humanity' (1952: 336–7). It demands respect for the freedom and dignity of each and every individual by each and every other. Thus the value of individual worth and dignity becomes a social value after all

9. See Chapter 10, below.

because it demands respect for all other individuals. It embodies concern for others, not the desire for gratification of the self. It is the value, *par excellence*, that can provide a secure basis for flourishing social relations of reciprocity and interdependence.

What makes individualism a unifying social value, therefore, is primarily its clear distinction from egoism or selfishness.[10] It does not authorise individuals' concern for their own welfare and aims beyond a similar concern for the welfare and aims of others. In this sense, almost paradoxically, individualism as a value is impersonal (1969b: 64); that is, unspecific to any particular individual but applicable uniformly to all. But it is a social value also in the sense that it is created by society. It is a 'social product, like all moralities and all religions. The individual receives from society even the moral beliefs which deify him' (1969b: 73). The word 'deify' is very deliberately used here. 'The human person . . . is considered as sacred, in what one might call the ritual sense of the word' (1969b: 61–2). In *The Division of Labour* he had already suggested that, in modern society, 'the individual becomes the object of a sort of religion' (1984: 122). Later he notes:

> The human person . . . has something of that transcendent majesty which the Churches of all times have given to their gods . . . Such a morality is therefore not simply a hygienic discipline or a wise principle of economy. It is a religion of which man is, at the same time, both believer and god. (1969b: 61, 62)

Durkheim terms this phenomenon the 'cult of the individual' (*culte de l'individu*), or sometimes a cult of man or a religion of humanity (1950: 199; 1957: 69, 172; 1969b: 63, 64, 70). He remarks that even in the earliest societies there was something sacred about mankind. But this was in regard to the body or parts of it. Now, in modern society, it is the individual personality that has become sacred. The idea of the soul suggests 'that, in a certain sense, there is divinity in us' (1915: 262). The very idea of personality derives from the combination of the ideas of the soul, originally reflecting a general sense of divinity, and the body, which individualises and separates human beings (1915: 270). Durkheim sees this sense of divinity as merely a particular form in which the power of the social world impresses itself on the individual's experience. Thus, he insists, personality is the combination of the expression of individualised wants and needs and of beliefs, sentiments

---

10. To emphasise the distinction Cladis calls this value system 'moral individualism'. But he admits (1992: 29) that Durkheim rarely uses this term. I do not adopt it here because it actually seems to weaken Durkheim's strong claim that individualism as such (rather than a particular variety of it) is a value or value system that has nothing in common with egoism.

and ideas that derive from the individual's interaction with the social world. It follows that, while human beings are individuated naturally by being born as biologically independent creatures, their personality or moral character as individuals is given by society. Thus the value of individualism, the respect for human worth and dignity, is not something inherent in individual human beings. It is, like all morality, an expression of social conditions; a creation of society.

It is this reasoning that allows Durkheim to solve the problem of how a value that stresses the inviolability of personal autonomy can also be one that unites individuals morally in modern society. The cult of the individual is the value system that society progressively evolves. It should be noted that nothing is said about any role for the division of labour in bringing about this evolution. What drives moral evolution here would seem to be a kind of gradual settling of a balance between the force of the social, embodied in beliefs, sentiments and general understandings, and the individualised force of personal, primarily biological need. The 'duality of human nature', as Durkheim (1960b) calls it in one of his last major essays, is precisely the interplay of these two forces. We have seen earlier that, for him, human nature is not static but evolving. Individualism is thus a value system that emerges gradually as both a framework for and an expression of human nature in this sense.

The cult of the individual as the heart of modern morality clearly embodies what we noticed earlier as the distinctively modern component of morality – moral autonomy.[11] But it affirms that the scope of individual freedom and the degree of respect for it is what *society* gives and prescribes. Individualism does not detach the individual from society, but treats individual personality itself as shaped by social life. Still less does the cult of the individual authorise individuals to deny that society exists as something beyond themselves, greater than themselves, and that they are merely a part of it. Individualism teaches, for Durkheim, that all personal rights, freedoms, dignities and opportunities are given by social life itself. Hence the cult of the individual empowers individual human beings and guarantees their self-respect through its insistence that others respect them. But it also teaches them responsibility to each other and to the society that makes possible everything that enriches their individual lives.

The idea of the cult of the individual provides for modern law a moral basis in shared values, or values that can at least be officially promulgated as uniting society. It seems to solve the problem left open by what I called Durkheim's early thesis of modern law: the problem of how this law can be rooted in popularly shared moral values that

11. See p. 63, above.

unite society. The argument, reflected in his later work, now seems to be not that the progress of the division of labour, driven by morphological changes in society, 'automatically' (cf. 1984: 302) produces restitutive law as a reflection of an underlying social structure. Rather, it is that modern conditions of social complexity, creating moral requirements of interdependence, make individualism objectively necessary as the unifying moral system of modern society. Hence, modern law must be founded on individualism if it is to correspond with the nature of modern society as a moral phenomenon, which sociology reveals and explains. The sociological analysis of individualism explains what essential form and content the central elements of modern law must have, and why.

The morality of the cult of the individual thus provides the grounding of modern legal rights. It makes individual rights secure, but it insists that these rights reside in society rather than in the individual as an isolated human being (Durkheim, 1957: 67). It makes duties meaningful by asserting that they are not merely necessary concessions to other individuals but are ties that link the individual duty-holder to society at large. Individuals are bound to society, and thereby to each other, in networks of responsibility. Far from responsibility being the weak, asocial bond that Fauconnet described, it is, in modern society, the most central expression of human nature. It is the moral tie that subordinates narrowly personal need to social expectations. It is the internal sense of regulation that provides a disciplining of desire at the same time as it widens horizons of aspiration. Thus, it is the key to defining personality, the very essense of individuality in modern society.

The nature of rights

What limits then, does the value of individualism put on the assertion of rights? How does the social character of legal rights define their nature and operation? Durkheim insists that rights do not come from birth; they are not inherent in individuals (1957: 57, 66–7); rights of individuals 'are not inscribed in the nature of things . . . on the contrary, the rights have to be won from the opposing forces that deny them . . . The state alone is qualified to play this part' (1957: 65). Davy, interpreting Durkheim, adds that individual rights 'are . . . bestowed by the state on the individual . . . to the precise degree that the separate outline of the individual becomes more clearly etched on the social background, in the natural progress of social life . . .' (Davy, 1957: xxxviii). Thus, rights are guaranteed by the state; it is the state's task to institute them (Durkheim, 1957: 57, 65). But the state here, as elsewhere, in Durkheim's view, must act as the agent of society as a whole.[12] Thus, rights and their limits are defined by society, acting through the centralised political agency that represents it for the purpose of regulation. They are not unconditional attributes of the individual who holds them, but of the society that entrusts them to individuals.

There is, however, a complex ambiguity here which is very important to Durkheim's conception of rights. Whether or not they are enshrined in law, rights must have a moral basis. If they are moral rights this is self-evident; if they are legal rights they are an aspect of law which, in Durkheimian terms, is a special form of morality.[13] The idea that rights are created and given by the state reflects the idea of a governmental morality underlying law which was considered earlier. It expresses, in part, the idea implicit in Durkheim's early thesis of modern law that law and its allocation of duties and entitlements expresses the objective moral necessities of modern complex society, necessities that must be worked out through governmental deliberation. In fact, there is no reason to suppose that Durkheim ever discarded this idea of a governmental morality underlying legal rights. The allocation and protection of rights is a means by which good government based on moral principle can be pursued.[14] But a different conception of a moral basis for modern law emerges in Durkheim's later work to coexist with the ideas of the early thesis. Thus, the popular morality of the cult of the individual seems to provide a simpler, more direct source of ideas of individual rights. In a 1906 discussion Durkheim spoke of rights and liberties as conferred on man by the 'sacredness with which he is invested' (1953a: 72). The cult of the individual, which declares the moral necessity of respect for all human beings, naturally sanctifies the idea of individual rights and liberties and indicates what the most important of these will be. Thus, freedom of thought – the very essence of autonomous personality – is the 'first of all liberties' (1969b: 65). A host of rights, concerned with protection of individuals and of their property and expectations, is derived from the same moral source.

12. His analysis of democratic conditions under which the state can do this is examined in Part 4, below.
13. Of course, rights are also a means of asserting interests. Perhaps an appropriate way to understand rights in Durkheimian terms is as the essential legal bridge between social values and private interests. Rights interpret social values as a matter of individual claims. They create individual interests as a derivation from these values. Alternatively rights can be seen as the device by which claims people might wish to assert can be judged against law's value system and translated into terms consistent with it. Thus, approaching matters from one direction, law has to make its moral value system relevant to the position of individuals by specifying their rights and duties; proceeding from the opposite direction, private claims have to be brought before law, via rights, if they are to be socially recognised. This view of rights is my gloss, not expressed as such by Durkheim.
14. See Chapters 10 and 11, below.

The ambiguity in Durkheim's views concerns the scope of the rights that the cult of the individual inspires. Are these rights determined politically by the state, or culturally as a pure expression of a popular morality evolving in the collective consciousness? The matter cannot be examined in detail until Durkheim's conception of the state has been considered in Part 4 of this book. But it is significant that he gives the state a kind of supervisory role in relation to the cult of the individual: the state must 'organise the cult, preside over it, ensure its regular operation and development' (1950: 104; cf. 1957: 70). This seems to be merely an aspect of the state's general task of clarifying and expressing in the form of regulation and policy the ideas and sentiments of society at large: the state acting as voice of the collective consciousness.[15] Hence it might be said that while rights are politically produced by the state, this is done on the basis of a kind of cultural authorisation, legitimising these rights in popular morality.

This ambiguous position – combining political and cultural sources of rights – makes it difficult to decide exactly how the idea of human rights fits into Durkheim's thinking (cf. Pickering, 1993; Thompson, 1993). Human rights are often assumed in modern legal thought to be rights that can be asserted, if necessary, *against* the state and its various agencies and officials. Durkheim sees the cult of the individual as an evolving moral phenomenon that reflects the progress of human nature and the shaping of personality in modern conditions. Thus, it clearly has a moral existence autonomous from the governmental morality that, according to Durkheim's early thesis of modern law, underpins restitutive law. So it would seem to provide a basis for rights that are more fundamental than mere political enactments. Durkheim himself was certainly deeply sympathetic to campaigns for recognition and protection of human rights. He was an initiator of the League for the Rights of Man and the Citizen, founded in France in 1898, and he helped to set up the Bordeaux branch (Lukes, 1973: 374ff.). But it is also apparent that he was unsure how deep-rooted ideas of human rights are (Durkheim, 1957: 60) and he realised how dependent they are on public opinion for support (1957: 67). He saw the spirit of humanitarianism spreading across national borders and inspiring a widespread moral movement. Yet he also doubted its power to control events in a world of nation states.[16]

Thus, on the one hand, modern law is driven forward by moral forces that reflect evolving, general, but far from universal, popular sentiments. On the other hand, its complex moral frameworks are

15. Cf. Durkheim's more familiar treatment of this role of the state in relation to punishment as discussed in Chapter 5.
16. See pp. 193–6, below.

located not in popular attitudes and beliefs but in governmental imperatives for effective management of society to promote and guarantee
solidarity. It seems that Durkheim was unsatisfied with his early conception of the morality of modern law as a wholly governmental morality
unconnected with popular sentiments. On the other hand, the popular
morality of the cult of the individual, strongly emphasised in his later
work, appears ultimately, in his thinking, to be put under a kind of
governmental tutelage of the state. In the following chapters it will be
seen that this ambivalent view of the interplay of popular and governmental morality informs much of his discussion of the various areas of
modern law. I shall argue, indeed, that Durkheim's ambivalence is justified. It reflects enduring tensions at the heart of modern law.

8

Contract

Apart from criminal law, contract is the most prominent legal field in Durkheim's work. In the categorisation of *The Division of Labour*, criminal law and contract law epitomise respectively repressive and restitutive law. Contract is thus a framework of organic solidarity. Equally, however, as presented in Durkheim's later writings, it is a major expression of the values of individualism. The ambiguity, identified in Chapter 7, in Durkheim's view of modern law is clearly present in his consideration of contract. Whether his early or later view of modern law is adopted, however, contract is the legal category that, for Durkheim, most directly expresses the essence of modern society. Thus, he devotes much attention to it. But we shall see in this chapter that contract law ultimately appears, in Durkheim's understanding and that of some of his closest collaborators, problematic in its relation both to solidarity and to individualism. Their work offers not only theoretical analysis of contract as a legal form but also critique of that form as it appears in modern society.

Two approaches to contract

Theories of contract often explain it as expressing a free interaction of individual wills, or as a legal embodiment of the morality of promising.[1] But the central aim of Durkheim's initial treatment of contract in *The Division of Labour* is to show it as an institution expressing the functional needs of society. Modern contract law does, indeed, seek to give effect to the intention of the parties to create legal relations and to do so on the basis of the specific terms they have agreed. But Durkheim and some of his followers try in their writing to show that contract as a legal idea emerged slowly as patterns of social relations changed through social development and as new forms of interaction became possible with changing moral sentiments and changing conceptions of personality recognised in law. In Durkheim's view, contract should

---

1. See, for example, Fried (1981), Atiyah (1981), Barnett (1986), MacCormick (1982).

express the reciprocity and interdependence at the moral heart of organic solidarity. 'The contract is indeed the supreme legal expression of cooperation' (1984: 79). According to his early account of modern law in *The Division of Labour*, a need was created for a regulatory framework to fulfil the division of labour, to make specialisation work, and contract is central to this framework. Contract is thus a social mechanism of co-ordination (1984: 302, 316). It is explained *functionally* in terms of the requirements of the division of labour.

By contrast, looked at in terms of Durkheim's later strong emphasis on the emergence of individualism as a value system, contract is explicable in a different way. In essence it is a legal expression of individualist values. It embodies the freedom of individuals to set their position in relation to others and negotiate social relationships voluntarily and consensually. If individualised and (to use Fauconnet's term)[2] 'spiritualised' responsibility provides the legal constraint most compatible with individualist values in the modern collective consciousness, the right to contract is the form of legal freedom most compatible with these values because it allows individuals to plan their destiny in relation to others. Contract can thus be explained *ideationally* in terms of the sentiments and ideas that are eventually fully expressed in the cult of the individual.

These two approaches – the functional and the ideational – are very different. The first is broadly that of *The Division of Labour*. The second is more apparent in Durkheim's later writing. The tension between them is illustrated in comments on the nature of contract made by Paul Huvelin (1907). Huvelin remarks that we often speak of wills meeting, concurring or agreeing on a particular object. The contractual obligation is seen as the outcome of some substantial meeting of two wills. But in reality this is not accurate. Historical evolution and logic combine, Huvelin asserts, to show that the source of contractual reliance (*créance*) lies in a unique will (1907: 41), able to create an obligation in someone else. The key development occurs when one person is able to impose an obligation on the other (for example, to repay a benefit or supply an equivalent). Huvelin shows this in his account, discussed in Chapter 6, of the emergence of private rights through the use of magical powers. These powers enable individuals to impose their will on others. The legal question is, therefore: what powers do individuals have? The question of the nature of the social relationships that might be formed as a result of the exercise of individual will comes later. Hence contractual rights and obligations need to be understood in terms of ideas of individuality and personality. We need to understand how these ideas came about.

If an approach such as Huvelin's is followed, therefore, ideational rather than functional analysis is needed. We could not understand how

2. See p. 108, above.

contract is able to develop to serve a social function of co-ordination unless we understand how the idea of the individual as an autonomous person able to contract comes about. On the other hand, it might be said that we could understand contracts functionally merely as legal frameworks to facilitate co-ordination or interaction without entering into questions about how contracting parties are able legally to impose obligations on each other.

Functional and ideational approaches thus have different emphases. And, as will appear, both are reflected in Durkheim's own work, in its different phases. As such, it is important to emphasise that both approaches see the source of contract as entirely social. Even if contract is the expression of will, the Durkheimian approach (reflected in Huvelin's or Durkheim's work) is that the very idea of individual will is something constructed socially, by collective beliefs shaped over long historical periods. The idea of individual personality, recognisable by law, has to evolve. Huvelin's (1900; 1907) thesis about magic is, as has been seen, an attempt to explain part of the process by which that evolution could occur.

Another of Durkheim's juristic followers, Emmanuel Lévy, arrives at conclusions similar to Huvelin's about the importance of individual personality and will as the basis of contract: 'What creates the contractual bond is the confidence (*confiance*) which the debtor's promise inspires in the creditor' (Lévy, 1926: 78). 'Contract is the practice of confidence becoming a practice of exchange' (Lévy, 1933: 145). 'The contract is the act that enables my right to manifest itself. I hold this right in my own capacity and through law, through my own [legal] personality created by society' (Lévy, 1926: 27). Again, therefore, it seems that contract is best understood not as a legal expression of interdependence (as *The Division of Labour* often suggests), but as an expression of collective beliefs about the individual's legal capacities.

If the starting point for analysis is individual will and the gradual evolution of beliefs and sentiments about the nature of individuality and personality the problem of explaining the contractual bond as a *reciprocal* relationship – a form of social interdependence – remains. How do wills come to bind each other? (cf. Durkheim, 1957: 178.) What ties these independent wills together? How does a social relationship of interdependence (and the moral institution of contract as a generalised form of social relationship) arise from the mere assertion of independent wills? (cf. Arnaud, 1975: 90.) This is a similar problem to that which Fauconnet encountered in understanding how purely individualised responsibility could express social solidarity.[3] As has been seen, for Durkheim, a solution is to recognise individual personality (and will and responsibility as aspects of it) as socially produced.

3. See pp. 107–8, above.

On the other hand, where contract is seen, first and foremost, in terms of its social functions, as expressing interdependence, the necessary framework of relationships determined by the division of labour, the converse problem arises. How do the social requirements of co-ordination and interdependence actually create individual rights? This is an aspect of the general question that Durkheim's early thesis of modern law provokes: where is the moral basis of restitutive law to be found? What is it that binds the parties to a contract individually to each other? What turns the social fact of solidarity, expressed in relations of interdependence, into individual rights and duties that have moral force for each contracting party? An answer would be that the state simply creates these rights and duties: they are a legal expression of what was called in Chapter 7 governmental morality, the morality involved in managing society effectively to promote solidarity.

But contract is not usually thought of in that way. Individuals are considered to have rights and duties under contract because they have chosen to make an agreement. On this view, contract law expresses not the governmental morality of effective co-ordination of social interdependence but the popular morality of individualism. Yet, it is also typically assumed that contract cannot be solely the expression of individual will. It must be controlled to reflect society's needs for the just co-ordination of social relations in general, so it is subject to overriding consumer regulations, implied terms, requirements of good faith and so on (Durkheim, 1984: 159). Thus, the ambivalence, examined in the previous chapter, between two kinds of analysis of modern law is present in possible approaches to the analysis of contract law. It seems that they need somehow to be combined.

Contract and status

Durkheim remarks that 'far from the contract being of early origin as an institution, it does not appear, and above all, does not develop, until a very late date' (1957: 175–6). He is able to say this with conviction even though the Durkheimian view of contract remains, as seen above, ambivalent. If contract expresses the growth of individualism and the flowering of the idea of the autonomous legal personality of individual human beings, this development occurs only after a long social and legal evolution. If contract expresses the needs of the division of labour, specialisation, social complexity and organic solidarity, it emerges only as these social conditions develop and flourish. It 'must have been built up by long endeavour' (1957: 179; and see Cohen, 1933: 70ff.).

The Division of Labour adopts a functional view of contract because its concern is with what law contributes to wider social processes. But in later lectures, dating from 1898 to 1900, Durkheim is specifically concerned with contract as an idea (Durkheim, 1957). He notes that contractual bonds arise from the will of the parties. But these bonds presuppose an already constituted legal status of the parties having capacity to enter into legal relations (1957: 176–7). In early society, a marriage contract, for example, presupposes an existing structure of families so that a woman of family X can, through marriage, join a man of family Y. 'Hence it follows that marriage, being of necessity a contract, presupposes an existing structure of the family that has nothing contractual about it' (1957: 177). Thus, as Maine (1861: 100) had argued before Durkheim, status (determining the nature and capacity of contracting parties) precedes contract. For Durkheim this is crucial because status can only be conferred by society. It is not inherent in the individual. Thus, although contract is an expression of will, what underpins the entire contractual situation is determined by society, not by individuals. As Lévy (1926: 99) puts it: 'All contracts have something collective about them.'

Hence, it is unsurprising that Durkheim, analysing contract ideationally, traces the origin of status – whether of persons or things – to religious beliefs. Religion in early or simple societies embodies beliefs that define the place of things, individuals and groups (for example, kinship groups) in society. It determines the social status of everything, especially by marking out the sacred from the profane. Originally, Durkheim asserts, bonds linking people were derived from the sacred character of the persons or things involved (1957: 178). Thus, in his view, it is important not to be misled by the idea of contract as the expression of the will of the parties. The expression of that will in meaningful legal form is only possible because society creates and defines ideas of personality and status, and so of capacity to act and to accept responsibility. He writes that contract is not sufficient in itself but presupposes a regulation of the contract that is social in origin (1984: 162, 302, 316). This claim applies, whether he is thinking, in *The Division of Labour,* of specialisation inspiring a governmental morality to regulate contracts, or, in the later lectures on contract, of ideas of personality and capacity evolving in the collective consciousness – what Lévy (1933: 11) calls 'the surrounding consciousness [that] . . . penetrates' contracts.[4]

4. In a comment written some years after both *The Division of Labour* and the lectures on contract, Durkheim claims that contractual obligations arise not from the will of the parties, as such, but from each party's declaration of will, on which the other party relies: obligation exists because, and in so far as, damage or loss would result if a declaration turns out to be false or is dishonoured (Durkheim, 1906a; cf. MacCormick, 1982). Here Durkheim links the role of individual will with the moral requirements of interdependence and solidarity which turn the parties' mutual reliance into a matter of obligation. But this still leaves open the question: under

Thus, for Durkheim, status defines the earliest social relationships – especially those within the family group. Contract's historic role is to make it possible to modify status. Thus, he suggests, it was natural that the earliest means of doing this would be by extending existing statuses, using symbolic procedures to do so. If status depends on blood ties, the mingling of blood can be a symbolic means of creating relationships (such as adoption) that have the force of natural status relationships (such as parent and child) (1957: 179–80). Thus the blood covenant, which involves mixing the blood of the participants, is a familiar means of creating bonds, like those of blood brothers. So is the sharing of food or drink: 'To eat the same food means to commune together or partake of the same source of life; it means making the same blood' (1957: 180).

Durkheim never fails to emphasise the importance of religious ideas and practices in the early evolution of legal bonds. He notes the early legal importance of formality and the use of ritual. 'When certain definite words, arranged in a given sequence, are held to have a force which is lost if the slightest change is introduced, we can be sure that they have or have had a sacred meaning and that they derive their peculiar powers from a sacred source' (1957: 187). Legal formalism 'is only a substitute for sacred formalities and rites' (1957: 182, 187). Thus, whereas Huvelin emphasises the importance of magic powers in making possible private rights,[5] Durkheim stresses religious practices. His concern is always to emphasise the social nature of law, reflected in its close ties with religion, rather than the private, utilitarian purposes which, for Huvelin, motivated the invocation of magic in early society. Yet, whereas Huvelin shows in some detail how private purposes could be given a kind of social force through magic, it is often hard to see how Durkheim thinks private legal relations could have evolved from religious rituals. He suggests that solemn rituals made declarations irrevocable; thus, one party could possess the other's obligation that was made secure in such a way. Gradually, ritual could be discarded as the declaration of will acquired force in its own right and under pressure of the needs of economic life (1957: 192–5). But this development seems vague and mysterious. Durkheim's difficulty here is surely his determination to see utilitarian calculation as contributing nothing to the idea of law.

what circumstances is an obligation to an individual held to arise from the fact of that individual's reliance (cf. Atiyah, 1981: 64–5)? In other words, when is a promise or other act of will directed to an individual considered a matter of social (legal) concern, so that society (not just the reliant individual) requires it to be fulfilled or its expected consequences realised? Presumably, for Durkheim, this depends on ideas of individual personality and individual status having been developed, at least to some significant extent, in legal thought, that is to say they have become socially recognised and valued.

5. See pp. 95–9, above.

Huvelin's approach seems more illuminating. He sees contract, in its most primitive beginnings, as acquiring its authority by means related to but apart from religion, in an individualised, private appropriation of collective beliefs, through magic (Huvelin, 1907: 45–6). Magic turns collective beliefs (about the supernatural) into private resources. Law inherits this authority from magic in so far as it concerns itself with controlling and authorising private claims. Thus, society as the author of all law eventually 'takes over' or replaces pre-legal sources of authority that initially made possible the assertion of private rights (Huvelin, 1907: 37). The approach explains how social beliefs can give individuals in early societies a purely private power to change their status in relation to others. It escapes Durkheim's disabling, implausible insistence that somehow religion must explain the social origin of all aspects of private rights. On the other hand, as noted in Chapter 6, the nature of magic as a source of pre-legal obligations or 'pre-law' (Gernet, 1951) remains somewhat unclear in Huvelin's analysis. What is the exact relationship between its social character (as a derivation from religion and a matter of collective beliefs) and its private character (as a resource to serve individual purposes)?

Social origins of contractual obligation

If Durkheim's own writing on the beginnings of contract is disappointing, further insights can be sought in the work of some close collaborators. Georges Davy (1922), for example, offers an anthropological account of the origins of contract. He seeks to explain how the idea of contractual obligation was established in social evolution. Like Durkheim, his focus is on the formal recognition of procedures used to bring about changes of status. Davy begins from the position that obligations in the most primitive societies derive from membership in a kinship group or clan and from alliance through marriage. To create relations with an outsider it is necessary to incorporate the stranger into the family group (for example, through blood covenant) (Davy, 1922: 49), or to marry into the stranger's family. Marriage alters the position of the families of the marriage partners. It creates a 'communion' between the families as a result of the sexual union and, typically, the woman being brought into the man's household (1922: 85ff.). It limits enmity between families, the rule of exogamy ensuring that the bride will come from a rival, external and thus potentially hostile group. Marriage also sets up a co-operative relationship between wife-giving and wife-receiving groups marked by exchanges of gifts and services (1922: 99ff.).

According to Davy, marriage in simple tribal society brings two 'contracts' into existence: one of succession by which the bride's father's rights and privileges will pass to his daughter's children through his son-in-law; and one of exchange of benefits between the kin of the marriage partners (1922: ch. 2). Thus, in the system of relations set up through marriage, specific obligations attached to individuals are created. Statuses are changed or produced. Marriage solves what Davy (1922: 109) calls the 'great problem of contract' – how to establish an *interval of time* between the creation of an obligation and its fulfilment. In a direct exchange of assets, each party's expectations are immediately fulfilled. But where one party gains only a promise from the other, for example to repay a debt or to perform services at some future time in return for a benefit received now, how is the obligation to provide a future benefit or service enforced? How does one person's will bind another's. Huvelin saw this problem as solved by the use of magic. For Davy, however, marriage provides the model of deferred fulfilment of obligations. Thus, among the North American Kwakiutl Indians, according to his description, the pre-nuptial agreement of the future bridegroom and the father-in-law involves both immediate and deferred benefits. The bridegroom makes an initial payment to the father-in-law and promises to produce children. The father-in-law gives his daughter to the bridegroom and promises that she will bear a child. On the birth of a child the father-in-law surrenders titles and badges of rank to his son-in-law, through whom these pass to the child. At the same time he makes a payment to the son-in-law which represents the return of the original payment received with substantial interest added. Thus, a transfer of immediate benefits ensures the later fulfilment of obligations (Davy, 1922: 102–14).

Davy emphasises that 'contract' at this stage is possible only in the context of membership in a family group. It is the institution of potlatch – or ceremonial gift giving – that frees it from this context (1922: ch. 3). Davy's evidence of potlatch is mainly from North American Indian (Tlinkit, Haida and Kwakiutl) societies. The potlatch can take various forms of ceremonial display of wealth but often involves an ostentatious transfer of property, accompanied by feasting or ritual, by a group or an individual to members of another group. The recipients must reciprocate this generosity at a later time. If they fail to do so they lose prestige. Thus, potlatch is used to demonstrate status (1922: 156–8). Davy distinguishes two forms of potlatch. The earlier is associated with status changes such as births, initiations, marriages and funerals. Thus, the Kwakiutl marriage agreement 'itself operated as a kind of potlatch' between father-in-law and son-in-law and their kin (1922: 270). The other, later, form of potlatch, however, is 'a simple commercial contract of loan functioning absolutely freely' (1922: 170). It involves an obligation to repay with interest, is not limited to occasions of change of status, is practised by individuals as well as groups and combines social and economic purposes (MacCormack, 1980: 170). According to Davy

(1922: 237–40), it is contractual in some sense because separate parties are identified in the procedures and brought into relation and an obligation – effectively that of creditor and debtor – is created by the acceptance of the gift; yet rights and duties here do not arise by agreement but through unilateral acts of giving and receiving.

Whereas the first form of potlatch is entirely a matter of group relations Davy sees the second as introducing the beginnings of individualism. It enables individuals to assert superiority over other individuals through the distribution of wealth. It facilitates the emergence of chiefs, not by right of birth but through control of resources; 'true feudal lords' or 'princes of commerce' (Davy, 1922: 250). Creditor–debtor relations thus come into existence between superior chiefs who distribute largesse, and inferior chiefs who pay tribute. Yet these relations are still, strictly, pre-contractual (1922: 231). Contract involves people transacting not as superiors and inferiors but on a basis of legal equality, in other words when pre-existing status no longer decides the nature of the relational bond.

What is of interest in Davy's thesis is not his view of social evolution, generalised from limited ethnographic evidence, but the image of contract that he presents. Like Durkheim and Huvelin he emphasises the way individuals come to be seen as having power to change their circumstances with socially sanctioned (legal) effect. Whatever the differences in the explanations offered by these writers, each sees social conditions, not individual desires, as creating this power in the individual, which is eventually recognised in law. For Huvelin, magic empowers the will. For Davy, social rituals create obligations which are the prototype of the debt owed to a creditor. The potlatch is made possible by the established organisation of society.

The essential point, common to all Durkheimian analysis, is that individual rights derive from social sources and are defined and limited by them (see Davy, 1922: 319–20). Private arrangements acquire legal and moral force only when they are aspects of a more general social structure or expressions of collective beliefs. The organisation of society (a structure of families interrelated by marriage) originally made possible the creation of individual obligations (Davy). Alternatively, collective beliefs empowered practices by which such obligations could be produced (Huvelin). Davy seems to offer a functional interpretation of the emergence of reciprocal obligations: the structure of society made it necessary for these obligations to exist. Huvelin, by contrast, provides an ideational explanation: collective ideas (underpinning magic practices) allow individuals to assert their will over others.

The institution of contract might be pictured here as an arch built with much difficulty. The pillars are slowly set in place in legal history as individual will gradually gains social power. Then, cautiously and experimentally, a span is thrown between the pillars (individual wills begin to be linked legally) as the possibility of reciprocal obligations is created and accepted in the collective consciousness and so further legal development occurs. The span consists of two ideas: first, that a person's acts may create an obligation in another (to reciprocate in some agreed way); and secondly, that a person's promise may create a right in another to insist on performance of that promise (cf. MacCormick, 1982). Huvelin's work, as has been seen, focuses on the way that individual wills are empowered. Hence its main concern is to explain the construction of the pillars of the arch. Davy concentrates on indicating ways in which the first efforts to create the span (the idea of reciprocal obligations) of the arch of contract are made in social development.

The morality of reciprocity

Davy does not delve deeply into the question of how the gifts of the potlatch create obligations of reciprocity. His focus is on the way that the status relationships of family and marriage provide a framework in which these obligations can initially be conceived. The potlatch, in some of its forms, is then just their extension beyond the family environment. But another of Durkheim's co-workers, Marcel Mauss, undertakes the task in his famous essay on 'The Gift' of showing the moral ideas that surround gift giving itself (Mauss, 1990). Mauss' study identifies what I shall call a *morality of reciprocity* – a morality creating an obligation to receive graciously what is given and to give adequately (but not necessarily a measured equivalent) in return for what is received. He emphasises the importance of things given as, in themselves, creating the obligation to receive and reciprocate.

Mauss (1990: 5) saw Davy and himself as co-workers in studying the 'archaic forms of contract'. But his focus is actually quite different from Davy's (cf. Gernet, 1956: 139). Davy studies a few key societies to identify a crucial stage of legal and social evolution. Mauss' aim is to identify principles of social organisation that are timeless and underpin even modern contractual life, although they are explicit only in a certain phase of social development (as in the societies of the potlatch). Mauss draws his evidence not only from Davy's tribal societies of the American Northwest but also from Polynesia, Melanesia and elsewhere to suggest 'a regime [of gift exchange] that must have been shared by a very large part of humanity during a very long transitional phase' (Mauss, 1990: 46).

For Mauss, the presentation and reciprocation of gifts is 'the archaic form of exchange', appropriate to societies of limited individualism. In these societies exchanges are no longer just between families or clans, but they have not reached the stage of 'purely individual contract, of the market where money circulates, of sale proper, and above all of the notion of price reckoned in coinage weighed and stamped with its value' (1990: 46). In this transitional phase, the 'force of things', which are often 'the magical and religious symbol of rank and plenty' (1990: 43, 44), drives the system of exchange. It draws people into this system, requiring them to participate. The system is an endless circulation of obligatory gifts. And Mauss argues that, in ancient European law, traces of this remain, for example in *nexum*, a very early form of Roman contract, or the Germanic *wadium* (1990: 48–9). Essentially, his argument is that the mere handing over of a thing creates obligations, even when in the formalistic procedures of early law the thing transferred is purely symbolic and of no value in itself.[6] Even the magical powers that Huvelin stressed rely, in Mauss' view, on assumed sacred qualities of the objects handed over; that is, on their being seen as separate from ordinary items of mere utility in everyday life.

It is not necessary here to examine in detail Mauss' images of the earliest ages of legal development. As always in considering Durkheimian uses of history and ethnography, it is important to ask what thesis about the moral constitution of social life the data are chosen to illustrate. Mauss' object is to show that the gift encapsulates the essence of solidarity and interdependence. The act of giving, in his picture, is a matter of obligation. The morality of reciprocity is universal and powerful. It fuses economic and social aspects. Thus gift exchange, embodying this morality, is pre-contractual, representing a stage of social development before the separating out of contract as the instrument of individualised economic exchange in a money economy. Making and receiving gifts is overlaid with ceremonial and social meaning. Contract, as such, in its later development is freed from these encumbrances to present itself as a pragmatic means by which individuals can realise their projects.

Mauss argues, however, that the morality of reciprocity must still underlie modern social life. The critical thrust of his essay is that, although this morality made possible the very idea of contractual obligation, modern contract in its individualistic heyday has presented itself as though it were wholly free of these moral origins. Legal codes have obliterated the sense of an unquantified obligation arising from the receipt of a benefit. In place of it they have put specific rights and duties defined by reference to criteria of agreement that privilege form over substance. Yet, nowadays, Mauss suggests, 'the old [moral] principles react against the rigour, abstraction, and inhumanity of our legal codes . . . a whole section of our law that is just emerging . . . consists

6. A comparison might be made with the doctrine of consideration in the English law of contract, which allows the transfer of a purely nominal consideration – 'a mere peppercorn' – to seal the contractual obligation.

of turning back the clock. This reaction . . . is perfectly healthy' (1990: 66–7). Modern law recognises that the consumer is not fully protected morally by abstract principles of freedom of contract. This development reinforces the old morality of reciprocity – the sense that an expectation of reasonable return for what is given (for example, as purchase price) must not be frustrated. Again, the expectation of artists of sharing in the full value of work they created produces a 'moral right' enforceable legally in some jurisdictions. And social protection legislation, in Mauss' view, is a legal recognition that wages paid to the employee do not exhaust the latter's right to a return for the contribution given to the employer (and to society) through work (1990: 67).

Durkheim, of course, sees such matters in terms of organic solidarity. Mauss explores the moral meaning of contract law by speculating on evidence from anthropology and ancient legal systems. The importance of his work in the present context is that it connects directly with Durkheim's own most clearly developed focus in considering contract law – the needs of organic solidarity. Mauss shows how obligation and right can arise not merely from individual wills but from social settings of reciprocity. But whereas Durkheim tends to assume in *The Division of Labour* that contract is self-evidently a framework of modern solidarity, Mauss casts doubt on the exactness of the fit between legal form and moral need. It is highly significant that it is the development of individualism that, for Mauss, pulls contract away from the morality of reciprocity and thus from the requirements of solidarity. It seems that, like most of the Durkheimians (see Pickering, 1993: 73), he did not really embrace Durkheim's view of the cult of the individual as the basis of a socially unifying morality. Hence his account of contract's prehistory raises the same basic question as does Durkheim's early thesis on modern law in *The Division of Labour*. Where does this modern law find its moral foundation? Mauss portrays its foundation as a morality of reciprocity. But he does not see modern law as firmly rooted in this morality: 'One might even say that a whole section of the law, that relating to industrialists and businessmen, is nowadays at odds with morality' (1990: 66). Hence, for Mauss, law must *recapture* its links with morality. And he sees tendencies towards this in the legal developments mentioned above: 'we are returning to a group morality' (1990: 68), as the state and its agencies act to modify the consequences of abstract contract principles.

Contract, individualism and solidarity

Mauss' prescriptions, in the final pages of his essay, seem to dissolve into wishful thinking. Somehow, it seems, law is getting back to its moral roots. 'The themes of the gift, of the freedom and the obligation inherent in the gift, of generosity and self-interest that are linked in giving, are reappearing in French society, as a dominant motif too long forgotten' (Mauss, 1990: 68). But this statement stands oddly alongside his other comments on commercial and industrial law as 'at odds with morality'.

The same ambivalence is very apparent in Durkheim's work. He makes much of what he sees as the developing idea of 'just contracts' (Durkheim, 1957: ch. 18). Things and services must be 'exchanged at the true and normal value . . . the just value' (1957: 211), which reflects the effort expended, the need for what is produced or done by each party, and the satisfaction afforded by it. This idea, already present in *The Division of Labour* (1984: 317–19) and further developed in the later lectures on contract (1957: 209–11), implies aspects of a morality of reciprocity such as Mauss explores. But it also implies respect for each individual's efforts as well as an 'objective' social valuation of the content of contracts. In the lectures, Durkheim proposes that contracts must be made by mutual consent and their consequences determined exclusively by the intent of the parties. In other words, moral substance must govern the contract rather than formality and abstract criteria.

From a lawyer's typical viewpoint, however, these ideas are very problematic: form and substance always have to be balanced, mutual consent and the intentions of the parties are often hard to determine, objective indicia of contract are necessary and the idea of just value is hard to operationalise legally. Durkheim's prescriptions for just contracts are vague. But it is easy to see why he treats contract in this way in his lectures. Contractual ties need to be *morally meaningful* to those involved with them. Individualism as a moral value requires that individual intentions and expectations be respected. Law must take full account of them. Durkheim's idea of just contracts, as fully elaborated, seems designed to reflect the morality of the cult of the individual – the only shared morality that he sees as underlying modern law. For example, gross unfairness in pricing is unacceptable. 'There is something about this exploitation of one man by another that offends us and rouses our indignation even if it is agreed to by the one who suffers it and has not been imposed by actual constraint' (1957: 210–11). In other words, the collective consciousness condemns such exploitation. The morality of individualism demands protection of the contracting party, just as, in a different way, it demands protection of the victim of crime and condemnation of the criminal.

It is clear, therefore, that Durkheim sees a popular morality at work governing expectations as to how contracts should work. But it is equally clear that this morality often does not prevail. 'Certainly the stronger succeed in crushing the not so strong or at any rate in reducing them to a state of subjection. But since this subjection is only a *de facto* condition sanctioned by no kind of morals, it is accepted only under duress until the longed for day of revenge' (1957: 11; cf. 1984: xxxii). Sometimes he writes of the 'moral anarchy' of economic life (1957: 15). Class conflict results from inadequate moral regulation of economic relationships.[7]

It seems that for Durkheim, as for Mauss, modern contract law has risked losing its entire moral basis. It has become a wholly economic rather than social matter. The fusion of social and economic functions of exchange, highlighted in Davy's and Mauss' accounts of the pre-history of contract, has disappeared. Thus contract appears purely as a utilitarian institution – a means of pursuing individual economic purposes not part of some larger pattern of the collective good. But economic functions, Durkheim insists, are not ends in themselves. They constitute merely one of the organs of social life which itself must be 'a harmonious community of endeavours' (1957: 16). The idea of just contracts suggests that the individual freedom that modern law enshrines in contract is not morally sufficient unless its exercise increases the well-being of all individuals.

In *The Division of Labour* Durkheim writes about just contracts in terms not of the values of individualism but of the regulatory needs of organic solidarity. There, the conditions by which contract law should operate are seen as merely part of a wider spectrum of requirements for regulation (1984: book 3). Insufficient regulation produces anomie – a failure of co-ordination, guidance or control and hence a lack of moral meaning in the face of limitless, chaotic pursuit of desires, or a lack of socially satisfying tasks to perform.[8] On the other hand, too much or too insensitive regulation can crush the relations of interdependence at the heart of organic solidarity and the fine balance that must be maintained among them.

Contractual relations are only one aspect of organic solidarity as described in *The Division of Labour* (1984: 316). But contract is the subject that most clearly reveals the ambivalence of Durkheim's thinking about modern law. Contract is the framework of commerce and industrial relations – the very fields where Durkheim sees the most serious problems of anomie and disruption in modern society. The contracted employee is treated as 'an inert piece of machinery' and 'no matter how one represents the moral ideal, one cannot remain indifferent to such a debasement of human nature' (1893a: 363; 1984: 306–7). Modern contract as an economic device denies the morality of reciprocity because it takes no account of the moral requirement to give adequately

---

7. See pp. 182–3, below.
8. See pp. 19–20, above.

in return for what has been received. Hence contract needs legal regulation to make transactions just in terms of popular morality; that is, to restore to contract something of the characteristics of a social rather than merely economic relationship.

On the other hand, contract law, as portrayed in *The Division of Labour*, is an area in which the governmental morality of proper organisation and co-ordination of social life directly focuses. Contract is a device that brings different functions into relations with each other. It thus facilitates agreement between people who have different expectations, values, beliefs and sentiments. It might be said that, in order to do so, it must operate on objective criteria legislated as a secure framework within which the different contracting parties must act. If it inquires too far into subjective intentions it may find irreconcilable differences between parties. If it attempts to legislate perfect fairness it may neglect the fact that fairness can mean different things from different standpoints. In this sense contract is not an expression of shared outlooks – whether about individual freedom and dignity, as Durkheim proposes, or encompassed in a morality of reciprocity, such as Mauss suggests. It is a framework facilitating transactions between parties having different outlooks.

Contract law, therefore, can be viewed from different Durkheimian perspectives. On the one hand, it must reflect popular perceptions of fairness and justice in bargains struck and in the treatment of contracting individuals. On the other, the law must be an efficient means of economic and social co-ordination between people with diverse expectations, perceptions and economic and social roles. The analyses of Durkheim and his followers suggest that contract, like modern law in general, stands uneasily between two moral influences. One of these reflects popular moralities of individualism and reciprocity. The other reflects a governmental morality presupposed by the task of managing social complexity. But the overriding message is that contract law as a moral force is concerned with more than economic relations. The economic, in this context, is merely an aspect of the social.

9

Property, inheritance and family law

Beyond contract and criminal law, Durkheim's writings discuss other areas of law – always with the same broad concerns in view: he tries to explore the various legal needs of solidarity and legal expressions of individualism as a modern value system. The fields that attract sustained attention in these further writings are property and inheritance rights, and rights and duties surrounding domestic relations. Durkheim's ideas on these matters are the focus of the present chapter. The tension between functional and ideational analyses, traced in Chapters 7 and 8, colours all his analyses here. But this tension appears in different ways in his discussions of property, inheritance and the family, allowing us to assess its significance further.

Property rights and solidarity

Durkheim distinguishes in *The Division of Labour* between negative and positive relationships regulated by restitutive law. Positive relationships are those 'affording co-operation'; negative ones involve 'a mere abstention' (1984: 72). Contract seems to epitomise such a positive relationship. The right of property is characteristic of negative relationships. Durkheim treats property as a relationship between a person and a thing (1984: 72). The legal bond of property links the thing to its owner irrespective of any third person. Durkheim describes the regime of property, somewhat puzzlingly, as the 'real' (that is, relating to a *res* or thing) form of solidarity and notes that it 'links things directly to persons, but not persons with one another' (1984: 72–3). What is puzzling is that it should be considered to express a form of solidarity of any kind, in Durkheim's view, since he immediately indicates that this solidarity is 'wholly negative' and is not an organic solidarity (1893a: 393).[1] 'It does not cause individual wills to move towards common ends, but only

1. Durkheim contrasts mechanical solidarity here with negative solidarity on the one hand, and organic solidarity on the other. The translation in Durkheim (1984: 331) seems incorrect on this point.

causes things to gravitate around those individual wills in an orderly fashion'; there is 'no active co-operation, no consensus' and this solidarity 'contributes nothing to the unity of the body social' (1984: 73).

It can be noted, initially, that Durkheim's view of property as a relation of a person to a thing is likely to seem odd to many lawyers. In the common law world, at least, lawyers typically think of property as a variable set of legal relationships between persons with respect to things.[2] This might be thought realistic because law does not merely focus on pre-existing things in relation to persons but can actually create 'things' – for example, copyrights – as benefits or assets defined and protected through the specification of legal rights and duties attaching to persons (Honoré, 1960: 179–84). All legal relations can be considered, therefore, as relationships between persons. But while the common lawyer's view of property emphasises its technical utility and flexibility (in constructing a great diversity of different kinds of property rights), Durkheim's conception of property may reflect more directly common-sense, popular views of its nature. Thus, his approach seems consistent with his view of law as a special field or aspect of morality – a refinement or expression of popular moral convictions. But it neglects law's role as a creative instrument of regulation, capable of creating and shaping the idea of 'things' as a technical means of defining legal relationships between people.

This oversight seems to underlie the difficulty Durkheim has in seeing the relationship between property and solidarity. Organic solidarity concerns relationships between people, seen in terms of roles and their positions in society as a whole. Relations of people to things can have no place in this moral structure. But it would have been possible for Durkheim to see property relationships as part of the means by which relationships of solidarity between people can be organised in modern society if he had put more emphasis on the variability of property rights as law constructs and defines them. In the French context this might not have seemed an obvious approach, since a tradition of continental European legal thinking about property sees it in terms of *dominium,* more or less absolute rights of an owner (*dominus*) over the thing owned (Bolgar, 1953). In English common law, by contrast, the tradition of thinking accepts that property can be fragmented in complex ways: many different kinds of proprietary rights can exist in relation to the same asset, especially where the asset is land (see, for example, Lawson and Rudden, 1982: ch. 5). Different people can have different kinds of proprietary rights coexisting in the same assets. The rights can differ in extent and duration. Thus property appears as a flexible device for organising very varied economic and social relations in connection with the use of valuable assets.

2. Grey (1980), Waldron (1988: ch. 2), and see Bolgar (1953: 213ff.) on French views.

Durkheim's approach, however, forces him to collect together a whole range of so-called real rights and assign them to the category of purely negative relationships as regards solidarity. These rights are those of 'property law in its various forms (literary, artistic, industrial, movable and immovable property) and its different modes' as regulated by the second book of the French Civil Code, and various forms of pledge (*gage, antichrèse*), special charge (*privilège*) or mortgage (*hypothèque*) relating or attaching to property (Durkheim, 1893a: 86; cf. 1984: 73). Durkheim adds to this collection of rights those of testate and intestate succession (inheritance). Other negative relationships bring into play the exercise of real rights, as where property is acquired or extended, or compensation for damage caused by its use has to be paid (1984: 74).

> To sum up: the rules relating to 'real rights' and personal relationships that are established by virtue of them form a definite system whose function is not to link together the different parts of society, but on the contrary to detach them from one another, and mark out clearly the barriers separating them. Thus they do not correspond to any positive social tie. (1984: 75)

It seems clear that these rights of 'negative solidarity' pose a difficult problem for Durkheim in the scheme of *The Division of Labour*. His treatment of them confirms the claim made earlier[3] that the classification of restitutive and repressive law is not seen by Durkheim as a comprehensive basis for analysing all kinds of law. Property law simply does not fit the classification. Although its sanctions are restitutive it does not have the normal functional characteristics of restitutive law: it does not help to bind society together in moral ties of interdependence. 'Negative solidarity' is thus, Durkheim admits, 'not a true solidarity, but rather the negative aspects of every type of solidarity' (1984: 75). Its relationship with organic solidarity is merely to presuppose that solidarity. Property is not possible unless relations of co-operation have been established (1984: 76–7).

Property and individualism

It seems clear that the framework of functional interpretation of law provided in *The Division of Labour* could offer no satisfactory means of analysing the nature of property rights. Unsurprisingly, therefore, in Durkheim's lectures dating from 1898 to 1900 (Durkheim, 1957) he

3. See pp. 70–1 and 85–6, above.

adopts a quite different approach concerned to trace the evolution of *ideas* of property. As in relation to contract, so in the analysis of property, an ideational approach vies with a functional approach. But, whereas the functional approach could offer important insights into the relations of law and solidarity in considering contract, it seems to have little to offer in the analysis of property rights. Indeed, the functional approach is silently abandoned in favour of ideational analysis. So it remains to ask how a Durkheimian approach can illuminate property as an idea, or as a set of rights and obligations rather than as a matter of functional relationships.

In the lectures, property, like contract, has unsurprisingly become for Durkheim an expression of the value of individual freedom. The earlier effort to link property with solidarity is discarded in favour of an analysis of the idea of private property as a vehicle of individualism. To have true liberty, to allow individualism to have a basis in social reality, the individual requires 'some physical sphere of action within which . . . [to] exercise a kind of sovereignty' (1957: 172). Durkheim links property directly with the cult of the individual. This cult makes the individual sacred and 'it is inevitable that this sacred virtue which invests the individual should be extended to the things he is closely and lawfully connected with' (1957: 172). The sanctity of private property is merely an aspect of the cult of the individual. Individual freedom requires that 'there must be some kind of region where the individual is his own master' (1957: 172).

Durkheim notes that recognising property as an essential element of the value of individualism merely explains why private property is treated as sacred. It does not explain what is necessary for a thing to be treated as owned or capable of being so treated (1957: 172–3). Certainly, the focus on individualism makes it easier to see property rights as expressions of will – vehicles for positive individual assertion – rather than, as in *The Division of Labour*, merely stabilising limitations on, or consequences of, relations of interdependence. This, in turn, suggests that property rights can be as varied as necessary to reflect the variety of expressions of individual initiative and will. Thus, in the lectures, Durkheim seems more ready than before to recognise that property is whatever human beings wish to make it. '*A priori*, no limits can be set to the power the collectivity has to endow anything that exists with the qualities requisite for juridical appropriation, or to take away those qualities' (1957: 138). Objects of property are determined by law, not by nature. Thus, although the 'idea of property first evokes the idea of a thing' (1957: 136), the earlier emphasis on property as a relationship between persons and things seems downgraded in the lectures, since things are what law (that is, society through its organised sanctioning) says they are.

Equally, the kinds of rights that can exist in a thing, an object of property, are now explicitly recognised as extremely varied. 'All that can be said is that wherever ... [a property] right exists there is a subject ... capable of legally exercising certain powers over the object that is said to be possessed, but without it being possible as a rule to say with accuracy what these powers consist of. They must always exist but we cannot say exactly what they are' (1957: 140–1). Thus, an owner may not have a right to dispose of the asset. Sometimes a non-owner may do so. And rights to use the asset may be held by a non-owner (1957: 145). Equally it is for law to declare who can and cannot be an owner (1957: 138). Durkheim still holds to the idea of property as the link between an object appropriated and the subject or person appropriating it (1957: 138). And in the first edition of *The Division of Labour* he had referred to the right of property as a '*complexus* of rights determined through a very great number of rules which complete or delimit each other' (1893b: 268). But when, in the lectures, property is thought of as an idea rather than a social function, it seems possible to recognise more explicitly the complexity and variability of that idea.

What then is distinctive about property rights? It is that only the owner (whether an individual or a collectivity) can use the thing owned, unless the owner gives permission to another to use it. 'A thing over which I exercise the right of property is a thing which serves myself alone. It is a thing withdrawn from common use for its use by a given subject ... no one other than myself can enjoy it' (1957: 141) [without my permission]. *Exclusive enjoyment* or possession, *withdrawal from common usage*, is, for Durkheim, the distinguishing feature of property (1957: 142, 146; cf. Gray, 1991: 268ff.). A property right must therefore be defined negatively, 'by the exclusion it involves rather than the prerogatives it confers' (1957: 142). The positive powers and privileges that ownership gives are too varied to yield a definition (1957: 146). A property right is 'the right of a given individual to exclude other individual and collective entities from the usage of a given thing' (1957: 142). The sole exception to this is interference by the state and its organs, which cannot be entirely excluded. But they can only intrude on property rights in special circumstances provided for by law.

The association of the sanctity of property with the cult of the individual implies not only the freedom that property gives but also its *limits*. We have seen that, for Durkheim, individualism is a product of society. It is the moral framework appropriate to complex modern societies, a shared morality allowing these societies to cohere despite the diversity of their members' experiences and understandings. Individualism is not to be confused with egoism, blind asocial selfishness, which is not a social value at all.[4] Hence property as an aspect of the cult of the individual is the vehicle of individualism, not egoism. It follows that society determines the limits of property and the meaning of its 'sanctity'. It does this, of course, through law. Property, therefore, is not a right that can be asserted *against law*. It is the creature of law and subject to whatever constraints and conditions law attaches to it. In all societies, Durkheim notes, 'the range of persons qualified to own is decided by the laws ... as is the range of things qualified to be owned' (1957: 138). More fundamentally the value of property is also socially determined. It is the value attributed to some thing (for example, a house or investments) by common opinion (1957: 125). Thus property is created and destroyed by opinion, in so far as it is part of a system of exchange (1957: 126).[5]

Durkheim's approach thus explains sociologically both the 'sacred' character of property and its various kinds of fragility. Although his lectures do not see property in functional terms, they interpret it as an expression of society's unifying moral code. Like contract, property is a social fact. If it is an expression of individual will this is only in so far as society allows individual wills to assert themselves. Property, no less than contract, must have a moral basis. Both must be made by law to serve as vehicles of individualism, not egoism.

The evolution of property rights

From all that has been said earlier about Durkheim's outlook on law after the early *Division of Labour* period, it is only to be expected that he would try to find the origin of ideas of property rights in early religious beliefs. Much discussion in the lectures on property is concerned with this somewhat esoteric quest, which involves using clues from ethnography, myth and early social and economic history.

The starting point for the inquiry is given by Durkheim's definition of property as that which is set apart from common use and rendered exclusive to the owner. The question is: what makes it possible to withdraw assets from common use and treat them as exclusively attached to particular owners? What evolution of ideas allows this to happen? Durkheim's approach is to emphasise, using ethnographic evidence from Polynesia, the importance of ideas of taboo – the setting apart of certain objects as sacred – in early or simple societies. Sacred objects are withdrawn from the common property of the group (Durkheim, 1957: 143).

4. See pp. 112–15, above.
5. This idea is the departure point for Emmanuel Lévy's radicalisation of Durkheim's legal theory, discussed in Chapter 12, below.

Access to sacred objects is reserved to priests or other specially authorised persons. 'The domain lived in by a priest or a chief was taboo to
the common people and could not be made use of by the common-
alty, but this very setting apart constituted the full property right of the
owner' (1957: 143). There is a close link, Durkheim suggests, between
taboo and the idea of sacred things in early Roman society.

> We can see how close the connection is between this concept and
> that of ownership. Around the thing appropriated, as around the
> sacred thing, a vacuum formed. All individuals had to keep at a
> distance, as it were, except those who had the required qualifications
> to approach it and make use of it . . . The origins of property are to
> be found in the nature of certain religious beliefs. (1957: 143–4)

And the declaration of things as sacred was a way of putting them
under the sole control of chiefs or priests.

Religious ideas, in Durkheim's view, thus originally made possible
the idea of things taken from common use and reserved or appropriated to special purposes and persons. Clearly, it would be impossible
to explain all the ways in which this evolution of ideas could occur
historically. But Durkheim devotes attention to a particular account of
the evolution of the idea of property in land. He notes that the idea
of the sacredness of boundaries is found in ancient Greek, Roman and
Indian society (1957: 150–1). There was, indeed, a Roman god of
boundaries – Terminus – and boundary land was sacred land. At the
edges of fields were places of sacrifice, while gates and walls were considered sacred (1957: 151–2; Fustel de Coulanges, 1864: 71–2). What is
the meaning of these practices and rituals? Durkheim insists that the
idea of the sacred here is not a matter of expediency. These customs
were 'far too primitive to have been expedients intended to preserve
worldly interests'; they constrained owners rather than giving freedom,
because the sanctified boundaries could not be changed (Durkheim,
1957: 153).

The historian Fustel de Coulanges, whose ideas on the significance
of religion as a source of law influenced Durkheim (Pickering, 1984:
56–8), explained these practices in terms of the cult of the dead – the
worship of ancestors (Fustel de Coulanges, 1864: book 2, ch. 6).
Durkheim rejects this explanation, however, because the sacred area
was not restricted to a burial area, and the most sacred places were not
the burial areas but the boundaries. The 'family cult' is much wider
than a cult of the dead. It encompasses protection of the harvest and
the fruitfulness of the fields. Indeed, the fields themselves are sacred
and it is dangerous to intrude on them without proper rites (for example,
the sacrifice of first fruits) being performed (Durkheim, 1957: 153–4).

Thus, every religion, writes Durkheim, is familiar with the practice of setting aside first fruits and offering them to the gods before people may touch the fruits for themselves (1957: 155). The sacred force of the fields is 'drawn off' to the boundaries, where sacrifices take place. Thus the link that people have to the fields depends upon the gods and the recurring sacrifices (1957: 157).

More generally, sacred property, controlled or supervised by chiefs or priests, becomes the model for *all* human property. It establishes property as that which is set apart, withdrawn from general use and appropriated under the exclusive control of certain persons. Thus, in origin, all property is social not individual. It becomes available for private appropriation as prestigious individuals – considered qualified to control things – emerge. These are initially the heads of families (1957: 165, 171). But also necessary to the development of private property is the emergence of an idea that personal or movable property is significant. Initially, only land was important and subjected to religious controls. These stressed its place in the natural order of life, its domination over individual human beings, its inalienability at the hands of the human custodians tied to it, its enduring nature and sacred attributes. Other objects had significance only in relation to land. But as movable property became important economically with the development of trade, property had 'a fresh nucleus . . . outside real estate' and free of the characteristics of landed property that had inhibited its alienation (1957: 166–8). Movable property bears the stamp of property's general origins, but modified to remove its ties to communal aspects of early property. 'From now onwards it is man who stands above things, and it is a certain individual in particular who occupies this position, that is, who owns or possesses' (1957: 168).

What should be made of these Durkheimian speculations, especially those relating to the earliest ideas about land? Perhaps they show, in the most acute form, a mysterious feature of much of Durkheim's ideational treatment of legal concepts. The functional analysis of *The Division of Labour* has entirely disappeared. In its place is an inquiry into the ancient history of ideas. Yet much of what Durkheim proposes about the significance of the earliest religious ideas of land and boundaries is unprovable; indeed, it resists any empirical assessment. The analysis, here as elsewhere, is pushed back to the very beginnings of social development where, inevitably, no convincing empirical inquiry is possible. What is offered ultimately is a set of ideas suggesting elements of a philosophy of law in society: a way of thinking about legal ideas, coloured by speculation on their origin. Durkheim does not merely write about myth in his account of the beginnings of property. He himself presents a myth of origins, unchallengeable because no evidence can be conclusive about the beliefs and practices of so remote a time.

Inheritance and the limits of property

Why does he take this speculative approach to the study of property? Surely, it is to argue further for what I called in Chapter 6 his philosophies of society and of law – to offer a particular moral perspective on the nature of legal and social phenomena. The theory of the origins of property in land should therefore be seen in much the same way as aspects of Durkheim's theory of legal evolution:[6] that is, it should be seen as social philosophical speculation coloured and inspired (rather than confirmed) by empirical generalisation about history. His tendency to use historical materials in this way did not disappear after *The Division of Labour* was written.

What then is the message Durkheim wants to convey through his speculations on the beginnings of property? He makes it explicit: 'Respect for property is . . . not . . . an extension to things of the respect that human personality imposes, individually or collectively. It has a very different source, exterior to the human person' (1957: 158). This source is *society*. Property may, like contract, be an expression of individual will. But, like contract, it must always be seen as a social phenomenon. It is given by society. That is, property is created by collective beliefs that establish its meaning and justify any legal significance things may have in the context of human relationships. Hence property must always be subject to the moral constraints that society, by its nature, demands.

Ultimately, however, the morality of property remains obscure in Durkheim's analysis. While, as we saw in Chapter 8, he and his co-workers offered many suggestions as to the moral constraints that surround, or should surround, contract, it is harder to see what Durkheim thinks these constraints are in the case of individual property rights. As has been seen, the early discussion in *The Division of Labour* offers no clear answers. In the later lectures, the approach is very different. The stress is on modern property as an expression of the cult of the individual, which 'depends absolutely' on it (1957: 172). With the cult of the individual, 'sacredness', which in the earliest history of property resided in things themselves, has now become an attribute of the individual, the property owner (1957: 173). In early times the question was who could own, on what conditions, subject to what constraints? Today the question is: what is owned? Previously the issue was about owners, now it is about the things owned. The 'sacred' character of the individual extends to things in some way closely connected with individuals. Thus, in understanding the moral significance of property, Durkheim suggests, it is essential to analyse the means by which

6. See pp. 91, 93, above.

the tie between persons and things is established: in modern society these means are contract and inheritance. So it seems that the general question of property's moral nature is side-stepped. Durkheim turns it into questions about contract – considered in Chapter 8 – and about the particular institution of inheritance, which is the one aspect of property on which he is prepared to express a strong moral view.

Certainly, powerful hints are given in Durkheim's lectures that property can never be considered an absolute right. The individual's right of property exists for society's purposes – that is, for purposes of exchange and co-operation (1957: 122–3). The cult of the individual sanctifies the individual in the abstract – that is, the equal right and dignity of *all* individuals – and therefore it may demand curtailment of the property rights of a particular individual to promote the rights of all (1957: 122). And the right to possess something, Durkheim writes, does not logically entail the right to dispose of it; 'the right to enjoy the things we possess has never been absolute; it is always hedged about with restrictions' (1957: 124). Hence the significance in the early history of property law of the estate holder's lack of legal power to alienate the land freely.

Durkheim's main concern, however, in stressing limitations of the freedom of the property owner is to lay foundations for his attack on rights of inheritance or succession. It is clear that, for him, rights of succession, whether testate or intestate, to property violate key principles of the necessary moral framework of modern society. By 'creating inequalities amongst men from birth, that are unrelated to merit or services, [inheritance] invalidates the whole contractual system at its very roots (1957: 213); 'distribution of things amongst individuals can be just only if it is made relative to the social deserts of each' (1957: 214); and 'one cannot have rich and poor at birth, without unjust contracts existing' (1893a: 378; cf. 1984: 319). Thus, the inheritance system undermines the possibility of 'just contracts', based on genuine equivalence. Yet this possibility was seen in Chapter 8 to be essential, in Durkheim's view, to a morally acceptable contract regime in modern society. The automatic right of inheritance is no longer appropriate because it denies the value of individualism that is necessary to modern society. Thus, Durkheim suggests, inheritance will lose its importance as a social institution more and more (1957: 175).

Intestate succession, among the surviving family of the deceased, is seen by Durkheim as a survival of archaic ideas of collective property; in particular, the right of family joint ownership (1957: 174, 216). In this family ownership, the rights of other family members are held in abeyance during the possessor's life, but reassert themselves as he is about to die. Thus the family – specifically, the heir as its representative – has the sole right to inherit. Only later does a right of testation arise historically (1957: 174). Thus, intestate succession reflects a view of the nature of property which is actually antagonistic to the values of individualism. It should, in Durkheim's view, be abolished (1957: 216). The position with testate succession is 'a more delicate matter' (1957: 217). We work for our children as for ourselves, and the right to pass to them what is ours is considered morally important. 'It is not unlikely that something would always remain of the right to dispose of property by will.' But it should remain only in weakened form: with limits on the amounts a testator can bequeath and with the right of testation limited to benefiting the children of the testator. 'The inequalities that would then continue would be so slight as not to affect seriously the operation of contractual equity (*droit*)' (1950: 241; cf. 1957: 217).

The difference here in Durkheim's treatment of testate and intestate succession reflects again the differences of emphasis between his two approaches to understanding modern law. If this law is to be seen, functionally, as a means of co-ordinating relations of reciprocity and co-operation for organic solidarity, inheritance regimes have no place in this co-ordination. They appear arbitrary. The wishes of the dead (in testate succession) cannot be appropriate to co-ordinate the collective organisation of the living. On the other hand, modern law can be understood, ideationally, as expressing the values of individualism. From that perspective, intestate succession again has no place in such a value system, being merely an automatic, non-voluntary and (in terms of merit) arbitrary reordering of property arrangements in the family. But testate succession is different. The right to make a will and determine the destination of one's property after death might be considered a supreme expression of respect for the autonomy of individuals – even to the extent of respecting their wishes after their death. Yet also, for Durkheim, it is essential to remember that individual rights are given by society to reflect society's moral requirements of collective life. Therefore, just as property rights in general can be curtailed for the good of society, so too testamentary freedom can be limited. The limitation will be that necessary to promote the morality of reciprocity that allows reasonable harmony in social relationships in complex modern societies.

Family, marriage and divorce

Durkheim's ideas on inheritance suggest that he sees changes in family structure as of great importance for the development of law's moral foundations. For him, the family, like the school,[7] can be treated

7. See p. 77, above.

in certain respects as a 'small society'. Here his nineteenth-century outlook on family life struggles with the attempt to conceptualise clearly the direction of social change affecting domestic relations.

As with all his other analyses of law, Durkheim's analysis of family law reflects tensions between the functional outlook of *The Division of Labour* and the ideational emphases of his later work. Thus, in his first book, the family is described in terms of the evolution in it of a division of labour. This is said to dominate its whole development (1984: 79). Family functions become separated and 'distributed among the various relatives according to sex, age and dependent relationships, so as to make each relative a specialised functionary in domestic society' (1984: 78–9). Family law specifies this functional differentiation: for example, it defines duties of husband and wife, relationships on termination of marriage, powers of a father, and legal consequences of adoption, or of administration by a guardian and relations with a ward (1984: 78).

Certainly, it is clear that much law in this area, historically, is concerned with the definition and protection of distinct statuses within family structures. But this legal differentiation hardly guarantees the kind of solidarity that Durkheim associates with the division of labour in modern society. Family statuses reflected in legal history have usually been those of domination and subjection. Sometimes, as Durkheim recognises, the regime of family life has had a severity carried to the harshest extremes (1984: lii). Yet as in the wider society, the division of labour in the family expresses, for Durkheim, a 'special solidarity' (1984: 78). Social differentiation in the family is thus no less 'normal' and morally appropriate than in the wider society. The natural social character of family life is undoubtedly, for him, that of a realm of harmonious co-operation and 'intimate benificence' (1984: lii; Davy, 1919: 198). The basis for this seems to be not equality between individual family members but an abstract association of interdependent, differentiated roles. Yet Durkheim recognises that these roles are not necessarily biologically determined. Adoption allows the creation of non-biological parental ties. Artificial kinship has been very easily created in many societies, though less readily in recent times (1984: xliv, 156–7). Also, the 'domestic division of labour' (1984: 78) does not, it seems, require specific unvarying roles, though Durkheim makes clear his belief that men and women are different by nature. Therefore, while their social roles in family life should be made of equal status, those roles will remain distinct (1952: 385).

In this context, functional analysis plainly militates against – or provides a justification for refusing – a complete recognition of freedom of action. The family as an institution is too important in the social structure of functional interdependence and co-operation to be left as a realm of purely individual choices. Creating and dissolving marriage, for example, require precise legal controls. Durkheim claims that entry (by marriage and adoption) into family relationships has become harder in the course of social development towards organic solidarity (1984: 155–7). The differentiated roles of marriage partners have social as well as individual significance. Thus, 'as domestic obligations are becoming more numerous they are taking on, so to speak, a public character' (1984: 157–8). But it might be said that, in *this* respect, family life is no different from other functionally defined spheres (such as commerce or industrial relations).

If the field of domestic relationships is looked at, not functionally but ideationally in terms of the development of the values of individualism that Durkheim sees as becoming ever more dominant as the moral underpinning of modern society, the emphasis changes somewhat. In lectures dating from 1898 to 1900, Durkheim notes the break-up of the family group under the influence of individualist values (1957: 218). It is no longer a stable social unit. The process of social development is towards ever greater freedom for its members and the ending of automatic family claims on the property of individuals. The family is no longer a permanent focus of group loyalty. It is reduced to a partnership of husband and wife except during the years of child rearing, and is dissolved by death in each generation (1984: xlv; Lukes, 1973: 184–5). In Durkheim's lectures, the idea of the family as a functional group, in which relationships are functionally defined, gives way to a different emphasis: on the family as seemingly almost anachronistic, or at least greatly reduced in social significance, as all morality increasingly focuses on the individual. The possibilities of individual autonomy and self-fulfilment (especially for women) sometimes seem unjustifiably curtailed in some respects by family structures. Does marriage then become a mere contract of individuals – no more than an expression of their personal freedom to join and leave partnerships with others?

Interestingly, Durkheim's answer is emphatically negative. If marriage has this character then divorce should be a matter of mutual consent. But he entirely rejects this conclusion. Of all the policy issues of his time, divorce was the one that seemed most to engage him and on which he took the strongest public stance (Besnard, 1993: 171–2). Divorce by mutual consent would destroy the regulation supporting the essential stability of marriage. 'A system of rules from which one can flee as soon as one has a fancy to do so ceases to be such' (Durkheim, 1906b: 189; and see 1952: 271). Consensual divorce would weaken marriage, undermine the parties' sense of mutual obligation and loosen the curb on unlimited desire (in this case sexual) which we noted earlier (see Chapter 2) as underlying Durkheim's concern with the necessity of regulation.

His approach to regulation of marriage and the family is no doubt influenced by a host of considerations that cannot be fully discussed here (see, for example, Besnard, 1973; 1993). But it illustrates neatly the point that evolving individualism – the working out of the value system focused on the cult of the individual – is to be understood sociologically, not philosophically. It is not a matter of a logic of personal freedom gradually extended to all aspects of individual existence, but of the conditions under which individualism corresponds to the sociological nature of modern society. The family as a 'small society' is a microcosm of society as a whole in which the dialectic between collective and individual well-being has to be played out. Durkheim's approach to family law shows, more clearly than his other legal analyses, that functional and ideational analyses cannot ultimately be separated. Structural requirements of organic solidarity need to be taken into account in understanding the nature of individualism.

The family – however attenuated and reduced in scale and scope it has become – is, therefore, for Durkheim, a functionally necessary part of modern (as of pre-modern) society. It is the locus of nurture for a new generation and ought to be a safe haven in which desires can be channelled into mutual affection. It needs, in his view, a stability which is not guaranteed merely by the freedom of individuals to transact freely with others or to act on purely individual preferences. Today, it is not just a voluntary group explicable in terms of the exercise of these preferences but a social institution that must embody highly developed relations of organic solidarity in order to ensure the individual freedom and dignity of its members.

So a centrally important point in Durkheim's legal theory is reinforced: however much law expresses the cult of the individual, this value system is powerful only in so far as it is required by the nature of social organisation. The question remains, however: if, as in many modern societies, divorce is (contrary to Durkheim's recommendations) easy to procure and increasingly common, must one say that individualism has flown free of the limitations to which organic solidarity, at least according to his analysis, requires that it be subjected? Of course, similar questions might be asked in the context of property rights and (as noted in Chapter 8) that of the struggle for 'just contracts'. In fact, modern divorce practice might be best explained as reflecting a recognition that legal constraints on exit from group membership (including family membership) contribute nothing to solidarity when mutual affection, convergent interest, the familiarity of custom or the ties of common belief have ceased to provide reasons for continuing social relations (cf. Cotterrell, 1997).

Part 4

Law, state and politics

10

The state and democracy

What place do government and the state occupy in Durkheim's legal theory? According to the arguments of *The Division of Labour*, while repressive law directly expresses shared beliefs and sentiments, a morality embedded in the collective consciousness, restitutive law has a different basis. No shared sentiments and beliefs underpin this law. What seems to be needed is a moral vision that does not reflect a collective consciousness of citizens but informs *government*'s efforts to co-ordinate society.[1] It expresses the needs of organic solidarity and underpins governmental expertise. According to this view, government and law actively shape the regulatory framework of organic solidarity (Durkheim, 1984: xxxiv).

As has been seen, however, in Durkheim's writings after *The Division of Labour*, he adopts a different approach, nevertheless prefigured in some of the ideas of his first book. He seeks a unifying moral basis of modern law and society in the values of individualism. But if these individualistic values underpin law in modern society, they do not *spontaneously* give rise to it. Law must be created and shaped deliberately, by legislative, judicial or administrative action. Moral leadership, interpretive wisdom, governmental skill and diligent administrative activity are needed to translate the morality of complex societies into law. They are required to enable law to co-ordinate effectively the social relationships and institutions of modern society. Government translates underlying values into specific regulation.

On the one hand, therefore, law may be thought of as fulfilling technical tasks of co-ordination necessary to organic solidarity, as in Durkheim's original thesis about modern law. On the other, it may be seen as following the evolving value system of individualism, as emphasised in his later work. But whichever approach is taken, an analysis of the nature of government and the state – as creator, interpreter and administrator of law – is essential to his legal theory.

Given these concerns, the inquiry is unlikely to be an orthodox exercise in political science. The social scientific study of political processes

1. See pp. 111–12, above.

is usually a study of structures, uses or modes of acquisition or transfer of power, but these are plainly not Durkheim's concerns. A Durkheimian study of the state and politics is a study of conditions under which the state can be a moral agent – that is, a force able to crystallise in regulatory form what he sees as the requirements of social solidarity. The questions at the heart of his inquiries about political processes are: how can the state contribute towards maintaining the moral climate on which solidarity depends? What kinds of political system are best suited to perform this function? And what is the relationship between political practices on the one hand, and moral conditions of social life on the other? This and the following two chapters examine these issues. This chapter considers Durkheim's general view of politics and the state.

The place of politics

Social science often sees law instrumentally, as a mechanism of governmental power, but we have noted that Durkheim sees it primarily as an expression of social values. Law is obviously, however, in modern society, an instrument of government. For Durkheim, there is no necessary conflict between seeing law in this way, and recognising its morally expressive character. The key to the reconciliation is in a particular view of the nature of government and the state which involves a drastic downgrading of the potential sociological significance of politics. Durkheim's sociological interest is in the state as a regulator and as a representative of society's central values. He is certainly interested in political values, especially those of democratic government. But he is largely uninterested in political practice as the struggle to gain and use power in the public domain.

Why should this be so? Various arguments related to the context of development of Durkheimian sociology have been offered. J.-C. Filloux (1993: 224) has remarked on Durkheim's 'horror of conflict', and W. P. Vogt has hinted that the Durkheimians' interest in the ethnography of 'exotic societies' might have been influenced in part by the fact that these societies could be studied 'free . . . from the heated political debates of the day in which [Emmanuel] Lévy and Jean Ray got ensnared by studying modern French legal issues.'[2] Certainly Durkheim's new science of sociology had best prospects of becoming established if it did not immediately become trapped in destructive political controversies. Yet Durkheim had taken 'solidarity' as the theme of his first book,

2. Vogt (1983: 193). Ray studied the French Civil Code, attempting to show it as an expression of the collective consciousness, a matter of shared sentiments and understandings at a specific historical moment, rather than of timeless legal reason. See Arnaud (1981: 139). Lévy's work is discussed in Chapter 12, below.

The Division of Labour, focusing directly on a concept that, although thoroughly reworked by him, had long been central to political debate in France. This hardly suggests a fear of political controversy.

It has also been suggested that he ignored political analysis to avoid internal university rivalries, for example with the law faculties, which had claimed political science as part of their academic field (Favre, 1983: 202–3). But if this is so, it is hard to see why he did not also avoid law (cf. Chapter 3, above). Biographical explanations have also been suggested, focusing on Durkheim's changed view of religion after 1895, and proposing that his early concerns with political analysis were replaced by an overriding focus on religion and a search for substitutes for the religious forces that had once unified society (Lacroix, 1981). References to political phenomena seem to become rarer in Durkheim's later work (Favre, 1983: 201). But the question remains: why? One ambitious 'contextual' explanation might be that Durkheim sought to attack clericalism in France and replace it with a modern philosophy of secularism. This involved establishing a new set of social beliefs to replace the religion of the Catholic state. But belief in the new 'civic religion' that sociology would foster (by revealing the moral foundations of modern society) would not be aided by a sceptical, scientific deconstruction of the state itself. That would go too far for Durkheim's project. Avoiding politics could thus have been a political strategy in itself (cf. Lukes, 1982: 23).

None of these reasons corresponds directly with those Durkheim himself gave for excluding the field of political practice from his sociological project. He claimed to see political facts as fortuitous, a 'product of contingent combinations' (Favre, 1983: 202), rather than sociologically fundamental, contributing to knowledge of the nature of society. Political science, although a well-recognised speciality in Durkheim's time, was, in his view, 'bastardised speculations, half theoretical and half practical, half science and half art'.[3] Law and morality are social facts of interest because they express the character of social institutions and significant patterns of social relationships. Presumably, however, in Durkheim's view, politics, seeing regulation as a contingent effect of the play of power rather than in terms of its social meaning, offers no such scientific potential for understanding society. What is of sociological interest is not the struggle by which political power is distributed, amassed, controlled or harnessed, but the regulatory use to which that power is put and the institutions supervising this use.

Thus, the *Année Sociologique* concerned itself with the institutional aspects of politics, with political organisation rather than public life

---

3. Durkheim (1890: 225). He makes the same criticism of political ideologies such as socialism or libertarianism. See Chapter 12, below.

(Favre, 1983: 204, 209). Durkheim was also interested in political geography, focusing on questions about the territory of the state. Otherwise, as Mauss put it (quoted in Favre, 1983: 211, 212), 'politics is not part of sociology'; it is an art, not a science, 'the practical art corresponding to sociology'. In fact, politics is applied sociology: strategies and tactics for realising in practice what sociology reveals scientifically. Thus, when the Durkheimians mapped out the divisions and classifications of sociology, no place was found for the study of politics in this scheme.

The function of the state

Given this outlook, it is unsurprising that Durkheim's writings show no interest in the state as a site of conflict. Instead he examines its capacity to be a force for morally significant regulation and especially the limits of that capacity and the problems arising from them. Under what conditions can the state provide regulation for organic solidarity? Or, to put matters in terms of Durkheim's later emphases, under what conditions can the state serve the needs of the modern value system of individualism? These are his questions.

The state is to be understood in the context of political organisation more generally. 'Political' implies the existence of an 'established authority' to whose actions individuals are subject (Durkheim, 1957: 42). Thus a political group is one in which a distinction or opposition has developed between governors and governed, between 'authority and those subject to it' (1957: 42). The nation is certainly not the only modern political group in this sense. The family is a political group as regards its governmental structure, but modern professional groups are not in so far as they are concerned with only one [occupational] aspect of life (1957: 26, 42). Thus it can be seen that, although Durkheim is not seriously concerned to analyse struggles for power in political life, his definition of 'the political' treats the distinction between rulers and ruled, power-holders and those subject to power, as fundamental. This is consistent with his view of regulation – at least his early strongly positivistic view, which, as has been seen, emphasises the coercive character of regulation as a social fact, 'external' to the individual. However, as has been seen, that view of regulation is gradually softened in his work by a concern with the moral meaningfulness of regulation to the regulated.[4] Correspondingly, as will appear, government is presented in Durkheim's later writings as something that must connect directly with the individual's understandings and convictions.

4. See pp. 62–4 and 77–8, above.

Political organisation is found in social groups of various kinds. Political society, however, is 'the complex group of which the state is the highest organ' (Durkheim, 1957: 48). It is formed by the coming together of 'a rather large number of secondary social groups, subject to the same one authority which is not itself subject to any superior authority duly constituted' (1957: 45). Students of legal theory will note similarities between this conception of sovereign power in political society and that of the jurist John Austin (1832: lect. 6). But it is significant that the relationship of sovereign and subjects which Durkheim postulates here is one in which groups, rather than individuals as Austin implies (Austin, 1832: 193–5), are subjects under the overall sovereignty of the state. Political society is a union of secondary or intermediate groups: that is, groups intermediate between the individual and political society as a whole.

Political society is not conclusively defined by a link to specific territory (Durkheim, 1957: 43–4). Nomadic societies may have a political structure, and in past times it was the citizenry rather than the territory that characterised the state when one state annexed another. Often the place of government (the capital) 'had an extreme mobility' (1957: 43). The political focus on a distinct, fixed territory is relatively recent. But size is some criterion of political society: 'there is no political society which does not comprise numerous different families or professional groups or both at once' (1957: 44).

Although Durkheim sketches this pluralistic, flexible view of political organisation as his general context, his real concern is with the modern state. Descriptively, the state consists of a certain group of individuals detached from the collective mass (1957: 82), a group (or a range of special groups) of officials entrusted as agents with representing the sovereign authority (1957: 48, 50). The state is defined *functionally*, however, not by reference to the authority that some people hold over others but by the distinct contribution that the state is required to make to society as a whole. The state's responsibility 'is to work out certain representations which hold good for the collectivity. These representations are distinguished from the other collective representations by their higher degree of consciousness and reflection' (1957: 50). Durkheim remarks that the representations worked out in the group of officials that make up the state 'are not the work of the collectivity' (that is, of political society as a whole) (1950: 86; 1957: 49–50). Thus, the state is functionally, as well as descriptively, distinct from the rest of society.

The function of the state as a special group of officials (for example, legislators, elected politicians, administrators, judges) is to *deliberate for society*, to work out and express on behalf of society at large what society can be taken collectively to think (and feel) about certain matters that are important to it. In this way, the state provides leadership in collective self-direction and regulation. Seen in this way, the state 'would therefore be directly deliberative, and only indirectly executive' (Davy, 1957: xxxviii). It is more important for the state to take the lead in directing the consciousness of the nation than to carry out tasks itself. Durkheim notes:

> The state does not execute anything. The Council of ministers or the sovereign do not themselves take action any more than Parliament: they give the orders for action to be taken. They co-ordinate ideas and sentiments, from these they frame decisions and transmit these decisions to other agencies to carry them out: but that is the limit of their office. (Durkheim, 1957: 51)

The familiar distinction between executive and legislature is, thus, in his view, misleading. The government *qua* executive is closely linked to actual executive agencies but should not be identified with them. Like the legislature, it deliberates and decides, and produces regulation, though in a different form from ordinary legislation. But the 'whole life of the state, in its true meaning, consists not in exterior action, in activity (*mouvements*), but in deliberation, that is, in representations' (1950: 87; cf. 1957: 51).

The state deliberates for society because more precise ideas are necessary to form the content of regulation than are supplied by the collective consciousness (1957: 50).

> In the main, that consciousness is diffused: there is at all times a vast number of social sentiments and social states of mind (*états*) of all kinds, of which the state hears only a faint echo ... The representations that derive from the state are always more conscious of themselves, of their causes and aims. They have been formed in a less obscure way ... Undeniably, there is often a good deal of obscurity ... but whether ... [the state's] decisions be ill motivated or not, the main thing is that they should be motivated to some extent. There is ... at least usually a semblance of deliberation, an understanding of the circumstances as a whole that make the decision necessary ... Hence we have these councils, these assemblies, these debates, these regulations, that ensure that these kinds of representations evolve only slowly. (1950: 86–7; 1957: 50)

Outside the state organs, public opinion is vague, disorganised and contradictory. Habit and preconceptions rule (cf. 1957: 83). The state focuses opinion in specific regulatory forms.

What should be made of this view of the state? Evidently, the normal conflicts, confusions, impasses, deceits, mendacity, personal ambitions and self-interest of political life have been largely defined away. What remains is the state as social 'brain' (Davy, 1957: xxxviii; Durkheim, 1984: 42, 164; 1957: 53). But the very fact that Durkheim's theory does not address the real processes by which the state 'thinks' – often in contradictory, confused ways because it is not an abstract entity but real people with diverse, conflicting interests that are doing the thinking – prevents him, appropriately, from making any sociological assumptions that the state actually produces morally appropriate policies and regulation. The point is merely that this is what the state *has* to do to serve the needs of social solidarity.

The state has a function to perform which can be specified sociologically. How specific political practices contribute or fail to contribute to the fulfilment of that function is a different inquiry. Thus, it is not that Durkheim is unaware of the political realities that might encourage us to think about the state in wholly different ways from the way he does. It is that his concern is with a specific, limited inquiry. Under what circumstances can the state have the best chances of realising the moral responsibilities attaching to it, and that justify its very existence? How can meaning be given to the idea of the state focusing the sentiments and understandings that make up collective experience? How is it possible for what Durkheim calls a 'government consciousness' (*conscience gouvernementale*) (1957: 81; 1950: 114) to be formed as a crystallisation of the collective consciousness? How can a governmental morality emerge to express and reflect the moral conditions of organic solidarity in complex societies?

The authority of the state

Durkheim presents his ideas on the state in his familiar evolutionary perspective. An important stage in early social development occurs when governmental power separates itself out in society and is successfully asserted by a particular person or persons accepted as having authority over the rest of society. Inevitably, Durkheim sees the source of this development in religion. The person who can interpret the sacred and mediate between it and the profane world of everyday life acquires power as a priest or chief. He harnesses the collective power of belief and thus gains authority over other people. The earliest societies did not necessarily have any governmental authority (1957: 46) but when such an authority emerges in social development the first and foremost task of those who govern will be to ensure respect for established shared beliefs, traditions and practices, in other words to defend the collective consciousness (1984: 42). The authority of the chief or priest becomes 'the symbol of that consciousness, in everybody's eyes its living expression ... Thus it partakes of the authority that the collectivity exercises over the consciousness of individuals, and from this stems its strength' (1984: 42, 43). Clearly, it is in the interests of those who govern to support the collective beliefs and traditions of society, since on those beliefs and traditions their authority depends.

How then does a governing authority acquire the capacity to act *autonomously*, to go beyond merely affirming and protecting society's established practices, understandings and beliefs; to become a lawmaker rather than merely a declarer of law? Durkheim remarks that, without breaking free of 'the source from which it derives and on which it continues to feed' government becomes 'capable of producing its own spontaneous actions' (1984: 43, 143). We have noted Davy's argument that the collective beliefs underlying potlatch exchanges make possible the acquisition and use of personal wealth by individuals, which underpins their autonomous chiefly power.[5] More generally, it can be suggested that holding power as a guardian of collective beliefs enables the power holder to derive material benefits and benefits of prestige. These benefits allow a chief or priest to assert his independent wishes, though these will usually need to be expressed in ways that seem congruent with the collective beliefs and understandings that guarantee his authority. Paul Huvelin, (1907: 7) draws attention to the doctrine of the divine right of kings as illustrating the idea of a ruler possessing unchallengeable power while deriving authority entirely from collective (religious) belief. Georges Gurvitch (1942), perhaps influenced by Huvelin's ideas on the importance of magical practices in providing early authority for individual initiatives, suggests that magic plays an important part in establishing the power of governing elites to act independently of collective sentiment. Those who claim access to magical powers are able to gain authority to act by 'usurping for themselves the social power belonging to the entire group' (Gurvitch, 1942: 121).

It would seem for Durkheim, however, that to maintain moral authority to act on behalf of society, a government must present its actions as expressing and realising society's shared beliefs and understandings or, more generally, the requirements of solidarity (cf. Durkheim, 1984: xxxii–xxxiii). Governmental authority (and so law) derives from a conceptualisation (initially religious) of society as a whole. This is why it seems obvious to Durkheim that early law is not primarily concerned with protecting individual interests.[6] Law and government in their earliest forms derive all their authority from the fact that they represent society, its collective beliefs and collective identity. In turn, law and government define and protect these beliefs and this identity. This reciprocity makes possible the birth of government.

5. See pp. 125–8, above.
6. See pp. 86–8, above.

Governmental authority thus derives, in Durkheim's view, from shared beliefs and sentiments. How then, does government acquire or maintain authority in modern society where collective beliefs no longer unify a society that has become complex and extremely diverse? For Durkheim the answer lies in mechanisms that optimise the quality of the state's deliberations on behalf of society. If the state is supposed to 'think' for society, the important question is how can it do this in conditions of social complexity and moral diversity? Under what conditions is it realistic to see the state's deliberations and decisions as made on behalf of *society as a whole*? What meaning can be given to this concept of the state as representative of society? Only if these questions can be satisfactorily answered can the state be regarded as having authority – that is, moral authority – in relation to society as a whole. This authority, in turn, is what enables the state to produce legitimate regulation for society by means of deliberate legislative, administrative or judicial acts. It enables the state to direct society.

Durkheim's theory of democracy seeks to answer these questions about state authority. But, because the theory proceeds on very different premises from most democratic theory, it is necessary, before considering it, to set out some background ideas that inform its use. Durkheim is not explicit about this background but it can be reconstructed by referring back to the discussion of morality and belief developed in Chapter 4. We noted there that Durkheim sees morality's character as having changed in modern society.[7] Early morality is purely a matter of obligations imposed. These are non-negotiable and morality is not understood in a reflective, critical way that would allow the individual some opportunity of evaluating its demands. More generally, the shared beliefs and sentiments of the collective consciousness are imperative and absolute. Durkheim portrays their character in early society as a universe of thought and feeling enveloping everyone, allowing no escape from the common thoughtways. It is easy to see, therefore, that, if governmental authority derives its authority from the collective consciousness in early society, it will be no less absolute and will be accepted unconditionally as long as those governing can rely on a popular conviction that their rule is ordained by the shared beliefs and sentiments that unite society.

In modern society, morality and belief have a different character. As has been seen, Durkheim stresses 'autonomy' as the specifically modern component of morality.[8] Individuals do not merely obey moral rules and accept beliefs as absolutely imperative. They reason critically with moral rules, evaluating them, considering their coherence and the rationality of the structure of values they represent, in the light of experience.

7. See pp. 62–4, above.
8. See p. 63, above.

Thus, it can be suggested that, for Durkheim, the moral authority underlying modern law relies not only on an acceptance of moral duty and
a sense of attachment to society, but also on a degree of active reflection by those subject to law's authority about the values and policies
represented in law. In short, it relies, unlike the authority of earlier law,
on active *communication and debate* about the meaning and significance
of the law, not just on a passive belief in its authority.

In modern societies, democratic processes can be considered to
provide mechanisms for this communication and debate. And, in fact,
Durkheim claims that democracy is the sociologically necessary basis
for government in modern individualistic societies (1957: 89, 90). I
suggest that reflection on his views about the nature of morality shows
why, for him, this is so. Democracy provides an institutional means by
which moral (including legal) issues can be debated, and legal-moral
ideas can be communicated and developed, in a process of refining or
negotiating their meaning prior to their enshrinement in regulation by
the state. Thus democracy is made *necessary* by the nature of modern
morality. As will appear, these emphases lead to an unusual view of
democracy as serving moral rather than political values.

Democracy

Durkheim's arguments about modern morality provide reasons why
modern government needs an authority not just passively recognised
by the governed, but actively, reflectively conferred by them. Democracy
provides, for Durkheim, the means of ensuring this active conferment
on the state of authority to speak for society (1957: 91). Most theories
of democracy centre on the problem of power. They treat democracy
as a means of ensuring the sharing of power, some accountability
of governors to governed or at least a 'market' in which citizens
'spend' their votes in choosing between alternative governments (e.g.
Schumpeter, 1952: ch. 22). In such theories, democracy concerns
specifically political values – addressing problems of power and conflicts
of interest. But Durkheim's democratic theory does not have this focus.

 Democracy, for him, is a means of working out understandings and
values for the benefit of society as a whole. It is not a means of compromising interests or tying the state to public opinion (Durkheim, 1957:
94). Rather, it is a system providing two-way communication between
state and citizens. It gives citizens the chance to reflect on laws and 'to
accept the laws of the country with more intelligence and thus less
passively', and it links the life of the state (its regulating activities) with
that of the citizens (1957: 91). It does not require that the state follow
popular views: the state must produce its own 'consciousness', more

focused and specific than that which fluctuating and often contradictory public opinion offers. But it makes state and people 'simply two aspects of a single reality. The state [in a democratic society] is a people awakened to a consciousness of itself, of its needs and aspirations – a more complete and definite consciousness' (Durkheim, quoted in Lukes, 1973: 550). Thus, the 'more that deliberation and reflection and a critical spirit play a considerable part in the course of public affairs, the more democratic the nation' (Durkheim 1957: 89). Democracy exists to discover and express unity, not to compromise differences.

Thus, for Durkheim, democracy is not, essentially, about representation (a political matter of controlling power and ensuring accountability), but about *communication* (a moral matter of promoting mutual understanding and interrelation of diverse values, experiences, sentiments and beliefs). The regulatory ideas produced by the state draw on and are influenced (but not controlled) by the diffuse ideas of public opinion – the collective representations or collective consciousness. At the same time the 'government consciousness' translated into regulation focuses and gives direction to the numerous, nebulous, disparate ideas, sentiments and beliefs present in modern society at large. Democracy thus requires much more than casting a ballot. It depends on a high level of awareness of political life: 'A democracy may, then, appear as the political system by which the society can achieve a consciousness of itself in its purest form' (Durkheim, 1957: 89).

The idea of democracy as a process by which society works out its values and beliefs in regulatory form tends to evoke notions of *direct democracy* (that is, direct participation of citizens in political decision making rather than participation through election of representatives to decide on their behalf). It raises familiar problems about the conditions under which direct democracy as a process of collective deliberation is possible (see, for example, Fishkin, 1991). But Durkheim makes clear that he is not an advocate of direct democracy. 'If everyone is to govern, it means in fact that there is no government. It is collective sentiments, diffused, vague and obscure as they may be, that sway the people' (Durkheim, 1957: 83). In fact, for Durkheim, direct democracy is not democracy at all. Democracy presupposes a separation of government from the governed. In direct democracy there is no such separation. It is thus, for Durkheim, not an ideal to aim for but (as in its ancient contexts) *anterior* to real political development (1957: 83). The problem for the democratic state to solve is how to develop governmental expertise to understand (but not necessarily intervene in) the widest possible range of matters, while maximising connections between this 'government consciousness' and the understandings and sentiments of the population at large.

Direct democracy, Durkheim suggests, replaces normal representative forms 'whenever the state and the mass of individuals are in a direct relation, without any intermediary being brought between them' (1957: 95). As a form of rule it may be impractical in all but the smallest political societies (perhaps, Swiss cantonal governments or Greek city states). But direct democracy is merely one form of the more general phenomenon of political populism. Thus, when 'the state stands too close to the individuals, it falls under their dominance' (1957: 95). When citizens elect representatives directly 'it becomes inevitable for those representatives to apply themselves almost exclusively to a faithful promotion of their constituents' views' (1957: 95). Instead of deliberating on behalf of society, they act as representatives of particular interests. Clearly, for Durkheim, populist democracy of this kind is a pathological phenomenon (1957: 99). It is a kind of abnegation of political responsibility – that is, the moral responsibility of the state. The state must be 'a mechanism that is complex and ingenious, the multiple cogwheels of a vast administration'. But populism 'represents a return to the most primitive of political forms' (1957: 99), one might say to pork barrel politics, an immoral politics because it denies the state's moral function – to work out representations that are not merely compromises but have meaning for society as a whole.

If populist politics dissolves the state into a chaos of conflicting interests, *absolutism* represents the opposite pathological political tendency. Political absolutism is greater, Durkheim suggests, the more the supreme power's relation to the rest of society is like that of a property owner, rather than a contracting party (1973b: 23). This is a revealing way of expressing matters since, as was seen in Chapter 9, property relations have little to do with organic solidarity, while contractual relations should be its supreme expression. Thus, it may be inferred that political absolutism has no place in modern society which depends on organic solidarity. On the other hand, absolutism is not a natural feature of early or ancient society either, but results from 'unique, transitory, and contingent factors' (1973b: 25). Again, Durkheim avoids any sociological analysis of structures of power. But he is prepared to assert that absolutism, like populism, is associated with an absence of intermediate or secondary groups (1973b: 22–3); that is, there are no vital collective organisations standing intermediate between the individual and the state. As will appear, secondary groups are the key, in Durkheim's analysis, to solving many problems of political organisation and effective regulation.

If democracy is, for Durkheim, the mechanism by which collective sentiments and understandings aid and authorise governmental deliberation, populism and absolutism are opposite ways of undermining this mechanism. While populism makes the state too undifferentiated from society, absolutism isolates the 'government consciousness' from society and so tends to make the state's deliberations blinkered and out of touch (1950: 117–8; cf. 1957: 84). The absolutist state relies on an authority given by collective beliefs or understandings but appropriates these understandings and beliefs from their social sources, focusing them in quasi-religious form (1957: 81–2; 1984: 144), or manipulating them by force. But, because Durkheim does not believe that force can, on any long-term basis, guarantee political power without collective convictions supporting this power (Lukes, 1973: 547–8), he seems to see populism as the more enduring threat to the democratic state. It is the kind of threat we have seen him emphasising in other contexts where he treats utilitarianism as the enemy of moral sensibility. In politics, populism turns the pursuit of moral vision into a mere balancing of interests, just as utilitarianism does this in moral life generally.

Legal obligation

The essence of law, as has been seen, is impersonal rule; that is, rule by *society* rather than by individuals over other individuals. This, above all, is why, for Durkheim, law cannot be explained merely in terms of the exercise of power. It is immoral, he declares, for a person to be subject to the will of a single other. 'It is only the abstract and impersonal rule that should command such deference of the human will' (1961: 145). Thus the idea of the Rule of Law (Durkheim does not use the term as such) enters the picture.

It is possible to see how this idea becomes essential to his legal theory both in the early thesis of *The Division of Labour* and through the later focus on the cult of the individual. In the early thesis, organic solidarity demands a moral framework residing not in popular convictions but in regulation devised by the state as society's moral agent. Leaving aside penal law, modern law embodies not popular morality but only what I have called a governmental morality.[9] Thus, the law embodying this governmental morality commands the citizen's moral allegiance only in so far as the state produces law through appropriate democratic processes. Democracy makes state regulation authoritative as law because it makes it possible to see this regulation as produced by society through its agent, the state. Thus democracy makes possible the modern Rule of Law; that is, the belief that law rules authoritatively and imposes a general obligation of obedience.

Durkheim's later emphases on individualism as the underlying value system of modern society make the link between democracy and the

9. See p. 112, above.

Rule of Law equally clear. Democracy, he remarks 'is the political system that conforms best to our present-day notion of the individual' (1957: 90); it recognises individual autonomy and choice, not least in shaping society's collective regulation. Democracy has 'moral superiority' because it treats citizens as rational assessors of their society's regulation as well as subject to it. Thus, while law expresses the values of individualism it is also the product of individual autonomy. The life of the state and of the citizen are brought into relation with each other (1957: 91). The main function of the modern state is to liberate individual personalities (1957: 62), to provide a realm of basic individual freedoms that enables citizens to escape the constraints imposed on them by particular groups that might otherwise repress them (cf. Merry, 1990: ch. 8). Thus, it is easy to see Durkheim's thinking as congruent in this respect with liberal theories that treat law as an expression of individualist values and a framework of neutral rules under whose protection a multitude of individual citizens' interests can be asserted.

We have noted, however, that communication, not representation, is the essence of democracy for Durkheim. By this emphasis he avoids the difficult question for liberal theory of how representative democracy can morally bind minorities who did not choose those elected to represent their interests in the fora of the state (cf. Durkheim, 1957: 107). If they voted for others or did not vote at all why should they be bound? If politics is merely a compromise of individual interests why must individuals accept a compromise in which they are not involved? And, in any case, why should such a compromise be adhered to even by those benefiting from it, if later their interests change? Merely balancing interests gives state action no moral authority (Durkheim, 1961: 260).

However, Durkheim's focus on politics as communication raises a different problem. And it is to his credit that he does not disguise it but makes it explicit and central in his analyses. How in complex societies can political life really be a conversation between governors and governed? How is political communication possible in these societies? This process of communication is essential because it is the means by which regulation is kept in touch with the conditions of social life, and individual citizens are enabled to assess legal regulation. Law must be inspired by social life rather than merely legislated by distant authorities. 'The true source of respect for the law', Durkheim (1957: 107) writes, 'lies in its clearly expressing the natural inter-relation of things.' Especially in a democracy law will only be respected in so far as it seems to have that quality; that is, in so far as it seems to reflect the conditions of organic solidarity. Thus, it would seem, legal obligation is not automatically produced by lawmaking even where the legal system is democratic in form. Confidence is inspired only when democracy as communication works well. 'Respect for the law depends on the quality of the legislators and the quality of the political system' (1957: 108). [Quote]

Ultimately, Durkheim recognises that possibilities for effective moral communication between the state and individuals are *limited*. The communication process cannot work adequately if it is seen only as communication between the individual citizen and the state. It is 'legitimate for every citizen to some extent to turn into a statesman' (1957: 108) to assess law and governmental acts in the light of the confidence (or lack of it) inspired by them. But there are limits as to how far this can really be productive. He seems to draw back from the idea that legal obligation could, in modern democracies at least, ever be conditional. The Rule of Law, it seems, must prevail. The state must demand unconditional allegiance to the law it creates. The citizen cannot become a legal expert, second-guessing the lawmaker's acts; this would not be practicable. Nor would it be authorised by the idea of the individual's autonomy because, as was seen earlier, individual liberty is, for Durkheim, given by and subject to society's rules (1984: xxxiii, 320; 1961: 54). Thus, there seems, finally, to be much more communication from the state to the citizen than the reverse.

The reach of the modern state has steadily grown more extensive (1957: 53). 'Today . . . we do not admit there is anything in the realm of public life which cannot become subject to the action of the state' (1950: 117; cf. 1957: 84). Yet, Durkheim suggests, it seems powerless to provide adequate regulation for social solidarity (1957: 218). The problems lie in its *remoteness* (1952: 389) – what might be called its moral distance from the regulated (Cotterrell, 1995: 305). It is important to note that Durkheim's fear is not the familiar one of the over-powerful state. As W. S. F. Pickering (1993: 57) remarks, he 'had a naive optimism about the modern state – that it is benign and did the best for its citizens. A thoroughly evil modern state was beyond his imagination.' Perhaps he merely did not want to contemplate what such a state might be. The problem Durkheim recognises is rather that, as society becomes increasingly complex, moral communication within it becomes more difficult. The state – charged sociologically with the task of producing moral order out of this complexity – becomes overloaded and unable to appreciate local moral conditions adequately (Durkheim, 1952: 374, 378; 1957: 218; 1984: 297). For Durkheim, the answer – first clearly mapped out in the preface to the second edition of *The Division of Labour* – is to devolve much regulatory power from the state to intermediate institutions reflecting the particular moral environments of the social groups in relation to which they exist (1984: xxxi–lix; and see 1952: 389–91).

It will be seen in the next chapter how Durkheim thinks this regulatory devolution should be organised.[10] But one of its consequences is that the concept of citizenship is transformed. Of course, citizenship is linked to the nation state – the political society as a whole. But organs of devolved lawmaking by groups become, in Durkheim's view, the appropriate focus for much of the active political involvement of the citizen. They 'will release the individual from the state and vice versa, and release the individual, too, from a task for which he is not fitted' (1957: 109), the task of actively engaging with a distant, unreachable, centralised government. The message, then, is hardly a complacent one. It is that, in certain respects, present representative democracy as a process of communication does not work. And without that process, much modern law, centrally produced by a distant state, has a deficit in moral authority.

10. See pp. 176–80, below.

11

Making and interpreting law

Durkheim's writings provide some resources for analysing the nature
of lawmaking and legal interpretation, and their theoretical problems.
He shows no special interest in examining the behaviour of particular
legislatures or courts, or the practices of administrative agencies or legal
professionals – in other words, the kinds of inquiries that are central to
much of modern legal sociology (Cotterrell, 1992: chs 6–8). But the
problems of lawmaking as a process of communication and deliberation, highlighted in the previous chapter, provide an important focus
for considering theoretically some of the workings of legal institutions.

Durkheim's approach in considering the institutional mechanisms of
law – the processes by which laws are created, interpreted and applied
in practice – is primarily that of functional analysis. He asks what the
roles of the various lawmaking and law-applying institutions are and
what general theoretical problems are implied in these roles. The overriding question is always: how can law be created and applied in ways
that enable it to fulfil its tasks as a special segment of morality, in other
words as an expression of the moral requirements of society?

The legislative function

How should we view legislation? Modern societies, Durkheim notes,
are characterised by ever more extensive lawmaking. Law is now a
conscious creation whereas in earlier times the 'whole of law worked
automatically in an unconscious way; it was a matter of custom' (1957:
86). 'Every day some new law is put on the statute-book, another is
taken off or some new modification is made (1957: 87). In part this
is because the 'present-day conditions of collective existence' demand
continuous regulatory change (1957: 90). Modern society, with its
complex, shifting patterns of interaction and co-operation between
individual citizens and social groups, demands complex, flexible and
regularly updated legal frameworks. But there seems to be another
reason for law's growth, too. If more and more details of social life find
their expression in legal regulation, 'that is because all these obscure

things come more and more to the surface in the clear region of the social consciousness, in other words the government consciousness' (1950: 121; cf. 1957: 87). Government's increased capacity to learn about the conditions of social life allows these conditions to find more sophisticated expression in regulation. Thus, democracy as communication makes possible a more detailed recognition of the conditions of organic solidarity. Presumably, the more effective the democratic communication process can be the more possibilities government has for regulating social life.

In so far as the ideas and sentiments that are diffuse in society become prominent through recognition in the governmental process they become, in Durkheim's view, more malleable. Presented in a clearer, more public way, they can be freely criticised and debated. They 'lose their powers of resistance and are made more accessible to change' (1957: 88). Thus, it is not only that democratic processes bring more regulatory concerns and tasks to government notice. The parliamentary processes of lawmaking and policy debate also create a faster flow of ideas and controversies that spark new regulatory possibilities. Yet in his lectures on the state Durkheim seems hardly to notice (because of his lack of concern with actual political practice) the forces of inertia that often constrain lawmaking, and the ideological factors that can keep issues away from the legislative agenda as well as drive them onto it.[1]

His concern is with a theory of the legislative function. In other words, what is important is the role that lawmaking as an act of government must play in society. He notes that legislation often departs from prevalent public opinion on particular matters (1957: 49). But he insists that it is not possible to legislate to shift people's moral beliefs towards some desired consensus or towards ideals chosen by the legislator. 'When the law forbids acts which public opinion considers inoffensive, we are indignant with the law, not with the act it punishes' (1952: 372). Legislation, to be effective, must reflect the moral climate already existing in society. For example, suicide is an act affronting prevailing values about the sanctity of life, yet it can also be linked to some socially approved or respected sentiments, such as those of altruism, loyalty or selflessness (giving one's life for others or a cause). In such a morally ambiguous area it is pointless, Durkheim suggests, to legislate to penalise suicide; 'our moral sensibilities will never be aroused by legislative measures'. The matter should be dealt with by subtly graded moral sanctions (1952: 371). These in turn depend on strengthening social groups that sustain individuals and provide a focus for them (1952: 373). On the other hand, legislation can support or undermine, symbolically, particular moral principles or stances. Thus,

1. But see pp. 182–4, below.

opposing the legalisation of divorce by mutual consent, he argues that facilitating divorce in this way would send a negative signal about society's willingness to defend the sanctity of marriage.[2]

Lawmaking is thus, it seems for Durkheim, a matter of carefully judging the moral impact of regulation, since law carries some moral authority solely by virtue of its source in the state.[3] In his early work, where the stress is on the state's role as co-ordinator of diversity in modern society, a medical analogy is sometimes used in considering governmental responsibility. 'The duty of the statesman is no longer to propel societies violently towards an ideal which appears attractive to him. His role is rather that of the doctor: he forestalls the outbreak of sickness by maintaining good hygiene, or when it does break out seeks to cure it' (1982a: 104). Sickness, in this context, is Durkheim's metaphor for an upsetting of the balance of social co-operation and interdependence on which organic solidarity depends.

His later work, however, sometimes implies an educational rather than medical analogy. The lawmaker may have something of the role of teacher, encouraging moral climates and sensitivities. At one point, writing of the cult of the individual, Durkheim suggests that the state should stand at the head of this cult, nurturing and promoting it (1957: 70). Because he often treats the school as a small society with regulatory needs related to those of the national society,[4] it is tempting to speculate on links between his view of the teacher's role in the school and the legislator's role in political society. Is this speculation justifiable? A society of children, Durkheim remarks, cannot be organised like one of adults because the child lives on feelings to a greater extent than the adult. Yet 'a class is a society' and 'academic institutions are like the corresponding social institutions' (1961: 203). Thus, Durkheim draws analogies between the 'government' of a school class and of a nation, and between the place of social rules and duties in both (1961: 148–9, 152).

The educational analogy would certainly suggest a paternalistic view of legislation, which is probably consistent with Durkheim's views up to a point. Classroom standards, he notes, depend on the teacher's resolution. The teacher's moral leadership maintains the class as an ordered social group. Discipline, understood as necessary and owed to a well-respected figure of authority (a rule-maker or rule-interpreter), creates collective morale, a spirit of unity and co-operation (1961: 150–1). Too much regulation is irksome and resented, and destroys initiative. It produces a reaction against all imposed discipline (1961: 153), perhaps like movements for wholesale deregulation as a reaction

2. Durkheim (1906b; 1952: 273); and see pp. 146–7, above.
3. See p. 69, above.
4. See p. 77, above.

to overregulation by law. Teachers, Durkheim insists, cannot force merit into their pupils by coercion or reshape them at will. Through their concern and respect for those they teach, they earn the respect of the pupils. So pupils are encouraged to *want* to follow the teacher's lead. Correspondingly, Durkheim condemns the assumption of 'legislative omnipotence' in political society, which assumes legislation can address the regulated without regard to who they are and what they think and feel (1961: 257–8). Of course, it might be said that the teacher's authority is personal while that of the legislator must be impersonal – invoking the Rule of Law. But, in Durkheim's view, teachers (no less than legislators) fail if the rules they impose are seen as theirs alone. Children must be taught to respect *impersonal* rules and to see the respected rule-giver in the classroom not as expressing personal preferences but as representing an abstract regime of regulation required to structure the small society of the class (1961: 247). Correspondingly, legal obligation in the democratic state is a matter of allegiance to abstract rules.[5]

We have seen, however, that for Durkheim modern morality is critical and self-reflective; the citizen's allegiance to law is to be reasoned acceptance. Certainly, in schools and political societies alike, the relationship of regulators and regulated should be one of mutual trust and respect. But the crucial point at which the educational analogy breaks down is surely that the legislator must usually assume the full moral maturity and autonomy of the regulated as the basis for the rules created in a way that the teacher of children cannot properly do.

Idealistic Making law, interpreting law

If the state is the social 'brain', legislative debates are, in Durkheim's words, 'a process analogous to thought in the individual' (1957: 80) – that is, the effort to come to a settled opinion after weighing conflicting ideas, feelings and tendencies. In his idealised view, speeches in the legislative chamber 'all have an echo in the whole of the society and modify the ideas strewn there' (1957: 79). It is as though, for him, factions and conviction politics can be treated as functionally inessential. No doubt, like populism, they are, for Durkheim, sociologically pathological[6] – disruptions of the deliberative process. Perhaps it operates despite them. Durkheim merely remarks optimistically that legislative debate ought to clarify minds and force debaters to become aware of motives swaying them and to account for themselves (1957: 80)

5. See pp. 163–5, above.
6. See p. 162, above.

What exactly is involved in this idealised process of making law? Perhaps the analogy with 'thought in the individual' can be taken further. Suppose I turn a matter over in my mind, weighing pros and cons, conflicting ideas, sentiments and commitments. Perhaps I reach a settled conclusion. The conclusion binds me for the moment because I now have it as a considered, reasoned basis for action. Thus it coerces me. It is more than a guide to action because it determines what action is appropriate, excluding a range of other possibilities. Similarly, if state legislation really is legislation 'on behalf of' society, it provides reasons for action that represent a crystallisation of society's collective reason from diverse sources of ideas and sentiments, mulled over in debate. Its coercive power lies in ruling out other possibilities of action. Just as the brain commands the organs of the body to obey its decisions on action, so the state commands the members of the social body to obey its regulation.

One final extension of Durkheim's analogy between the thinking of the state and of the individual might be made. Suppose I ponder conflicting ideas, values, attitudes or sentiments jostling for supremacy within me, and come to a settled view on a particular matter. In the same sort of way the legislature ponders similar conflicts, deliberating to reach a view that will be enshrined in particular legislation. Now, suppose I spend my whole life pondering difficult issues and conflicting ideas, contradictory perceptions and attitudes, irreconcilable values and beliefs. Some of these ways of thinking I inherited from revered sources of influence. Others I learned from experience or reflection. Slowly, through honest deliberation, I work towards conclusions. Over time I clarify what I believe, what I think I know, and the limits of my knowledge and belief. Because the process of reaching understanding seems never ending, I learn to tolerate what I cannot appreciate and to recognise the fallibility of my own views. I try to make my conclusions consistent, but I recognise that the process of trying to reconcile the ideas and convictions that pull me in different ways will not be completed. Perhaps, eventually I come to feel that some of my views have been well tested. They seem strong and settled. I take them to be the core of what I believe. But I try to continue to learn from experience. And the mix of stability and flexibility that I recognise in my views makes me the person I think I really am. It gives me my moral identity.

Could it be suggested that a somewhat analogous process characterises the state's action in 'thinking' for society and building a body of legal regulation? In other words, law is built slowly, haltingly, with difficulty (and, one hopes, some humility) in a process of wrestling with inherited and accumulated collective convictions, attitudes and understandings and their ongoing confrontations with experience. Durkheim makes no such explicit claims about the process of deliberately building law. But his analogy between the state's 'thought' and the thought of an individual implies some such view. Certainly, for him, the 'thinking' state cannot make rules arbitrarily. Rather, it must creatively make sense of the diversity of popular experience – wrestling with moral conflict like an individual seeking consistency in personal values and understandings. In this way, I suggest, Durkheim sees the state making law that expresses society's moral identity.

If matters are seen in this way it seems that no sharp line in Durkheim's thinking should separate legislation from judicial development of law. As has been seen, Durkheimian democracy is not a formal system of political representation but a communication process by which regulators learn of social conditions, and citizens critically assess and, in some sense, 'own' regulation.[7] It is not self-evident that legislatures alone can be democratic in this sense, or that they necessarily are. Perhaps judicial lawmaking might have some democratic attributes in Durkheim's specific sense (cf. Collins, 1986). He does see the judicial role as one of deliberating on behalf of society in a manner somewhat similar to that of the legislature. But if courts are

> organs of rational reflection . . . these are less central organs than are legislative assemblies. [They are] centres of the collective conscious-ness, [drawing on and focusing social understandings and senti-ments,] but secondary centres. They are not set up in a way that embraces the social life in its entirety . . . so they represent only very imperfectly and incompletely all that occurs there. They are aware only of certain needs, certain currents; and the scope of their legisla-tive influence must be limited because their information is limited in scope. (Durkheim, 1904: 270; cf. Lenoir, 1994: 32–4)

Judicial development of regulation from customary practices is a less productive source of law, Durkheim notes, than it was in the past (1904: 270). Nevertheless, judges must stay in touch with popular senti-ments: if they condemn acts that the public does not condemn, for example, their judgements 'would lack both influence and authority' (1961: 243). Presumably, too, if they fail to condemn acts that in popular opinion are utterly obnoxious.

The fundamental sociological distinction between judges and legis-lators as lawmakers, then, resides not in whether or not they are elected (a matter of purely political authority) but in their differing capacities to understand and deliberate on the diversity of social experience, so as to 'think' in regulatory terms for society as a whole (a matter of moral authority). Legislatures are better organised than judiciaries,

7. See pp. 160–3, above.

Durkheim suggests, to perform this task. Yet judges have an active role in shaping and focusing diffuse social sentiments and ideas (1904: 269–70). Perhaps his view of judges is too constrained by the positivist view of law made explicit in his early writings, which diverts all attention from judicial interpretation because 'a legal rule is what it is and there are no two ways of perceiving it' (1982a: 82). By contrast, for the Durkheimian jurist Emmanuel Lévy, anxious to draw radical potential from Durkheim's sociology, judicial interpretation could not be ignored. Lévy insists that if judges, like legislators, 'think for society' they must be genuinely knowledgeable reflectors of social opinion, chosen for their ability to appreciate all social milieux (De Tourtoulon, 1908: 231). They must be able to compare realistically, for example, employers' and employees' conditions in relation to the employment contract and to assert a moral regulation embracing both (Lévy, 1933: 133).

Officials, experts and citizens

Can anyone else, apart from the judicial, legislative or other agents of the state, have any role in making or interpreting law? When Durkheim discusses lawmaking processes in his lectures on the state he portrays law ideationally as deriving, at least ultimately, from popular understandings and convictions and reflecting social experience. The official lawmaker's role is to transform into regulatory form the ideas, sentiments and experiences diffuse in society at large. But what is important, even where law is seen as the expression of collective representations, is that these are *collective* phenomena. They are not expressions of any particular individual's views, nor need they correspond with the views of any such person. Hence Durkheim gives no sense of a *community* making its law by deliberate collective act. Rather, law as an expression of collective representations expresses what state lawmakers – ideally aided by social scientists – can identify as the content of these representations. Thus, in modern society, even if individualistic values drive legal development, the state supervises this process (Durkheim, 1957: 70; Pickering, 1993: 56–7). Presumably through the deliberative activity of all its branches, executive, legislative and judicial, it elaborates society's beliefs and values. Small wonder that Lévy (1926: 118) writes of judges as having a 'religious' function.

The lawmaking and law applying role of the state appears in a different way in the context of Durkheim's early functional thesis about modern law in *The Division of Labour*. When he stresses there the co-ordinating role of the state in regulating for organic solidarity, law and morality seem even more clearly matters for expert elaboration. The governmental morality of organic solidarity is not even understood in the consciousness of many ordinary citizens.[8]

Thus law and government, despite Durkheim's insistence on their necessary embeddedness in morality and social experience, are, for him, entirely matters for professionals and experts, at least in modern society. Steve Fenton writes:

> [It is] apparent that Durkheim has an affection for all types of 'fonctionnaires' – public officials, whether they be teachers, lawyers, judges, administrators, direct or indirect agents of the state. [He] places his faith in their goodwill, their conciliatory functions, their understanding and their 'neutrality' in enabling them to carry out the functions of the state as arbiters of common good. (Fenton, 1984: 46–7)

Durkheim distinguishes the state as a deliberative body from the administrative apparatus required to put into effect the results of its deliberations. But his image of modern society is one in which the numerous areas of social life that are given distinctiveness by functional specialisation are organised through intricate structures of administrative regulation. A growing army of lawyers and administrative officials is required to provide this organisation in practice. But Durkheim has little to say about the nature of their activities or responsibilities (Vogt, 1993: 90).

This is, perhaps, the most frustrating aspect of his entire legal sociology. He has no significant interest in the workings of the administrative state or the professional practices of lawyers and officials. It should be noted in passing, however, that it is certainly possible to draw on aspects of Durkheim's sociology, beyond his concerns with law, to provide insights into legal processes, such as courtroom trials. This is, for example, the case with his ideas on the functions of ritual, which form part of his sociology of religion (Pickering, 1984: part 4). His elaborate analysis of ritual might well suggest resources on which legal processes draw in influencing people who are brought into contact with them (cf. Garfinkel, 1956).

Towards the end of his career, he began to develop important ideas about the role of symbols in social life. Collective ideals 'can only become manifest and conscious by being concretely realised in objects that can be seen by all, understood by all and represented to all minds: figurative designs, emblems of all kinds, written or spoken formulas, animate or inanimate objects'; for example, sometimes 'a rag of cloth becomes invested with sanctity and a tiny piece of paper can become a very precious thing' (Durkheim, quoted in Lukes, 1973: 423, 424;

---

8. See pp. 110–12, above.

cf. Durkheim, 1953c: 94). The cloth that is a national flag symbolises the nation; the 'tiny piece of paper' may be a parchment that states ancient laws or constitutional principles, carrying them from a distant past to the present. Such objects and the ritual acts in which they play a part can focus popular sentiments and beliefs, symbolise collective representations, convey ambiguous, complex meanings that are neverthless collectively sensed. It can be suggested that many legal processes should be understood, at least partly, in these terms, as ritual performances: for example, the use of oaths in connection with testimony and some formalities in connection with legal acts, and various courtroom procedures, perhaps especially perhaps those surrounding confession, judgement and condemnation.

But it would be necessary, in using Durkheim's ideas on ritual to analyse legal processes, to reason entirely by extension and analogy, as I did earlier in comparing his ideas on education and the legislative function. This is because (unlike many later writers) he does not suggest any direct comparability between priestly rituals of religion and the formalised practices of modern legal systems.[9]

Any analysis of law in action that can be constructed out of Durkheim's writings thus remains limited and speculative. Clearly such an analysis is of little concern to him. So he provides few clues as to what might be problematic about legal practices and, especially, as to how they relate to the popular understandings and convictions – the collective consciousness or collective representations – that he sees as underlying them, providing their authority and, in general, supplying material from which regulation is formed. For a radical Durkheimian jurist such as Lévy, the way forward is to look more closely at these popular understandings and convictions and to treat them as more than just social sources of inspiration or information on which experts might deliberate to produce regulation. Instead, as will be seen in the next chapter, Lévy considers the possibility that, in certain circumstances, the changing popular convictions that provide the foundation for law can burst asunder the established structures of regulation created by the state and its legal experts.[10]

In Lévy's view, the state (relying on its retinue of legal experts) does not necessarily have the final say as to how the collective consciousness or collective representations are to be turned into specific regulation. Ultimately legal ideas depend for their validity on the fact that people accept them: 'Our belief in the law is our true law' (Lévy 1926: 69). Whereas Durkheim assumes that the state will 'think' for society as a

9. See, for example, Fenn (1982), Hepworth and Turner (1982), Levinson (1988). As noted earlier, Durkheim does, however, see early legal formalism as derived from or substituting for religious ritual: see p. 124, above.
10. See pp. 190–3, below.

whole and largely avoids looking at the political obstacles that might arise in doing this, Lévy is acutely aware of these obstacles. What if the state fails to recognise important collective representations, social sentiments or convictions? Then, at a certain point, the communication between society and state which Durkheim's idea of democracy emphasises may become urgent and noisy; certainly more so than might be preferred by those officially involved in the state's regulatory deliberations. The popular convictions of particular sections of society may become specific and focused rather than diffuse. They may demand a hearing and require radical legal reform. And because law ultimately depends on popular conviction, in Lévy's view, the demand will have to be met. Here, as we shall see later, is an important means of radicalising Durkheimian positions. But it is not apparent in Durkheim's own work.

Durkheim's position is set, it seems, by the consequences of the positivist view of law made explicit in his early work. Although modified, this view is never repudiated: law is an objectively identifiable social fact (Durkheim, 1982a: 82). It is not, therefore, essentially, a matter for negotiation, argument or interpretation. It derives from deliberation, but this is, for Durkheim, merely the mechanism by which one social fact leads to another. Thus, following his early thesis in *The Division of Labour*, the social fact of organic solidarity leads (via the state's deliberations) to the social fact of restitutive law. Alternatively, adopting the emphases of his later work, collective representations (popular understandings, beliefs and so on), as existing features of modern society (social facts), give rise via the state's deliberations to modern law as a social fact. Individual agency is not absent from this scenario. But few means of analysing it are offered. The consequence is a mechanistic view of the process of creating and interpreting law. The Durkheimian academic jurist can supply law-creating elites with useful knowledge and inform citizens of social realities (Lukes, 1973: 330–2). Yet, as Lévy insists, the jurist 'is a man of action', an interpreter who wants more than science (quoted in Aillet, 1923: 472). Of his own role as a radical legal scholar Lévy remarks: 'I wanted to grasp directly the convictions (*croyances*) [underpinning law] and to express them in a language which supplies social transformation with the power of [legal] tradition' (Lévy 1909: 32). The object, in other words, ought not to be just to observe the legal world, but to be a part of it and have some means (supplied by sociology) for changing it.

Devolution of regulation

In one area only, Durkheim shows himself acutely sensitive to fundamental questions about how legal processes work. In this area, he identifies serious problems and, on the basis of sociological analysis, advocates reform.

In complex modern societies, social life is diverse and moral understandings are varied. But the state must produce a network of legal regulation that encompasses all this diversity. The task may be impossible. Perhaps the state is too remote from the specific local conditions of particular social groups or functional aspects of social life (Durkheim, 1952: 374, 378; 1984: 297). For example, Durkheim notes that, over time, the 'relationships between capital and labour have . . . remained in the same legal state of indeterminacy. The contract for the hiring of services occupies in our [French] legal codes a very small place, particularly when we consider the diversity and complexity of the relationships it is called upon to regulate' (1984: 303). And contracts of employment purport to regulate basic social relationships in a great variety of work situations. Nevertheless, employment protection, health and safety regulation, and, more generally, conditions of stability and trust in working relationships are needs that may be met in different ways in different contexts.

An occupational activity, he suggests, can be effectively regulated only by a group close enough to it to know how it operates, what its needs are and how it is likely to change (1984: xxxv; 1975a: III, 217–20). And, while industrial relations often appear merely as an arena for conflicts between opposed interests (of capital and labour), Durkheim postulates a situation in which, as in his idealised state, such conflicts are replaced by collective deliberation on values and rules. These serve the entire group of people involved in a certain industry or a certain sector of commerce, providing this group as a whole with meaningful regulation to which all can freely give considered allegiance. Thus, occupational groups, embracing both management and workers, ought to be, in Durkheim's view, able to create, to a certain extent, regulation for themselves, which is meaningful precisely because it is created within the group and tailored to its collective experience and understandings. Organised social groups can thus be, for their members, 'a moral force capable of curbing individual egoism, nurturing among workers a more invigorated feeling of their common solidarity, and preventing the law of the strongest from being applied too brutally in industrial and commercial relationships' (1984: xxxix).

This last quotation suggests that Durkheim seeks not just better informed but also more humane regulation. The assumption is that these go together. The reduction of what I earlier called moral distance[11] between regulators and regulated, by making intermediate groups responsible for regulating their field, should allow regulation to be

11. See pp. 165–6, above.

created where required (thus avoiding the pathological situation of anomie or lack or regulation). It should also allow the creation of regulation sensitive to the character of social relations of interdependence and supportive of them.

His arguments do not seem to be necessarily limited to occupational groups, though he puts most stress on these groups because of their importance in commercial and industrial spheres. Not every group, however, in his view, can be an effective source of regulation for its members, and many social groups in commercial and industrial spheres wholly lack the requirements for this. What is needed is 'a defined, organised group' that can relate as 'a public institution' to the state (1984: xxxvi). The group's authority depends on its structure: its coherence and the intensity of contact between its members; the frequency and intimacy of their interactions and sharing of ideas and sentiments (1957: 8). A highly developed group can exert moral discipline – as in the ethical codes that well-established professional groups enforce on their members. But the only occupational groups able to do this effectively are those that include all who work in the same activity (1984: xxxv). Thinking back to the old idea of the medieval guilds, Durkheim terms such groups *corporations*.

He does not view trade unions or employers' organisations as corporations in this sense since they represent only particular interests, not an entire section of economic or social life (1984: xxxv–xxxvi). No doubt they may promote solidarity among their members but in relation to society at large they function merely as pressure groups for collective interests. Because of this 'it is always the rule of the strongest [between these groups] which settles conflicts, and the state of war is continuous' (1893a: vii; 1984: xxxvi). It is obvious that Durkheim's concern is only with groups which can be seen as small societies in themselves, having a collective life extensive and rich enough to give rise to a shared moral experience. Any such group is likely to be hierarchically structured, with internal variations in economic, political or other power. No doubt it also asserts collective interests externally. But he has no sociological concern with groups defined solely by their economic or political interests as against others, since, in so far as they are politically organised to represent *only* these interests, they are not part of any network of solidarity in society as a whole.

Functional groupings, such as those focused on a particular industry or occupation, are, in Durkheim's view, potentially more significant than those based on locality (1957: 102–3). The life of occupational groups, as he envisages it, 'is, in certain respects independent of any territorial boundaries' (1984: li). And the activities people engage in are often more important to them than where they live. Hence occupational associations have increasing potential for regulatory authority, Durkheim suggests, while the corresponding authority of territorial associations is declining. Local government provides only a weak focus for regulatory devolution. Its boundaries and jurisdictions have little moral influence; 'we see in them only conventional labels without meaning' (1952: 390; 1984: liv).

Thus, secondary groups take on special regulatory importance as 'corporations' in Durkheim's thinking. If they are to assume some of the state's regulatory functions they must be democratic like the modern state, with 'the elective principle' operating in them (1975a: III, 208). The logic of regulation through 'corporations' thus seems identical with that of the state's lawmaking. The same processes of communication and deliberation operate, but Durkheim assumes that communication is likely to be more effective in devolved regulation because of the smaller moral distance between regulators and regulated. About the likely quality of deliberation, however, he has little to say.

The structure of lawmaking that he envisages thus seems to be one in which 'corporations' as public institutions are themselves regulated by the state and, in a sense, become the primary members of political society, for which the state must deliberate. The state must pay heed to the sentiments and experience of the secondary groups, not dominating them but providing a regulatory system linking and uniting them morally to ensure organic solidarity. The vitality of secondary groups he sees as the best bulwark against excessive state power (1957: 63). The state as protector and champion of the cult of the individual guarantees individual freedoms against the potential repression that groups might exert over their members (which implies that in the industrial sphere it must keep a balance between capital and labour). But within this framework the secondary groups acquire much devolved regulatory authority. Each would have an administrative council, 'a kind of miniature parliament' (1957: 37), nominated by election. It would regulate labour relations, provide social security, technical and adult education, sport and recreation (1957: 37; 1984: liii; Lukes, 1973: 540–1). And as the family has ceased, in modern times, to be an extensive, enduring network by means of which property relations can be managed, the secondary groups might take on some economic functions it once monopolised, such as the transmission of property between generations (1984: lvi).

Durkheim thus presents his image of the legal regime of the future in vague outline. What he sketches is not a corporatism in which the state absorbs and uses secondary groups as its agents; nor is it a radical pluralism or syndicalism in which the state is merely an umpire in a negotiation between secondary groups. It is not a liberal individualism that sees the individual as the sole object of law; nor a collectivism treating all legal relationships as centred on groups. Instead, it seeks finely to balance rights and duties between groups and individuals and to divide regulatory authority carefully between the centralised state and more functionally specific groupings.

Many problems remain unaddressed. What is this balance and how is it to be stabilised? How are secondary groups to be defined and recognised? Are individuals to have a choice of membership (Durkheim suggests membership might be compulsory)? And what is the position of those who have no relevant group? Why must occupational groups (rather than other groups) have such prominence? And what of multiple membership by individuals in different groups, and possibly temporary, rapidly shifting and fluid memberships? The whole scheme points towards a static condition of society, and so seems out of date in many respects. Yet, I shall suggest in Part 5, the broad idea of a balancing of different kinds of legal authority and different kinds of legal participation still has something to recommend it.

12

Political action and political ideals

Durkheim's advocacy of the devolution of regulatory authority from the state to intermediate groups shows that he was aware that communication between the regulated and the regulators might be very problematic. An inadequate inflow of information to the state could defeat democratic intentions. But Durkheimian sensitivity to problems in the input side of lawmaking does not seem to be accompanied by any corresponding sensitivity to problems in the output side – that is, the process of deliberation leading to the formulation of law. Durkheim usually assumes that law will be made by well-motivated elites: office-holders in the state or, in the case of devolved regulation, the administrative councils of the 'corporations'.

Is organising regulation, then, purely a managerial matter? Is law nothing more than official administration of social complexity? What has happened to the intimate link between law and morality that is central to all Durkheim's thought about law? Is it that, in modern conditions of organic solidarity, morality, no less than law, becomes a matter for governing classes to elaborate and shape – a purely governmental morality? I have suggested earlier[1] that, in important respects, this is indeed Durkheim's image of modern law and its moral basis. But it has been seen also that a different emphasis appears in his work after *The Division of Labour*: a stress on the importance of a popular morality of individualism as the basis of all modern law. Thus modern law, as presented in his later writings, appears to recover its roots in popular values and sentiments, at least to some extent. The link between law and belief, which in *The Division of Labour* is a central feature only of early law and a declining, residual feature of modern (penal) law, reasserts itself. Not only that, but shared popular ideas, beliefs and sentiments take on much more significance (as collective representations) in his later writings, being treated as, in themselves, potentially causal forces in society.[2]

1. See pp. 109–12.
2. See pp. 11 and 109, above.

Thus interesting questions present themselves. In what way do popular currents of ideas, beliefs and sentiments influence modern law? If public opinion on moral or social matters changes, by what means can these changes in opinion change law? How far are popular movements, rather than legislative elites, able to exert influence by and through law? Broadly speaking, how can law be affected by such movements and their political ideals?

On the whole, Durkheim might seem to be trying to create a body of sociological knowledge that would head off such popular influence. This is not to dismiss his work as conservative. His sociology is intended, among other things, to show the legislator and statesman the *need* for change and how this should be implemented. But, as we have seen,[3] it is aimed at advising governing elites, not encouraging popular movements. This chapter, however, will try to show that Durkheimian legal theory has critical implications (developed notably in the work of Durkheim's collaborator, the jurist Emmanuel Lévy) which link its theses to transformative political action and political ideas.

Law as an obstacle to solidarity

In Durkheim's era, the most important political struggles were in the industrial sphere, focused on the endless conflict of capital and labour in the workplace. Reading Durkheim, one senses that the matter was never far from his mind. Economic life, he writes, is a field of 'moral anarchy' (1957: 15; cf. 1984: xxxi–xxxii). 'For a whole century, economic progress has mainly consisted of freeing industrial relations from all regulation' (1952: 254). But employees should not be treated like machines and nothing in the social logic of modern society requires them to be (1984: 307). Production

> is not all, and if industry can only bring output to this pitch by keeping up a chronic state of warfare and endless dissatisfaction among the producers, there is nothing to balance the evil that it does ... Society has no justification if it does not bring a little peace to men – peace in their hearts and peace in their mutual intercourse. (1957: 16)

The imagery of war and peace (anomie and regulation) is familiar in Durkheim's writing on modern industrial life. Elsewhere, he often invokes a climatic image: modern society lacks warmth; social relations that do not contribute to solidarity have a moral coldness that chills all

3. See pp. 175–6, above.

social life.[4] And sharp class differences prevent justice in contractual and property relations (1957: 213). In Philippe Besnard's view, Durkheim's critique amounts to 'a vigorous and almost vehement condemnation of the ideology of industrial society' (Besnard, 1993: 180).

Yet all these situations he sees as exceptional, pathological conditions to be remedied by proper regulation. The potentially unlimited desires of all parties in industrial or other social relations need to be controlled, so that instead of merely pursuing private interest as far as the pursuit can go, these parties see interests as defined in relation to collective values and understandings enshrined in law. Thus, people should be enabled by (external and self) regulation to pursue their interests in co-operation with, rather than antagonism towards others.

Durkheim sees many factors upsetting this ideal situation. Whether the size of modern enterprises militates against solidarity depends on how they are organised (1982b: 174; 1984: 305–6). Anomie is avoided when interdependent groups or units are sufficiently proximate with easy and frequent interactions, when their relations are sustained over a substantial period, and when the operations of each unit are visible to and understood by the others (1984: 304–5). What is essential is to create or sustain conditions in which moral distance is minimised. In such circumstances regulation can evolve and adapt to meet changing circumstances. Hence the importance of devolving some regulatory authority to 'corporations'.

More serious problems arise when it is not a lack of regulation that needs to be remedied, but the *wrong* regulation, that is regulation imposed by coercion rather than evolved spontaneously out of, or in relation to, social circumstances (1984: 310ff.). Regulation of this kind produces what Durkheim calls a forced rather than a natural division of labour. It may, presumably, be caused by failures in the processes of communication or deliberation that produce regulation. Discussing in *The Division of Labour* the problems of such a forced division, Durkheim seems to realise that political processes might produce an impasse that could only be overcome by radical popular action. Nevertheless, as Hans-Peter Müller (1993: 99) states, interpreting Durkheim: 'Force points to a crisis in the system, a constitutive defect in a society's system of rules, which can only be eliminated by radical changes in the rules themselves and can by no means be left to the healing power of time.' The only solution, as Durkheim (1984: 311) notes, would be to change the established order of regulation and create a new one. Thus, whereas anomie may indicate a transitional state of absence of relevant rules, forced regulation 'indicates an illegitimate order, whose unjust rules systematically create an asymmetrical division

4. Durkheim (1915: 425; 1952: 381; 1961: 233, 239; 1975b: 186, 187; 1984: lii).

of power which favours a small elite at the expense of the mass of society' (Müller, 1993: 99). More generally, forced regulation would seem to be regulation aimed at promoting the interests of some individuals or groups by entirely suppressing the interests of others.

Thus, his writings clearly point to situations in which law is a problem rather than a solution (Durkheim, 1984: 310), where regulation frustrates possibilities for solidarity rather than providing or supporting them, where rules are maintained only by force (1984: 312). Hence he seems to see, if perhaps reluctantly and very much as a peripheral matter, the possibility that popular sentiment might legitimately be turned against existing law, to demand regulation appropriate to the requirements of solidarity. This seems to provide an entrée into Durkheim's intellectual world for a more traditional sort of politics than that which he usually assumes: in other words, for politics as a struggle around power, a matter of insisting on regulatory change rather than providing input into deliberations about it.

A context of law reform

Durkheim's discussion of the forced division of labour suggests that, even from his standpoint, law might need in some – albeit rare – circumstances to be recognised as an object of politics, something to be fought over, rather than an expression of popular or governmental morality. This is because law in practice sometimes fails to fulfil its role as such an expression and must then be *made* to fulfil it. So it might be necessary to consider the nature of popular movements for legal or governmental change and the conditions that encourage them. In fact, he could hardly ignore politics in this sense, writing in an era when popular political demands were insistent and important legal changes reflected some of these demands. Towards the end of the nineteenth century legal developments occurred which provide the context for Durkheimian views on the politics of law. In France at this time it was possible to observe a 'revolt against the fundamental principles of the Code Napoléon' and the hitherto dominant interpretations of it (Arnaud, 1975: 78–9). This was so especially as regards the Code's treatment of individual rights, for example property rights, with limited concern for their social effects, and the assumptions it enshrined about social roles and legal statuses (for example, of men and women) (Arnaud, 1975: 81, 94–5).

Progressive legal argument around the right of property involved treating it as one example of individual rights, these rights being seen in a broad social and legal context (Arnaud, 1975: 95). The rapid development of commerce, industry and public services in an increasingly

Political movements towards legal reform

complex society seemed to make this an appropriate legal approach.[5]
A doctrine of abuse of rights developed to limit the anti-social use of
private rights (Arnaud, 1975: 95–6; Gutteridge, 1933). Ideas of legal
responsibility changed, putting more emphasis on social or enterprise
responsibility for misfortune such as industrial accidents (Arnaud, 1975:
96–102) and, if these changes are interpreted in Durkheimian terms,
more clearly recognising interdependence as a basis of individual
welfare. Durkheim's follower Célestin Bouglé (1935: 102) observed that,
in the view of many jurists, 'traditional individualism in France' (which
ignored collective concerns and saw only egoistic individuals interacting)
'was on the way to becoming bankrupt.' A frequent claim in the decades
around the turn of the century was that French law was becoming
'socialised'. The jurist J. Charmont wrote that to 'socialise law (*droit*)
is to make it more comprehensive, larger than before, to extend it from
rich to poor, from owner to wage earner, from men to women, fathers
to children, because, in sum, it is to make it benefit all members of
society' (quoted in Arnaud, 1975: 89). Social welfare law and a political movement for what came to be called 'legal socialism' emerged.

All of this is, in some respects, merely one version of the familiar
story of the growth of the welfare state in modern Western societies.
But the closeness to Durkheimian viewpoints on law and society of
some political arguments and ideas is clear. Drawing on the ideas
of legal writers, Bouglé, in a book on 'Solidarism' (the political movement advocating a philosophy of social solidarity or mutual support as
a basis for social welfare), wrote of 'quasi-contractual' links between
individuals from the time of their earliest nurturing in the natural associations of social life (such as the family and the state). These links
implied rights and duties of mutual support between individuals. And
the legal structure of mutual support could, in modern conditions,
extend across the whole of society, accompanying the various kinds of
voluntary links established by contractual agreement (Arnaud, 1975:
87–8). Hence law that might have been thought of as an expression of
egoism through the sanctification of private rights in the Civil Code
could be seen instead as a framework of interdependence, embracing
all members of society linked in forms of association providing the
networks of modern life.

From Durkheim's perspective, such an analysis would point merely
to an ongoing process of legal development dictated by the character
of modern society. On this view, law inevitably reflects and supports
the continuing development of organic solidarity. If it fails to do so it
must eventually lose its authority and meaning as socially relevant
regulation. On the other hand, the analysis might suggest that the legal

5. See pp. 26–7 and 37, above.

equilibrium of interdependence and solidarity, even if sociologically explicable, is still something that has to be fought for politically by social groups. In other words, the ideas, sentiments and experiences of particular groups will not necessarily be automatically recognised in law-making processes. Collective representations may have to battle for social dominance and expression in legal regulation. Both of these implications of the analysis could be regarded as Durkheimian. The first puts little emphasis on popular political action; the second makes it central. To examine each of them it is necessary to look first at Durkheim's own ideas on socialism as a social and political movement corresponding in certain respects with (but to be distinguished from) sociology, and then at more radical ideas on the possibility of a Durkheimian politics focused on law.

⟶ Durkheim's ideas on Socialism.

A cry of misery

For Durkheim, much political activity is uninteresting because it is ill-informed and directed to purposes that either cannot be accomplished or can only be accomplished at a cost that makes it self-defeating. When everything becomes a matter of ignorant controversy and division, democracies descend into chaos, he notes. What results is a situation of

> constant flux and instability . . . If only this state of affairs led to any really profound changes. But those that do come about are often superficial. For great changes need time and reflection and call for sustained effort. It often happens that all these day-to-day modifications cancel each other out and that in the end the state remains utterly stationary. Those societies that are so stormy on the surface are often bound to routine. (1957: 94)

This statement shows clearly why, for Durkheim, politics as a rational activity is dependent on sociology. Conviction politics and the politics of special interests need to be replaced by an informed politics, grounded in detailed knowledge of social conditions, sensitive to the array of sentiments and ideas current in society, and aware of the vast variety of social experience. His scepticism about politics is not the outlook of a social conservative, in any thoroughgoing sense, but of someone frustrated by the pointlessness of much political action which, for all its noise and energy, changes little or brings about consequences very different from those intended.

Durkheim's writings on socialism (by far the most important progressive political movement of his time) provide a sustained expression of this frustration. Mauss (1958: 34) writes that Durkheim was loathe to embrace socialism because of its association with violence, its class character and 'its political, even politician-like tone'. This explains why he distanced himself from socialist political movements. But there is no doubt that he was sympathetic to many of socialism's egalitarian and liberating ideals. According to his friend Hubert Bourgin, Durkheim acknowledged that he was a socialist: 'He considered that a society transformed by the methods and practical applications of the sciences, including his own, was ripe for a great legal reconstruction . . . and it was this reconstruction . . . which he called socialism' (quoted in Lukes, 1973: 321). Socialism would be sociology turned into politics: not a revolutionary or class-based political movement but a carefully considered, progressive transformation of society by an informed, democratically-empowered elite acting on detailed empirical knowledge of social conditions and social experience to remove gradually all obstacles to solidarity. Socialism thus had to discard all 'its out-of-date slogans', or become a 'new socialism' (Durkheim, quoted in Lukes, 1973: 321).

Perhaps, like many present-day social democrats or democratic socialists, Durkheim saw this approach as the only realistic and productive one for socialism. But, unlike most of them, he defined this realistic socialism traditionally in entirely economic terms, though not in terms of state ownership of the means of production. 'We denote as socialist every doctrine which demands the connection of all economic functions, or of certain among them, which are at the present time diffuse, to the directing and conscious centres of society' (Durkheim, 1958: 54). Commenting on this definition Durkheim stresses that 'connection' does not mean 'subordination' but rather a partnership between state and economy. Nevertheless socialism is 'essentially a process of economic concentration and centralisation' (1958: 89). It remains somewhat unclear, assuming Durkheim's sympathy with socialism, how such centralisation and concentration of economic matters would coexist with the regulatory decentralisation discussed in Chapter 11. Lukes remarks that Durkheim 'had little interest in the economics of socialism' (Lukes, 1973: 321). Presumably, however, it is to be assumed that the state's economic task would be to co-ordinate the functional roles of the various 'corporations' or occupational groups. These groups would be the units of economic life and the organisational centres for everyday economic activities. Socialist philosophy would judge the success of any such economic organisation of society, shared between state and corporations, in terms of its contribution to socialist aims. For Durkheim these aims would centre on promoting the freedom of all citizens by removing sources of arbitrary inequality (such as socially unjustifiable inheritance rights and large discrepancies of bargaining power between economic actors).[6]

6. See Chapters 8 and 9, above.

Durkheim's critique of socialism is thus not that its ideals are unacceptable but that its political methods are counterproductive. The social scientist cannot accept 'these premature solutions, these vast systems so summarily sketched out' (1958: 42). Yet it is not at all clear that some of his own prescriptions, for example for devolution of regulation to occupational groups or 'corporations', are immune from similar criticisms. Ultimately the main problem Durkheim sees with socialism as a political movement may be that it sends distorted communications into the deliberative processes of lawmaking, legal interpretation and administrative regulation. 'Socialism is not a science, a sociology in miniature – it is a cry of misery (*douleur*), sometimes of anger, uttered by men who feel most keenly our collective malaise' (1928: 37; 1958: 41). The Durkheimian message here is straightforward: the cry *must* be heard by the lawmaker; remedies must be sought for the malaise; but the communication of social information may well be distorted. Socialism 'expresses a state of society . . . It does not express this accurately' (1897: 244). The rule-maker must deliberate rationally on the best available, broadest social knowledge. To legislate for emotion is to fall into all the traps of 'mere' politics – whether the politics of conviction or of vested interests, of absolutism or populism. Sociology, it seems, mutes the cries of despair. It hears them only as part of the great hubbub of voices conveying collective ideas and sentiments and reporting the diversity of social experience.

A radical jurist in Durkheim's world

A much more radical Durkheimian view of the relationship between law and popular political movements is possible, but it is found not in Durkheim's own work but in that of one of the law professors who co-operated with him over many years as a member of his sociological circle. Emmanuel Lévy was a colleague of Paul Huvelin's in the law faculty of the University of Lyons, and taught there for some three decades. Indeed, it was Lévy who introduced Huvelin to the Durkheim group.

Lévy is an unjustly neglected intellectual figure. His difficult, aphoristic and often enigmatic writings are hard to find and he is rarely mentioned in modern French legal writing, although his place in the history of legal sociology is noted (Carbonnier, 1994: 118; Chazel, 1991: 37; Arnaud, 1975; 1981). In legal and sociological literature published in English he remains almost completely unknown (cf. Vogt, 1983: 194). Yet he is an important contributor to Durkheimian legal theory. As a genuinely radical or critical jurist long before these terms became familiar he sought to give Durkheim's ideas an uncompromising political reading, harnessing them to the cause of socialist activism in France during the first three decades of the twentieth century.

Lévy sees law as expressing and dependent on collective sentiments and convictions diffuse throughout society. Thus his emphasis is similar to Durkheim's to the extent that Durkheim links law with a collective consciousness or collective representations. 'From the viewpoint of scholarship,' Lévy writes, 'I found in Durkheim confirmation of this: we live through beliefs (*croyances*)' (Lévy, 1933: 168). André-Jean Arnaud notes that 'Lévy reduced the whole reality of law to a flow of living, moving convictions (*croyances vivantes et mobiles*) existing in advance of any legal classification' (Arnaud, 1975: 161). It is these convictions or beliefs that make law possible and give it meaning.

But Lévy does not treat collective sentiments or beliefs as forces acting 'externally' on individuals as coercive social facts. Rather than adopting directly Durkheim's view of the collective consciousness, he sees individuals as sharing their ideas and attitudes when they respond to the same experiences and influences – thus a continuous movement arises between individual and collective beliefs and outlooks (Arnaud, 1975: 162; Gurvitch, 1934: 173–6). This is an important aspect of Lévy's approach because it shifts emphasis from the idea of collective representations or a collective consciousness seeming merely to bear down on individuals, controlling them. Instead it suggests that individuals, joining together and sharing their ideas and sentiments, actively create collective convictions which then orient their individual lives. The individual as a potential political actor – but in concert with others – assumes a place in Lévy's thought which remains largely unfilled in Durkheim's (Gurvitch, 1934: 174–5). It can also be noted that Lévy's emphasis on the causal importance of popular convictions as the driving force in producing law is much closer to Durkheim's later ideational orientation[7] than to his early thesis which sees legal change as brought about by changes in social structure (morphology) (Gurvitch, 1934: 174). In some respects Lévy follows directions of analysis that remain merely implicit possibilities in Durkheim's later ideational outlook on law.

What then is the essence of Lévy's argument? Like Durkheim, he sees law as part of a continuum with morals and collective beliefs in general. Without these popular convictions supporting it, law lacks social meaning and authority. Underpinning civil law are notions of trust or reliance (*confiance*) and good faith (*bonne foi*) (Arnaud, 1975: 162; Carbonnier, 1994: 118), which, in turn, reflect the needs of social solidarity. In Chapter 8, the Durkheimian emphasisis on shared moral convictions as the foundation of contractual obligation was noted. More

7. See pp. 108–9, above.

generally, for Lévy, the universally accepted idea of credit or security (*créances*) – reliance, for example, on a debtor's promise or on the stable value of property in many different forms – underpins development in private law and shows its basis in popular convictions. Thus law is founded on beliefs and assumptions widespread in society: for example, the belief that agreements are to be fulfilled, credit satisfied and property respected. The state makes law, but Lévy, like Durkheim, sees the state as essentially the agent of society in doing this. All rights rest on conviction: the conviction of the right-holder, confirmed and supported by the convictions of people generally. The state, defining legal rights, officially expresses these collective convictions, but what are ultimately important are the 'convictions of all, whether sanctioned by the state or without the state' (Lévy, 1909: 9; 1926: 132). Thus, property rights, contractual rights and legal liability depend on social beliefs.

Law is a *measure* superimposed on these beliefs. Legal rights are 'measured convictions'. Rather than remaining diffuse they become, in law, precise and calculated (1926: 177). In this way an official measure of belief represented in law is distinguished from other matters of conviction. Time and money are the criteria of this measuring (1933: 150–1, 164–6). Thus, penal law is a system of tariffs (the amount of the fine, the period of imprisonment and so on). Similarly, civil justice requires an accounting when credit is redeemed, compensation paid, and it specifies when this is to be done. 'Justice postulates a calculability . . . in justice everything is made to tally' (1926: 177; 1933: 166). Law thus involves also the intellectualisation or rationalisation of popular convictions, 'cooling' them by 'making them pass through a logical intermediary' (Gurvitch, 1934: 175). The parallel with Durkheim's deliberating legislator or legal interpreter seems clear.

The credit right of labour

The most important part of Lévy's analysis attempts to explain how law is changing generally in modern society and how the logic of this ongoing transformation accounts for law's 'socialisation', discussed earlier in this chapter. If law is founded on popular convictions it is necessary to understand how and why these convictions change. Lévy notes that, gradually, the enforcement of legal liability has evolved so that it is directed more and more against the wrongdoer's assets rather than his person (his body). Thus, while individuals assert rights, duties are enforced primarily against what they own (1933: 38–9). In practical terms, obligations take effect only if the obligated individual has assets. Limited liability companies separate assets that can be the object of commercial liability from the individuals who direct commerce. Thus liability attaches mainly to capital rather than to individual capitalists. 'So as not to be obligated oneself one becomes a right holder in a group that extends our [legal] personality' in the form of corporate personality (1926: 98–9).

But the major modern change, in Lévy's view, is that an immense variety of credit rights is replacing traditional forms of property rights. Securities (*valeurs*) are taking the place of possessions (1926: 132–9). Traditional forms of property rights are thought to have stability and permanence with a 'solid basis in the past', that is in a chain of preceding holdings (1909: 11), and with the support of the state. But modern life depends increasingly on many forms of reliance (*créance*) or rights to security (*droit à des valeurs*) – for example, insurance, guarantees, credit assurances, documentary promises – that are 'temporary and variable', depending not on the past but on expectations about the future (1909: 11) – in other words, expectations about future conduct by others. They are based much more directly in public confidence than are traditional property rights. For example, the credit rights represented by shares in a company depend for their value very directly on beliefs about the present conditions and future prospects of the company and of markets generally.[8] And, Lévy notes, these matters are not necessarily in the control of the state. It cannot guarantee the value of credit rights to the extent that it protects traditional forms of property (1909: 13–14; 1933: 54–5). 'The fortune in securities is as international as landed property is national' (1909: 11; 1933: 56, 81–2). Thus, he suggests, the forms of value that law protects or embodies have become more flexible with the proliferation of credit rights or securities, but also much more vulnerable to shifts in the beliefs that underlie all legal entitlements. The 'regime of securities abandons the [concept of] the perpetual individual right. Value obeys the laws of the market, the market rate. It is not isolated like property, as if it were something acquired; it is subject to influence, it changes, is declared, is mobile' (1933: 77). Popular convictions play a major part in determining directly the value (indeed the very existence) of such rights (1909: 11; 1933: 56).

Lévy sees a qualitative legal change here, but perhaps there is only an extension of law's perpetual dependence on collective beliefs. However, the extension does seem to remove any need for material objects (such as land or tangible assets) to which rights to assets are attached and which help to stabilise them. Shares and other 'paper securities' are obvious examples of this extension. But intellectual property rights in general are also credit rights in Lévy's sense, constructed purely

---

8. On the historical process of detachment of the share as 'fictitious money capital' from any basis in traditional forms of property see Ireland et al. (1987).

to embody value reflecting popular convictions about the worth of particular enterprises, ideas or creations (Lévy, 1909: 15).

One consequence of the spread of credit rights, in Lévy's view, is that rights in general take on a more collective character. This seems to be because their nature now depends more directly on collective convictions, rather than on, for example, the state's enforcement power supporting particular individual right-holders. For example, a creditor's position in a bankruptcy may depend on the will of the majority of creditors in deciding on a settlement (1909: 12). Most importantly, the fact that wealth in modern society has increasingly taken the form of capital, itself an accumulation of credit rights, has made it vulnerable to fluctuations in market confidence, which is an expression of collective beliefs (for example, about the economy or market conditions). Capital is thus usually organised collectively in corporations or groups *co-operating* to minimise risk. Correspondingly, labour organises collectively. When an individual employee asserts a credit right to recompense for his labour, this right is weak, but it becomes strong when asserted as part of the collective credit right of labour. When employees organise themselves to assert their rights collectively their action can have direct and major effects on the confidence underpinning the credit rights of capital. Thus, the idea of rights as social rather than individual becomes more familiar.

In essence, Lévy sees the shift to credit rights as having opened up for the first time the possibility that employees, having only their labour power to sell to the employer, nevertheless become powerful creditors, the holders of significant credit rights (arising out of the contribution of their labour) confronting the credit rights (for example shares) that constitute capital. The individual alone has only a fragile credit right against the employer because it exists only if he works, and there is no legal right to work (1909: 15; 1933: 42). But when the credit right of labour is asserted collectively it can, in fact, *destroy* the credit rights of capital (for example, strikes can destroy the value of a company and its shares).[9] As noted earlier, the state, in Lévy's view, cannot guarantee the value of the credit rights of capital to the extent that it guarantees traditional forms of property rights (1909: 13–14). Thus, he argues, organised labour is able to use to its advantage the forms of legal right that have flourished in modern society. In effect, labour can

9. Lévy (1909: 27). He does not address the point (which one can imagine Durkheim raising) that such a destructive use of the credit right of labour could ultimately also destroy its own possibilities of profitable realisation. Lévy's claim is presumably that the strike is a final and potentially drastic sanction if employees' rights are denied, not a normal means of asserting these rights. Indeed, in his analysis, a strike sweeps away old rights and clears the way for new ones, because it marks a disruption of collective convictions that made the pre-strike regime of rights stable as between the parties affected by the strike. See Lévy (1909: ch. 4).

'cash in' its credit rights against capital. And, he claims dramatically, the credit right of labour will gradually but inevitably 'absorb' that of capital (1933: 28). The collective right of labour corresponds directly to labour's part in the process of production and the collective convictions that support a just return on contracts while the collective credit right of capital depends entirely on the security of stored up capital (1933: 29–31). What this seems to mean is that capital is ultimately dependent purely on popular (but perhaps fragile) convictions that its accumulated 'paper' entitlements (for example, the recorded value of bank account balances, the quoted value of investments, the benefits of employment or other contracts) should be respected.

Lévy's Durkheimian outlook asserts itself particularly when he declares, despite his emphasis as a jurist on rights, that the worker in modern conditions acquires first and foremost not a right but a *function* (1909: 28). Legal rights arise as a by-product of the relations of interdependence that social solidarity demands. Thus, reflecting Durkheim's view, he insists that the protection of employees' rights is not the prerogative of trade unions, supervising collective agreements for their members: 'It is the occupational group (*profession*), it is the industry, which has the right to contract, to act; the occupational group of which the union is only the variable, mobile, changing expression ...' (1909: 26). Despite Lévy's militant socialism, he couches his analysis ultimately in a Durkheimian framework that treats law and rights as expressions of relations of solidarity. It is the necessity for these relations that gives rights whatever force they may have. Yet, crucially, unlike Durkheim, he claims that these relations of solidarity may need to be fought for through direct action (especially strikes by employees against employers). Thus, the industrial strike is the ultimate means of asserting the credit right of labour. In Durkheimian terms we might say it is one of the most forceful means of legitimate communication by the regulated to the regulators.

Legal allegiance to what?

Lévy's writings remain ambiguous about the place of the state in determining legal rights and duties (Gurvitch, 1934: 182–4). 'Only the state guarantees to individuals or removes from them their rights ... it is the [enacted] law (*loi*) that gives and that takes away; in other words the will of the state (legislators, administrators, judges)' (Lévy, 1909: 9). On the other hand, the proliferation of credit rights seems to Lévy to have the inevitable consequence that the state cannot fully control or channel the popular convictions on which law depends for its social meaning and authority. They cannot even be kept insulated within national boundaries. There are some parallels with this ambivalence about the state in Durkheim's writings. We noted earlier that, in discussing the growth of values of individualism, he sees an international current of belief in human rights developing, spilling beyond the boundaries of nation states.[10] Yet, unlike Lévy, he remains unconvinced that international movements of ideas and beliefs are strong enough, for the present, to begin to displace the nation state's legal dominance.

It is interesting that both Lévy and Durkheim (but especially Lévy) have some sense of the emerging transnational currents that, long after their time, have tended ever more noticeably to reduce the state's monopoly of legal controls on social life. But Lévy's view is ultimately unclear. The state 'keeps in the background; one might say that it is everywhere' (Lévy, 1933: 81). It 'exists, above all, among those who want to control [popular] convictions by violent compulsion', yet where convictions clash violently, for example between managers and workers, as in strikes, often arbitration rather than crude coercion is used (1933: 72, 81). It seems the nature of the state's power to regulate is in some respects problematic or controversial.

One can see why, still following a Durkheimian analysis, this may be so. Lévy's work, unlike Durkheim's, introduces explicitly the idea of conflict between popular convictions, clashing and competing collective representations, and ultimately a fragmented collective consciousness. Division and diversity in society reflected in diversity and conflict between popular sentiments, understandings and beliefs may be more prominent than unity. How then is the state to 'think' for society? We can assume that Durkheim's answer is still that the state must elaborate values and principles in regulatory form that can bridge the disagreements and sow harmony in place of discord. This is not an ideal for political practice to follow but a necessity dictated by the sociological insight that solidarity is the moral mechanism that makes social life both possible and efficient in complex societies, no less than simple ones.

But if sociology can tell the legislator and administrator how they must function, what can it tell the citizen? In a society of diverse beliefs, conflicting sentiments, contrasting social experience, how is the citizen to view law? Why should law claim the allegiance of all, and on what basis, by making what kinds of claim to authority? Is it enough to say to the citizen that law is made for the general good, that it is not merely a compromise of interests but an elaboration of principle, that law expresses what society collectively believes? Where law seems not to reflect popular belief or sentiment is it enough to say that this is because law is created to provide the moral framework objectively required for the co-existence of individuals and groups in conditions of interdependence?

10. See pp. 117–18, above.

In the final years of his life Durkheim became increasingly concerned with the question of the bases on which a shared popular allegiance to regulation could be created. The cult of the individual is, of course, one such basis, for he sees this as the unifying value system in which, in modern society, it remains possible to believe. Yet does it provide a basis of allegiance to the law of the *nation state*? The state must stand at the head of the cult, writes Durkheim, as its protector and exponent (1957: 70). But the values of individualism are not confined within national boundaries. Thus, the claim of state law to monopolise the regulatory expression of the rights of the individual may not remain permanently secure. Morality (including law as a special form of morality) is a matter not only of duty but also of attachment to social groups.[11] But which groups? Allegiance to the nation state as the moral agent of regulation is weakening: 'Doubtless we have towards the country in its present form . . . obligations that we do not have the right to cast off. But beyond this country, there is another in the process of formation, enveloping our national country; that of Europe, or humanity.'[12] European nations are in certain respects 'all part of the same society, still incohesive, it is true, but one becoming increasingly conscious of itself' (1984: 76–7). Elsewhere he writes of 'the great human community' and of a 'universal consciousness and a universal opinion' that goes beyond national boundaries (quoted in Lukes, 1973: 552). The dream of an ideal of human brotherhood 'cannot be satisfied unless all men form part of one and the same society, subject to the same laws', a 'society that embraces all societies'; nothing proves that such a world society is impossible (1984: 336–7).

Yet for the moment it is impracticable and what is required is a form of allegiance to the nation state which the state earns by acting as local agent of the idea of a united, universal humanity (1957: 74; 1961: 77). Thus the transnational values of individualism are harnessed to the only practical focus of regulatory power, the nation state.

Still the nagging problem remains. Is the cult of the individual enough to unify citizens morally? It is here, with the final problem which lies only partly answered at the end of Durkheim's career, that we should end this account of his work on law. The question that haunts his last book, *The Elementary Forms of the Religious Life* (Durkheim, 1915), is whether in modern society it is possible to find a focus of belief that can take the place of the old forms of religion of pre-modern societies. The 'old gods are growing old or already dead' and nothing has yet replaced them (1915: 427). This is surely the real significance of Durkheim's frequently repeated metaphor of the 'coldness' of modern

---

11. See pp. 62–3, above.
12. Durkheim quoted in Lukes (1973: 350); and see Durkheim (1961: 77–9).

society. Great collective celebrations, ceremonies, pageants or shared national experiences may rekindle for a time the popular sense of shared destiny and common commitment. But people 'cannot celebrate ceremonies for which they see no reason, nor can they accept a faith which they in no way understand' (1915: 430). A vacuum of absent belief may lie at the heart of modern life. Nothing is more urgent than to fill it, but without any illusion that one can or should return to the past (1952: 169, 375). Sociology shows that the past is, indeed, 'a foreign country' where 'they do things differently.'[13] Durkheim's sociology of law does not explain how the vacuum may be filled, but it shows how modern law can be conceptualised in relation to belief, as a liberating rather than authoritarian moral force. It remains to attempt an overall assessment, in the final part of this book, of this single-minded, elaborate attempt to find the moral essence of law.

13. L. P. Hartley, *The Go-Between*, Prologue.

Part 5

An overview

13

The moralistic perspective

What overall view should be taken of Durkheim's achievement in the study of law? I shall argue, in this and the following chapter, that despite the inadequacies of his legal theory, which are serious, it has two general virtues that make it an important and powerful contribution to the understanding of law. The first of these is its particular effort to analyse law in moral terms – its moralistic perspective. The second is its effort to develop this approach sociologically. This chapter is primarily concerned with Durkheim's moralistic perspective. The next considers more directly some implications and problems of his sociological outlook.

Alongside these virtues – and perhaps inseparable from them – are important failings. But they are not, in the main, the failings of omission (such as to address questions of power, to account fully for legal or penal history, or to embrace theoretically all areas of law) with which Durkheim is often charged. Where he appears to leave seemingly very important matters wholly out of account in his analyses it is wise to assume that, in the main, this is deliberate, and to ask the reasons. What is important is to inquire why he approaches matters in the way he does, and how enlightening his approach is in its own terms as well as by comparison with other approaches. In other words, it is important to see Durkheim's theory not as a failed attempt to produce a sociology of law or legal theory that would follow an agenda set by his critics, but as an attempt to set an agenda that is wholly his own.

Two virtues

A first virtue that can be claimed for Durkheim's legal theory is its effort to view law consistently in terms of its actual or potential *moral worth*. For Durkheim, law must justify itself morally. It must have value and importance not merely in terms of its utility as a political instrument but as a part of the collective moral life of the society in which it exists; we might say that it must take its place as a part of culture. Indeed, it seems that for Durkheim law can justify and present itself in no other way.

Today, this seems a strange theoretical approach to law. Modern legal theory has tended to discard the requirement that law be grounded in or an aspect of morality. In general, only various kinds of natural law theory – now somewhat marginalised in Western legal thought – continue to insist on emphasising a moral essence of law as a central focus for legal theory (e.g. George, 1992). So Durkheim puts forward an agenda that is unusual and difficult in relation to modern legal thinking. He asks us not to think of law politically, in the usual senses of the term; if law is a political instrument, then it is one devoted exclusively to moral tasks. He requires that we see law in this way even though modern law often seems, doctrinally, to be no more than a mass of technical rules, and, functionally, merely a governmental instrument for resolving clashes of interests as and when they arise. For Durkheim, law has to tame and transform interests, redefining them as a matter of social values.[1]

This Durkheimian approach is a virtue because it challenges us to think of law as something worth giving loyalty to, in circumstances in which it seems increasingly hard to see why this loyalty should be given whole-heartedly. His view of law as a special kind of morality necessarily reduces the difficult question of the nature of legal obligation (e.g. Raz, 1994: ch. 15) to one of moral obligation, but he explains the latter in a way that prevents this obligation being manipulated by political authorities for authoritarian ends. Thus he tries implicitly to solve the problems which positivist jurists have long associated with attempts to make law and morality analytically inseparable (Hart, 1958; cf. MacCormick, 1992). Treating law as having its basis in morality does not give states and their leaders *carte blanche* to propound a national or state morality to support tyranny or totalitarianism. Nor, conversely, does it make each citizen his own lawmaker. The morality that can provide the basis for law is given not by political authorities or lawmakers, nor by the individual preferences of citizens, but by the nature of society itself. And in complex modern Western societies that morality *must* be one that privileges and protects individual autonomy and dignity in a context of social solidarity.

The second virtue that can be claimed for Durkheim's legal theory, following from the above, is that he makes his inquiry about law as a moral phenomenon a *sociological* one. The polemical thrust of his ideas on law is expressed in his refusal to accept theories that deduce law's moral basis through speculations that cannot be readily seen as grounded in systematic empirical study of social life. For example, although Durkheim (1960b) recognises general features of the human condition that sociology should recognise, he refuses to postulate an

1. See pp. 112–13, above.

unchanging human nature as a basis of speculation on law and morality.[2] He denies that morality is a system to be deduced from first principles. As we have noted, Durkheimian morality is historically specific and not necessarily systematic. It develops out of belief patterns present in societies. In modern societies it is demanded by the empirical complexities of social experience. While the sociologist who records these beliefs or this experience can portray morality as a social phenomenon, Durkheim insists that morality is not legislated by great thinkers or somehow immanent in humanity or in human life in general.

His way of going about his inquiries enables us to treat morality as, in essence, philosophically modest yet sociologically fundamental. Morality may be irrational or ignorant in its demands in particular times and places. It may derive from beliefs whose substance seems to defy all rational justification or explanation. On the other hand, modern morality may codify the principles and values on which a complex society has to be organised if there is to be reasonable harmony between individuals and groups within it. Morality is a network of ideas, intuitions and convictions about how we should live in relation to others, a web of understandings and convictions expressed in the form of obligations and attachments. But in its modern forms, as noted earlier,[3] it also includes, for Durkheim, very importantly, sources for criticising its own prescriptions. Modern morality turns back on itself and engages in self-questioning. Thus, we do not merely follow moral duties but reflect on them as autonomous individuals, confronting the teachings of duty with the lessons of our own experience and reflection. Morality has the possibility of becoming rational, or rationally grounded, in a way that was not necessarily true of it in earlier times. At least, its rationality is very different from that of earlier times. Thus, Durkheim gives important resources for considering law's moral foundations.

Individualism and rights

Among the most important of his reflections on the moral bases of law are those that seek to clarify the nature of individualism as a value system. His legal theory shows that individualism in this sense can explain the main orientations of modern law, as well as providing bases for criticising some of its aspects.[4] In addition, however, as has been seen, Durkheimian sociology offers an elaborate explanation of the

2. See pp. 19–20, above.
3. See pp. 63–4.
4. For example, aspects of contract (Chapter 8, above) and inheritance law (Chapter 9, above).

nature and sources of this value system.[5] It attempts to explain why individualism has emerged as the dominant system of shared values in modern society, why that system is not merely desirable but also necessary as an essential foundation of social complexity in modern societies, and why no other value system can compete with it in these circumstances. These claims are of great significance for contemporary, sociologically oriented, legal theory because Durkheim links them with issues about law that remain vitally important a century after he wrote.

Perhaps the most notable of these issues concerns human rights. Questions of the nature and significance of human rights have acquired, particularly since the Second World War, an international prominence much greater than in Durkheim's time. Through his sociological account of the cult of the individual it becomes possible to see why human rights have become increasingly central to the trajectory of modern legal development. As individualism becomes more clearly established as the only value system that can be a focus of shared moral allegiance in modern society, it might be said that it finds its 'purest' expression in human rights discourse. Durkheimian individualism demands respect (and legal protection) for the dignity of all other individuals. It requires a reaching out to others, a collective concern for individual well-being. And it seems plausible to claim that this moral imperative now seeks full legal expression primarily through movements and institutions for the protection of human rights.

It cannot be said that a 'rights culture' in which individuals invoke rights as a matter of course is necessarily consistent with Durkheimian individualism. A highly litigious society, in which individuals or groups feel a widespread need to assert legal rights aggressively to protect and promote their interests, might be better seen as mired in widespread egoism in Durkheim's sense. But a general collective effort to give rights to personal dignity and well-being to *others* might well be a powerful expression of Durkheimian individualism. Perhaps this effort, recognisable in the work of some national and international human rights movements, signifies the value system of individualism extending its reach and becoming a shared moral culture, explicitly recognised and valued as such in popular consciousness. Some of the continuing controversy around the place of certain collective rights in human rights discourse and about the cultural relativity of human rights (e.g. An-Na'im, 1992) can be understood, up to a point, in Durkheimian terms. These controversies may reflect the need to define individualism as a *social* value system; that is, one deriving not from some abstract transcultural notion of the 'individual' but from the conditions of social life in particular historical and geographical contexts. Perhaps Durkheim's

5. See Chapters 7, 8 and 9, above.

detailed analysis of individualism as a value system in a specific legal and sociological context provides some partial resources for clarifying issues here.

The relationship between law and individualism is surely one of the most important areas in which Durkheim's moralistic perspective can contribute to contemporary legal theory. And the explanation of the fundamental nature of this relationship in modern society is one of the most valuable products of his sociological perspective on law and morality. But we should note that a Durkheimian analysis does not suggest that individualism will permanently remain the value system of modern law, that counter-currents will not dislodge this value system in certain respects or, indeed, that it will retain its character in unchanging form. Legal theory and the sociology of law certainly should not assume that modern society has reached a finished state in which its values have lost all capacity for further evolution (cf. Fukuyama, 1992). A Durkheimian sociology of morality can forcefully suggest, however, why certain tendencies in legal development in particular conditions seem to take on an air of necessity or even inevitability in the legal systems of societies that share those conditions.

Of course, no sharp line can be drawn between philosophical and sociological views of morality, as Durkheim himself ultimately recognises. But a sociological approach favours a certain emphasis. It requires that if moral principles are to be justified this must be done by reference to the nature of the particular society in which these principles arise, in other words by reference to the nature of society as a phenomenon taking different forms in different historical settings. Morality is not timeless but historical. As such it is relative, yet not a matter of preference. It reflects the nature of social life in particular times and places. And it is for sociology – the systematic, empirical study of social phenomena – to clarify that nature. This is why, for example, Durkheim's analysis of individualism as the basis of modern law is not a 'communitarian defence of liberalism' (Cladis, 1992) or a liberal kind of communitarianism (cf. Miller, 1993), for these phrases invoke the timeless terminology of political philosophy and its intellectual controversies. Durkheim's attempt is rather to explain sociologically what law as a system of principle, in a particular time and place, viewed in a certain perspective, must be.

A constructive analysis of Durkheim's legal theory, then, will focus on these aspects of it and the problems that arise in relation to them. My argument may seem paradoxical. On the one hand, it is that Durkheim's legal theory is inadequate; it entirely leaves out of account matters of great importance to an understanding of law. On the other hand, I suggest that Durkheim's legal theory is powerful and enlightening. It addresses matters that are important and yet neglected. It forces us to think of law in ways that are valuable, today no less than when he wrote.

This is, in fact, no paradox. All legal theories offer merely partial perspectives. Each theory highlights some matters while ignoring others. A theory is produced from a certain standpoint and reflects a certain range of experience. It may persuade us that matters should be seen from its perspective and that, for the moment, other perspectives should be ignored. Perhaps this is because it develops impressively the image that it presents – sharply, carefully, in illuminating detail. It enables us to make sense of a certain picture of law, to see this picture as informative and interesting, conveying important knowledge, even though we know that it is presented from one viewpoint only, and that the phenomena portrayed would appear differently from another perspective. To evaluate theories should not be to criticise them for giving one picture of experience rather than another. It should be to ask how illuminating is the picture offered. How much does it allow us to see, and how clearly? And how can we go beyond it, locating it in relation to insights provided by other theories? In other words, how can we broaden the perspective that the theory offers, not trivialising or dismissing it, but fitting it into a broader picture, albeit one that may never be complete?

Power and force

A familiar substantive criticism of Durkheim's legal theory is that, focusing so firmly on morality, it ignores questions about power. Examining this criticism is essential to any assessment of Durkheim's moralistic perspective on law.

Steven Lukes and Andrew Scull (1983: 24) remark on Durkheim's 'extraordinary neglect of the phenomenon of power'. Steve Fenton sees Durkheim's work as marred by 'a vast underestimation of the compelling coercive facts of social and political life'; he tended to confuse analysis of social relations with an exposition of moral forms they should ideally take (Fenton 1984: 99). As regards conflict, power and unpredictability, 'the truly extraordinary thing about Durkheimian sociology is that it can find no place for them', writes Lukes; power 'is the massive blind spot' in this sociology (Lukes, 1982: 23).

In fact, as will appear, Durkheim certainly does not ignore problems of power or the role of force in society. But he usually thinks of power in a functionalist manner that treats it as a resource. In this view, power is a means of getting things done, the motor that drives legal regulation and ultimately makes it effective. It is self-evident that, in normal conditions, the legislator has a certain power to make laws, the judge to interpret and apply them, the police to enforce them. In general, where Durkheim does not see power as a problem this is because he usually treats it as _legitimate_ power. In other words, he thinks in terms of authority – the authority of legislator, judge or administrative official in the state, and he assumes that legislative, judicial or administrative power must be exercised in ways that confirm power's legitimacy rather than undermine it.

This takes us back to the emphasis on law's relationship with morality. In considering where law obtains its authority, its legitimate power to command, Durkheim assumes that this authority must come from its moral character, the fact that it expresses moral needs of society. The authority of law (and therefore of those who make, interpret and apply it) is moral authority (Durkheim, 1978a: 80).

Durkheim does not, however, always regard the exercise of state power over the citizen as unproblematic. In one very important case, he clearly sees this power as _not_ legitimately exercised. This is the case of the forced division of labour.[6] Here state power is a problem precisely because law and regulation do not express society's moral needs for solidarity. Rather, they coerce the citizen without moral justification. In modern society law must enable social relations of interdependence to flourish, enabling individuals and groups freely to find their place in the network of these continually developing and changing relations. If law fails to do this, coercing people into some relations or prohibiting them from entering others without reference to the needs of solidarity in society as a whole, it becomes mere coercion. Law is reduced to pure force.

In a host of ways one can see that, for Durkheim, to reduce law to force is actually to deprive it of all its legal character. Of course, he defines law, and distinguishes it from morality more generally, in terms of its sanctioning methods. Yet a close examination of his definition of law shows that, for him, the means of declaring a judgement or a rule – that is, of making the particular kind of moral pronouncement that a legal judgement or a legislative declaration represents – provides law's fundamental hallmark.[7] Indeed, he recognises force as a very serious problem when he thinks of it as coercion without legitimacy; he certainly does not ignore it. Rather, he sees it as law's perpetual enemy, a phenomenon that, lacking all moral attributes, can only be destructive, arbitrary and unjust. From one viewpoint, Durkheimian sociology appears almost _entirely_ concerned with finding the means of abolishing force from social life, replacing it with moral regulation that makes it unnecessary and incapable of wreaking disruption[8] or perpetuating injustice (as in coercive commercial and industrial relations).

6. See pp. 183–4, above.
7. See pp. 60–1, above.
8. As in feuding, which can never lead to stable social relations: see pp. 87–8, above.

Many instances where he opposes law to force in this sense can be noticed in his writings. In presenting the legal evolution thesis he insists that private vengeance must not be mistaken for a legal process.[9] Again, the purpose of punishment should not be deterrence, for that would merely coerce the convicted offender or other potential offenders rather than express law's moral judgement. More generally, law degenerates into force for Durkheim, I suggest, whenever legal rules or decisions are created solely to compromise opposing interests. Then, law is reduced merely to a participant in a struggle between opposing forces. When these forces are locked in irresolvable conflict, both sides may be coerced into a truce. But unless law puts in place a moral rule serving the general welfare, one to which all parties can and must give their allegiance, it becomes just a counter in the battle, a factor to be taken into account in the struggle, an obstacle to be avoided or a weapon to be wielded; in any case, mere force.

As we have seen, what is at stake is law's authority. If law justifies itself only by achieving a compromise of interests, why should that compromise have continuing validity once the specific balance of force has altered, once the circumstances that made the compromise accept- able have changed? Of course, law can aid private or group interests or limit them. It does this always. But this is, for Durkheim, surely not the essence of law, as his effort to distinguish law from arbitration or mediation shows.[10] Legal authority is different from negotiated compro- mise. So the problem of force, or of law being subsumed by force, haunts Durkheim's legal theory.

Nevertheless, he certainly debars himself through the methods he uses from considering some of the most important problems of the use of power in legal processes. His legal theory, as has been seen, is largely unable to examine the nature and practices of judicial and other inter- pretation of law. The positivist method he relies on, and which I shall criticise in the next chapter, produces this lacuna in his work. A legal rule, he declares, is what it is and there are no two ways of looking at it.[11] But, of course, there are many ways of looking at it and interpretation is a form of power. It is Durkheim's failure to take account of this that accounts for some of the most serious inadequacies of his legal theory.

When he does notice interpretation in legal contexts what he refers to is 'deliberation'. The state deliberates in making law; judges also deliberate in applying it. Clearly, creative processes are occurring in this deliberation but they are of interest to Durkheim in only one respect. They are processes through which the sociologist's scientific knowledge of society can be used practically to inform regulation. He seems not

9. See p. 88, above.
10. Cf. pp. 86–7, above.
11. See pp. 12–13, above.

only to assume goodwill on the part of all involved in these deliberative processes but also that the processes are not, in themselves,
problematic. They are just a conduit to express principles of social solidarity in the form of public regulation.

A focal meaning of law

What of problems of *private* power in society? Durkheim, we have seen,
is unequivocal about abuses of economic power in commercial and
industrial spheres.[12] Without proper regulation, the stronger crush the
weaker or reduce them to subjection, he writes. And this subjection
being 'sanctioned by no kind of morals ... is accepted only under
duress until the longed for day of revenge' (1957: 11). Thus, force
does not create peace. His attack on inheritance rights and his insistence
on the need for 'just' contracts, involving fair equivalence of benefits
and duties between the parties, reflect his awareness of the problems
of economic power lacking moral justification. Thus, Durkheim in
no way ignores problems of power, though he tends to treats them as
exceptional and abnormal. But a valid criticism of Durkheim's approach
to power is that he is uninterested in its *mechanisms*, or the fact that
the compromising of interests always accompanies the use of these
mechanisms. All of this, it seems, is mere politics – 'a thing so small
and mediocre' (cf. Lukes, 1973: 47). Is this lack of interest, then, an
unforgivable omission?

It would surely only be so if it were impossible to offer a plausible
theory of law except in relation to these mechanisms and this compromising of interests. Here Durkheim's thought can be usefully contrasted
with that of his contemporary, the German scholar Max Weber, the
other classical founder (with Marx) of modern sociology. Weber writes
that law has lost all its fundamental moral characteristics in modern
conditions. In 'the great majority of its most important provisions it has
been unmasked all too visibly, indeed, as the product or the technical
means of a compromise between conflicting interests' (Weber, 1968:
874–5). Thus, Weber presents as central to law what Durkheim's theory
treats as peripheral: the mechanisms of power by which conflicting
interests are compromised. For Weber, modern legal thought stresses
formality and procedure rather than substantive moral commitments.
Moral arguments around law sometimes become intense, but then they
are entwined with politics, as one group or another seeks to harness
law to its interests, to its efforts to acquire and use power over others.[13]

12. See pp. 182–3, above.
13. For a classic study see Gusfield (1963). For recent illustrations see Kellough (1996),
    Cuklanz (1996), Silverstein (1996).

As between Durkheim's and Weber's images of modern law, it is surely Weber's that has carried the day and influenced or, at least appeared compatible with, much modern Western sociologically oriented thinking about law. In modern liberal legal thought, law is presented as a framework in relation to which the diverse interests of individuals can be formulated, pursued and, in Weber's sense, compromised with each other (Bobbio, 1987: 113, 144). How this compromising is done may be a matter largely of procedure: the mechanics of democratic election, the procedural forms of the administration of justice, the routines and formalities of bureaucracy. Law provides a framework for politics. In other contexts, which liberalism condemns, law is merely a cloak for violence, even further removed from moral principle.

Recognising these lessons of legal experience does not amount to declaring Durkheim wrong. It rather inspires us to ask what enlightenment his moralistic approach offers in the light of evidence that seems hard to relate to it. One way of answering this question is to treat Durkheim as offering a *legal philosophy* informed by reflection on history and by systematic, empirical observation of society. In considering Durkheim's ideas on legal evolution I suggested that this is, at least up to a point, a fruitful approach to his work. Such a legal philosophy chooses a certain perspective on law and develops it. The perspective in this case is one 'in which legal obligation is treated as at least presumptively a moral obligation . . ., a viewpoint in which the establishment and maintenance of legal . . . order is regarded as a moral ideal'. It adopts a 'focal' meaning of law or 'the central case of the legal viewpoint', which does not necessarily deny that law can be seen in other ways (Finnis, 1980: 14–15, 277). These various quoted phrases are taken from a very different legal theory from Durkheim's but they capture the idea of looking at law in a way that does not attempt to account for all its empirical features, all the ways it presents itself in social experience, but emphasises how that experience might be considered in relation to law, making sense of it in a certain way that is philosophically illuminating.

In Durkheim's case the illumination lies in requiring that law be envisaged as potentially meaningful in moral terms to the widest possible range of citizens and in the widest possible range of circumstances. As we have seen, this brings certain matters to the foreground of attention: regulatory processes of communication and deliberation that have to take full account of the diversity of citizens' social experience; an effort to link law (though not uncritically and automatically) with general patterns of collective sentiment and belief; recognition of the centrality among law's functions of promoting ties of interdependence between groups and individuals; the identification of law's central modern value as that of mutual respect of people for each other as autonomous individuals; examination of the bases of allegiance to the nation state as a source of legal regulation; and elaboration of the character of morality – combining duty, attachment and autonomy – as the foundation of law. We might not accept that law *has* to be seen in these terms. We might even think that the perspective relates as much to what law could or should in some ideal sense be as to what it presently is.

I think that this emphasis on a 'focal' meaning of law is a productive way to view Durkheim's project of legal theory. But it must be emphasised that it is not the way he justifies his project and it is probably impossible to reconcile with the positivist outlook that colours much (but not all) of his sociology. Indeed, I shall argue in Chapter 14 that the rigidities of this positivist outlook undermine the power of his legal theory in some very important respects. Durkheim never admits that his (focal) meaning of law as a moral phenomenon might not encompass important aspects of legal experience. According to the Durkheimian mantra, law is what it is and there can be no two ways of understanding it. So he presents as the result of observation what he wants law to be, never admitting that we might have to settle for less.

A coherent view of morality?

Various writers have noted changes in Durkheim's views on the sources of morality over the course of his career (e.g. Alexander, 1982: 296). Ernest Wallwork sees Durkheim's early view as being that moral rules vary systematically from one society to another but that the validity of these rules for any given society is necessarily judged against universally acknowledged values. Among these values are those of social solidarity, protection of the nation, welfare of society's members, altruism and security of the individual from attack. But, according to Wallwork, the arbitrary nature of these, taken as universal values, led Durkheim gradually to abandon this approach in favour of the view that society's well-being is the only intrinsically desirable object of human conduct. Consequently, despite his rejection of a utilitarian basis of morality,[14] Durkheim explains morality in terms of a kind of social utilitarianism – what is beneficial to society (Wallwork, 1972: 163–8). The whole matter remains ambiguous. Utility here must be a matter not just of facilitating society's survival but its moral integration (Cladis, 1992: 24–6). But is morality useful to society merely because, whatever its substance, it expresses collective convictions that unite society's members? Or must its utility reside in the contribution its particular

14. See pp. 55 and 71–2, above.

rules make towards organising society so as to promote and protect social solidarity (cf. Wallwork, 1972: 175)?

Seeing this matter in the context of Durkheim's legal theory the problem relates closely to that of integrating what I have called Durkheim's early and later theses about the nature of modern law. On one view, appropriate law and morality must be *created* for modern society, governmental morality is for experts to elaborate and law is for the state to enact; law derives, as a practical matter, 'from above', from governmental elites and their advisors. We might say it is a matter of planning for solidarity. On another view, law and morality *reflect* the convictions that social development itself inspires; they derive 'from below', from currents of thought and belief, collective representations, diffuse in social life. Ultimately, I think that Durkheim never resolves this polarity of outlook in his legal theory. Nor could he because it reflects obliquely the polarities of modern law itself. Law is *voluntas* and *ratio* – coercive enactment and shared understandings. It appears both as the authoritative expression of public power over individuals and as the product of their collective reason and experience (Cotterrell, 1995: ch. 15). A sociology of law has the task of exploring and relating these polarities.

Because Durkheim's legal theory tends to treat law's authority as derived entirely from morality[15] it cannot, I think, fulfil this task. As we have seen, Durkheim has no interest in considering law's political authority, its *voluntas*, in any terms other than those of morality. But he does offer an important way of thinking about law's *ratio*. His legal theory portrays law as a rationalisation and systematisation of moral experience, that experience being, in itself, unsystematic, particularistic and evolving.[16] A major part of the task of legal interpretation (or 'deliberation' in Durkheim's sense) is thus the task of putting ever-changing moral experience into systematic form, imposing form on it so that it can be expressed as rational doctrine. But because Durkheim's legal theory refuses to see a political dimension of law apart from morality, it cannot recognise that law's *ratio* is also concerned with rationalising and systematising the exercise of power as a purely bureaucratic matter, the kind of rationalisation and systematisation that Weber emphasised in his studies of modern law.

Evolving morality clearly yields patterns that law can recognise as its own guiding principles. It is, at least, clear that several different *kinds* of moral principles are presented in Durkheimian analysis as

15. We should recall, however, some limited suggestions in his work as to how law gains autonomous authority. One is the implication that regulation can be, in itself, a possible focus of belief or allegiance in a quasi-religious sense (see pp. 50–3, above). The other is the idea that the collective consciousness to some extent gives the state autonomy to create regulation as it sees fit (see p. 69, above).
16. See pp. 55–7, above.

underlying modern law and that the relationships between them need analysis. His later work treats individualism as a value that promotes social cohesion.[17] But does a concern for the dignity of individuals in general actually yield the principles of interdependence or reciprocity necessary to organic solidarity? Does it foster co-operation or just a respect for other people's projects? Does it require outreach to others or merely an active concern for their right to autonomy and their efforts at self-fulfilment? Jean Piaget (1932: 339) makes an interesting attempt to reconcile these alternatives: 'What we love in others', he writes, interpreting Durkheim, 'is not so much the individual as the possibility of a bond of affection, not so much the friend as the friendship.' In affirming the dignity of others we want them to be able to reach out to us, which becomes possible when their own individuality is secure. Yet individualism as a value system does not seem to *guarantee* this outreach.

In examining contract law we noted the idea of a morality of reciprocity emerging from Mauss' study of gift relationships.[18] If the emphasis, as in Durkheim's early thesis on modern law, is on the needs of organic solidarity, such a morality seems appropriate to meet at least some of these needs. Yet it is a morality requiring that one freely give, receive and give in return. It does not necessarily *calculate* exchanges. Nevertheless, law calculates and measures, at least up to a point;[19] if it is to provide co-ordination (for example, ensuring the ability to plan and to predict the outcomes of transactions) it must do so. On the other hand, if law is a special kind of morality it must, to some extent, reflect the specificity of moral judgements in particular circumstances.[20] Hence the age-old tension between law and equity – between consistent application of rules and the doing of justice in each case. Durkheim does see law as a universalistic system that organises and rationalises particular moral responses (Alexander, 1982: 99, 263). But nowhere in his work does he recognise adequately the interpretive tension, familiar to all lawyers, between two values that law serves: the value of rule-governed consistency or predictability and the value of moral responsiveness to the particularity of circumstances.

Contract requires that obligations be met according to the terms of the contract, no more no less. Yet when Durkheim writes about 'just contracts' it is the need for justice in the circumstances of each transaction that he emphasises, and so the value of fluid principles – of fair equivalence and equality of bargaining power.[21] Again, the morality of

17. See pp. 112–15, above.
18. See pp. 128–30, above.
19. See p. 190, above.
20. See pp. 55–6, above.
21. See pp. 131–2, above.

reciprocity in its implication of indefinite rather than measured obligations to repay, and positive obligations to give, seems to relate more
easily to fiduciary responsibilities or general duties of care recognised
in law than to the exactitude of many modern economic exchanges
(cf. Cotterrell, 1993). Indeed, Mauss recognises that purely economic
concerns of modern contract are very different from the fusion of social
and economic purposes that relied on the morality of gift exchange.
The problem, as I shall argue in Chapter 14, is that Durkheim's conception of solidarity, at least as a focus for legal regulation, is too rigid and
undifferentiated.

The example of contract here highlights the difficulty of accommo-
dating economic transactions and calculations in Durkheim's moralistic
framework of analysis. So does that of property law. Property is the
basis of economic exchange, yet we noted how unclear Durkheim seems
to be about its moral basis.[22] Ultimately, both contract and property,
in Durkheim's analysis, are best understood as legal expressions of individualism. But this gives them a different moral justification from that
typically suggested by claims of 'sanctity of property' or 'freedom of
contract'. Property and contract, seen in terms of Durkheimian individualism, are means by which the dignity of the individual can be
legally protected and expressed. This is a much more modest justification for the protection of rights to property or the enforcement of
contractual obligations than would be provided by many liberal asser-
tions of the freedom of individuals to engage in transactions, pursue
projects of their choosing and secure profits as the opportunities to do
so arise. Indeed, the Durkheimian morality of individualism would seem
to limit this freedom. In the case of inheritance rights, as has been seen,
it might even take it away.[23] I do not wish to suggest that these
moral judgements on contract, property and inheritance regimes, which
Durkheim's approach inspires, are inappropriate. But they are based
on a reasoning that hardly analyses in detail the meaning of solidarity
in different contexts and the variety of legal relations that might be
conceptualised from such an analysis. We shall return to this matter in
the next chapter.

For the moment, we can note that because the pursuit of private
interests as such can never appear as a moral purpose for Durkheim,
and because law can *only* be understood in terms of moral purposes,
the somewhat surprising result is reached that an 'economic analysis of
law' – at least one drawing substantially on classical economic liberalism
– is, from the standpoint of Durkheim's legal theory, a contradiction
in terms. For him, it would be a misreading of law's social nature to

22. See pp. 142–3, above.
23. See pp. 143–4, above.

analyse it theoretically in relation to essentially utilitarian calculations. Putting the matter in less polemical terms, an economic analysis of law would deal only with certain *effects* of law; the concern of legal sociology would be with law's *essence*.[24]

Durkheim can be heavily criticised for failing to concern himself with the utilitarian consequences of law, its economic effects and applications; that is, with the whole matter of law's role in the compromising of interests. This is a main reason why his 'focal' meaning of law is inadequate for understanding legal experience. Nevertheless, he does show how law can be coherently viewed in a way that does not make its economic aspects central. And he makes the strong claim that if we try to make these central we lose all real sense of law's ultimate claims to moral authority.

Can we believe in law?

Something more must be added on this question of law's authority. Is it impossible in the context of contemporary Western law to treat seriously Durkheim's claim of a necessary link between law and religion? To do so it is necessary to see clearly that what he wants to emphasise with this claim is the necessity of collective belief as a basis of law's authority. 'Religion' is, in this context, a cipher for some such belief which links people together in an organised group, whether it be a nation or some other collectivity. The reference to religion is a reference to some social source of this belief and to the rituals, traditions and ceremonies that express and reinforce it. As noted earlier, there is something to be said for the view that law has become, at least in some modern societies, an important focus of belief.[25] But Durkheim's claim would be that this belief in law is not self-founding or self-sustaining politically (cf. Luhmann, 1985: 206), though law's procedures may serve ritual functions that support it (Tyler, 1990). Law relies on, as well as promotes, a faith in society itself.

If, therefore, something is to be made of Durkheim's claim today it is surely as a reminder that legal rationality originates historically from sources that are hard to see as rational in any modern sense, and that, even in modern conditions, some kind of faith ultimately guarantees law's technicality and 'rational strength'. Again, this idea seems at odds with much modern legal theory, which focuses on law as a rational structure of rules or norms, or a practice of rational interpretation or

24. Everything depends on perspective, of course. For Hans Kelsen (1991: 301), sociology of law deals with certain effects of law (on behaviour) while the concern of legal philosophy as a science of law is with its essence.
25. See pp. 50–3, above, and, for example, Levinson (1988) and Grey (1984: 21–5).

argumentation. Durkheim's view of law here might be seen as religious in a very specific sense. Whereas Weber (1948: 138–9) was convinced that the 'disenchantment' of the modern world, including its law, had been accomplished (not necessarily with entirely welcome results), Durkheim seems to suggest that this process of disenchantment can never be completed. Just as the religious believer scorns the arrogance of assuming that mankind needed no creator, so Durkheim seems to scorn the view that law can be presented as self-justifying:

> Beneath the letter [of the law] lies the spirit that animates it: there are the ties of all kinds binding the individual to the group he is part of and to all that concerns the group . . . all these social sentiments, all these collective aspirations, these traditions we hold to and respect, giving sense and life to the rule . . . (1957: 28–9)

A century after Durkheim wrote, this reads partly as a hankering after the past 'enchantment' of law and society that Weber saw as destroyed by the rationalisation of the modern world and partly as a fierce assertion that we delude ourselves if we think that law can do without its 'spirit' – the moral convictions that give life to it. Most of all, however, consistently with Durkheim's own ambition both to record law's moralistic character and to enhance it, we might now see his statement as a kind of programme: to put at the forefront of legal theory forms of analysis that aid the effort to make law morally meaningful in the lives of those it regulates. But it is necessary, finally, in the last chapter, to assess how far Durkheim's particular approach to sociology provides resources for doing this.

14

The sociological perspective

How far should Durkheim's distinctive sociological perspective be seen as important, and what problems does it raise? Certainly, it is no longer necessary to defend the value of some kind of sociological analysis of law. Sociology of law has become, in the century since Durkheim wrote, a rich, well-established field. Social scientific researches on law – often now called socio-legal or 'law and society' studies – have become an important part of legal scholarship in many countries. But Durkheim's writings on law have only a limited influence on current work in this field. In Chapter 13 it was noted that, if Durkheim and Max Weber are compared as classical founders of sociology who devoted much attention to law, Weber's legal outlook seems much more in tune with contemporary social scientific thinking about law than Durkheim's. Indeed, 'today the vein seems rather exhausted' even in France (Carbonnier, 1994: 103–4). Durkheimian approaches have been marginalised.

This final chapter explores some main reasons for this. But it attempts also to suggest how Durkheim's particular sociological approach to the study of law can be built upon; to affirm that, in certain respects, the pursuit of this approach is, indeed, an important virtue of his legal theory. In Chapter 13 it was suggested that the sociological explanation of the prominence of individualism as a value system expressed through modern law is a major contribution of his work. I shall argue, in this chapter, that his effort to explain the nature of social solidarity as a basis of law and as its *raison d'être* is also of enduring importance. But his ideas provide only a starting point for theoretical analysis of law in this respect.

Positivism and its discontents

To reach Durkheim's sociological virtues it is necessary to confront some serious limitations of his analytical methods. The sociological positivism that he advocated early in his career carried important costs for his legal theory. In particular, as has been seen, it prevented him from

treating law clearly as a matter of interpretation, with all that this interpretive approach might entail.[1]

Durkheimian positivism parallels but does not correlate exactly with
what lawyers understand as *legal positivism*. The latter has several meanings, one of which is closely related to the sense of positivism associated
with Durkheim's sociology. Thus, legal positivism treats law as a *datum*
– something 'posited' or put in place, typically in the form of established rules. As such, its existence in a given time and place can be
observed. Thus, law might be identified positivistically through the
formal processes by which particular rules come into being: for example,
rules may be recognised as legal if they have been established in a recognised legislative process or by judicial pronouncements in certain
contexts of adjudication. The positivist jurist uses 'tests' of what is law,
treating law as a normative, institutional or social fact,[2] rather as
Durkheim's index thesis proposed the use of law itself as an objective
test or measure of other social facts. These tests identify law not as a
timeless idea but as it appears in particular historical settings.

Another familiar aspect of legal positivism, however, is its insistence
that law and morality should be treated as analytically distinct. Law
should not be confused with morality, even though the two often
interrelate (Hart, 1958). This, of course, is somewhat different from
Durkheim's (1893b: 276–7) position which treats the study of law and
morality as practically inseparable and insists that morality and law
must be the concern of a positive social science embracing them both.[3]
Thus Durkheim is able to treat law objectively as an *aspect* of morality,
differentiated only by relatively loose, practical criteria.[4] A consequence
of this, as has been seen, is that, for him, legal obligation is a kind of
moral obligation; if we understand the basis of the latter, we also have
the key to the former (Durkheim, 1978a: 80). By contrast, for legal
positivism, legal and moral obligation must typically be treated as distinct
and the basis of legal obligation is sometimes considered controversial
or obscure (Raz, 1994: ch. 15; Watson, 1988: 125–6).

In other respects, too, legal and sociological positivism do not
necessarily coincide. Thus, an insistence on the analytical separation of
law and morality, typical of legal positivism, might be adopted in a
social scientific approach that rejects or supplements positivist sociological methods. Such an approach might treat social phenomena not
just as facts to be observed but as actions to be *interpreted* in the light

1. See pp. 12–13, 173, 176, 206–7, 211, above.
2. Hart (1994: 109–10), Watson (1985: 32–3), MacCormick (1974), Lyons (1984:
   ch. 2).
3. Nevertheless, he presents the sociology of law and the sociology of morality as distinct
   divisions of sociology. See Durkheim (1978a: 83).
4. Focused on the requirement for recognised institutional means of publicly declaring
   or affirming society's norms. See pp. 60–1, above.

of the *subjective meaning* of those actions for the individuals who act. Thus, law might be seen in terms of certain kinds of actions oriented towards norms. Viewed in this way, it could appear as a matter of various forms of reasoning or decision making to be understood in terms of the typical kinds of meaning that it has in the minds of those who reason or decide. This is the way law tends to be approached in Weber's sociology (Weber, 1968: part 2, ch. 8). His sociological method is interpretive in this sense rather than positivistic. Yet he adopts the premise that law in general should be treated as analytically distinct from morality (Kronman, 1983: 8–10).

It should be stressed that Durkheim's sociological positivism has certain benefits for the study of law. It makes possible a clear focus on law as something external to the individual, exerting coercion (Durkheim, 1982a: 51). It emphasises that law is a social phenomenon which in some sense has an existence independent of the human beings who create, interpret or apply it (Carbonnier, 1994: 102). And it insists that law must always be seen as a concrete historical phenomenon, to be understood empirically in its specific time and place. Some modern legal sociology wholeheartedly accepts such a positivist approach (Black, 1976; 1989). Indeed, it might well be said that Durkheim's greatest influence on current legal sociology, and perhaps on current methods of social scientific research generally, is through his clear statement of principles for a strict sociological positivism, as in his *Rules of Sociological Method*. Essentially, what has remained most influential from this programme is the idea that social phenomena should be observed and recorded objectively, without the intrusion of the researcher's own values, and that social phenomena lend themselves to measurement in various ways. Thus, for example, a study of the work of courts might be based on measurement of court caseloads over time, quantifying, from court records, cases dealt with in various categories and observing changes in the work of courts over a certain period (e.g. Friedman and Percival, 1976; Sanders, 1990).

The effort to treat law as objectively observable social fact might, indeed, be taken much further than Durkheim himself does. For him, law is always a matter of rules, and so observation of law is the identification (and, in *The Division of Labour*, quantification) of rules that have been enacted, codified or otherwise officially recorded in some recognisable way. But a stricter sociological positivism than Durkheim's might treat rules as not observable phenomena at all and seek rather to regard the social facts of law as being the observable behaviour of officials or citizens as this behaviour relates to certain governmental functions categorised as legal. From such a positivist standpoint law is to be treated not as rules as lawyers think of them but as 'governmental social control', an external, measurable force operating on individuals (Black, 1976).

The price to be paid for this sociological positivism is high. It is that law cannot be understood in terms of the meaning it has for those who interpret it (Cotterrell, 1995: 183–93). These interpreters are, of course, not just lawyers, judges or administrators working in a range of settings but citizens in general. Durkheim's sociological positivism cannot really grasp the nature of 'legal experience' (cf. Gurvitch, 1935), the meaning of law for those who participate (for example as officials, advisors, litigants, offenders or merely law-abiding citizens) in legal systems. Thus, it condemns the sociologist to take a purely 'external' view of law. 'The first and most basic rule', Durkheim advises in his *Rules of Sociological Method* (1982a: 60), 'is to consider social facts as things.' There is no doubt that law is sometimes treated as such (as an obstacle, threat, resource to be harnessed, distant force, symbol, locus of power or security) by those who live in its jurisdiction. But, for lawyers, legal scholars and lay citizens in many contexts, law is a world of meaning: a matter of arguments, understandings, interpretations, problems and solutions. In this sense law is not something that exists as a thing. Rather it is a matter of modes of reasoning and acting, strategies and pleas, rhetoric and justification, conflicts of view and meetings of minds, and techniques for building or protecting authority, or disguising the lack of it. A sociology that cannot recognise these aspects of law sees only a limited part of it. At the same time these aspects of law need to be understood sociologically, in historical context.

Hence sociological positivism affirms a sharp divide between internal and external views of law (cf. Hart, 1994: 88–91). It accepts that sociology can only take an external view; yet this is surely self-defeating. There is no sharp line, indeed no line at all but only a difference of emphasis, between internal and external views of law. The lawyer sometimes views law predictively as a matter of social fact with coercive force, something to take account of as a fact of social life. So does the non-lawyer citizen. But this 'taking account' of law typically involves interpretation of its normative meaning, since (except in societies where the doctrine of the Rule of Law has no place) this interpretation will provide some information as to when and how those who have the authority to apply legal rules are likely to do so. Indeed, while it is easy to envisage the legal point of view of an 'insider' who reasons with rules (and may also need to assess the likelihood and consequences of them actually being enforced or invoked), it is very hard to envisage realistically that of a legal 'outsider' who sees law *only* as social fact, without engaging in any interpretation or understanding of the nature of law as a matter of ideas. Presumably it is only when, in Durkheim's terms, law gives way wholly to force[5] that legal interpretation becomes, for practical purposes, irrelevant.

5. See pp. 205–6, above.

Sociological positivism, as advocated by Durkheim, is thus disabling to legal theory and sociology of law, unless treated as a limited method requiring much supplementation. It forces the legal sociologist to view law in ways that are for many (but not all) purposes unrealistic. And it is surely significant that Durkheim's work shows much evidence of his seeking gradually to escape the rigours of this positivistic outlook. When he emphasises not only duty but also attachment to groups and autonomy as elements of morality,[6] it seems that he is seeking to grasp morality as a subjective outlook, the way of thinking and feeling of a moral person. His earlier idea of morality, as rules commanding the individual, reflects much more clearly the positivist approach to morality as a social fact external to individuals and coercive of them. There is a similar significance in the change in his view of punishment from his early position, treating it as a social process by which the collective consciousness is affirmed, to his later account of it as a kind of communication between society and the offender.[7] Surely, here too, Durkheim's thought evolves towards treating the subjective meaning of social phenomena for the individuals involved in them as of great importance. In general, positivism retreats from Durkheim's legal theory as he seeks to analyse the values that give law meaning for citizens and inspire their allegiance to it. Yet ultimately, the positivist outlook limits his legal theory in important aspects. For example, the process of deliberation, so important to his picture of the creation and interpretation of law, remains wholly mysterious in his description because he does not examine the motivations and meanings that inform it. It remains an unanalysed process by which law is put in place as a social fact.

The organisation of organic solidarity

Positivism stands opposed to any effort to appreciate the meaningfulness of different perspectives on experience, including law as a field of experience. Yet even Durkheim recognises, to some extent, such different perspectives. Durkheimian law, as a special segment of morality, reflects, to some extent, popular convictions and beliefs and collective experience. Yet modern society, as *The Division of Labour* was at pains to demonstrate, is characterised by a diversity of convictions, beliefs and experiences. Different perspectives on social life reflect these different experiences. In part, regulation is uniform and society-wide, reflecting social experience that is shared or uniform and convictions and beliefs held in common. In part, however, regulation needs to be

6. See pp. 62–3, above.
7. See pp. 77–8, above.

differentiated to correspond with the functional differentiation of various occupational groups. In order to reflect different perspectives and experiences regulation must, in Durkheim's plan, be decentralised to the 'corporations'. It follows, therefore, that there is a regulatory perspective on social life reflected in state law, and different perspectives reflected in the regulation created by the 'corporations'.

Durkheim's positivism and functionalism, strongly present in the approach of *The Division of Labour*, limit his ability to recognise these different regulatory perspectives. Thus, organic solidarity is founded, for Durkheim, on *functional* interdependence. Since some of the most obvious functions to be fulfilled in modern society are economic it is unsurprising that, alongside individuals, occupational groups appear in his work as the most important functional units. Hence, Durkheim sees functional organisation as requiring state-wide co-ordination and supervision of occupational 'corporations' together with the freedom of the corporations to regulate their own internal collective life. But apart from these groups the only others to which Durkheim devotes sustained attention are families. The regulation of families is, for him, as important as that of occupational groups. Yet, whereas he has strong views about the role of the latter and how they should be regulated,[8] his work is ambiguous and unclear about the role of the family as a domestic group.[9] It even seems unclear how the family relates to organic solidarity and individualism (Alexander, 1982: 267–9).

Consequently, the sense of social differentiation in modern society is limited in Durkheim's work, for all his emphasis on the complexity and variety of modern societies. Organic solidarity as the moral condition of modern society depends largely on interdependence between functionally distinct groups and these are identified, almost exclusively, as occupational groups. Hence, although there is a strong sense of the need for a pluralistic structure of regulation in modern society (that is, a plurality of sources and systems of regulation made possible by devolution of authority to 'corporations') this is a very one-dimensional structure. Even the familiar concept of devolution of regulatory authority to geographical localities – as in local or regional government – is marginalised in Durkheim's discussions.[10] Rather like the family as an active, self-regulating group, the local government area as a basis of regulatory jurisdiction seems, for Durkheim, outdated. He suggests that individuals do not, in modern society, feel a strong sense of attachment to locality, hence local government cannot be strongly empowered morally to create regulation. For Durkheim, the local mayor and the

8. See pp. 176–80, above.
9. See pp. 144–7, above.
10. See pp. 178–9, above.

paterfamilias seem to be similarly anachronistic as regulators. But he pins great hopes on the assemblies of the occupationally based corporations as having regulatory authority.

If we try to construct a picture of a pluralistic organisation of law-making or regulation in modern society from these ideas the result is surely very incomplete, problematic and strange. Jeffrey Alexander (1982: 305) remarks on 'the unrealistic, highly utopian proposal for reorganisation that crops up throughout Durkheim's career, the "occupational group"', and suggests that it springs from his 'residual' fear that modern collective life does not have the resources to guarantee order and cohesion. The emphasis on occupation groups seems to arise from the emphasis of Durkheim's functional approach on the interdependence of occupational roles and the consequent need for their co-ordination. Yet nowhere 'in his analysis of the development of modern society does Durkheim offer any evidence that such guild organisation is on the historical agenda'; the occupational group 'is a magical formula' for creating social cohesion, 'one whose political implications or actual historical possibility are never explored' (Alexander, 1982: 305).

This is harsh but largely just criticism. The problem seems to be that a one-dimensional view of the nature of organic solidarity gives rise to a similarly one-dimensional set of prescriptions for guaranteeing it through law and devolved regulation. It is only really in the context of the theses of *The Division of Labour* that the concept of organic solidarity is explained. The problem of co-ordinating the complex variety of moral experience, ideas and beliefs appears there largely as one brought about by economic complexity and the differentiation of productive social roles. Moral variation is easily associated in this context of analysis with occupational variation. Certainly, Durkheim's proposals for a pluralistic organisation of regulation through occupational groups do not arise solely in the context of analysis of the concept of organic solidarity. In his later book, *Suicide*, these proposals are introduced as a means of making regulation sufficient and meaningful in the variety of particular moral contexts of life. We have seen how Durkheim's work increasingly emphasises the importance of the individual's subjective experience of morality as related to a sense of attachment to a social group and as a matter for critical reflection. So the need to make regulation morally meaningful to individuals in the context of social groups to which they feel a sense of attachment appears pressing. Yet the template set by the focus on the division of labour in Durkheim's first book seems to colour all his later discussion of the differentiation of modern society into social groups. Apart from the state, and the self-disciplining individual, only occupational groups have any real prominence as sources of regulation in his theory.

I think that the strength of Durkheim's approach here is in its recognition that centralised state law is insufficient to meet the need to make public regulation meaningful to citizens. Regulation has to be seen as a pluralistic process in modern society, dependent on a variety of sources of regulatory authority. Indeed, we might as well extend the concept of law (though Durkheim seems ambiguous on this) to include the regulation produced by organised groups. Then law itself is understood pluralistically as a variety of types of regulation, only some of which have their source in the state's deliberative processes. An important aspect of Durkheim's sociological perspective is that it points towards a pluralistic view of law, which frees the concept of law (as enacted public regulation) from exclusive association with the regulatory processes and agencies of the state. Durkheim recognises clearly that state law is incapable of fully expressing the needs for morally meaningful public regulation that exist in complex modern societies. He is acutely aware of what I have called the problem of moral distance[11] which makes the state and its legal processes remote from, alien to and unwelcome in the lives of many citizens. The primary virtue of Durkheim's sociological perspective is that it highlights this problem and begins to explore ways of solving it by recognising the diversity of social experience of different social groups.

Varieties of community

Where then does Durkheim fail? The failure is complementary to the virtue. Durkheim's positivist approach enables him to identify regulation as a social fact wherever it may be produced – in the family in ancient times, in the modern state's deliberative processes or in the projected assemblies of occupational 'corporations'. At the same time, his functional outlook enables him to see clearly that modern society can be conceived as a complex organisation of interdependent elements. Thus co-ordination, reciprocity and the promotion of mutual support and respect for others (whether individuals or groups) are revealed as appropriate objectives of modern regulation. But Durkheim's positivist outlook debars him from exploring the variety of subjective experiences of solidarity that are possible for people involved in group relationships. And his functionalist outlook deters him from considering that group relationships are not necessarily organised to meet social functions related to the well-being of society as a whole.

Thus, we noticed in Chapter 13 an important ambiguity in Durkheim's thought as to the kinds of moral principles actually presupposed by the

11. See pp. 165 and 177, above.

idea of organic solidarity – or, more generally by the need for integration and co-ordination in modern society.[12] But what exactly *is* Durkheim's image of solidary social relationships? Are they, for example, exemplified by the relationship of two companies contracting with each other on the basis of a mutual appreciation of their corporate tasks and of the convergence between these? When Durkheim describes contract as the legal form that most clearly expresses the requirements of organic solidarity it seems that he has some such idea in view. But how does a contract that is inspired purely by the parties' pursuit of their own interests become a vehicle of morality and solidarity, when, as we have repeatedly noticed, Durkheim insists on excluding the pursuit of interests from his conception of specifically moral action? In fact, we have seen that a mere instrumental agreement for co-operation may not be enough for Durkheimian solidarity unless it adheres to certain principles of justice and fairness[13] and these principles relate not to the effectiveness of the agreement as an instrument of co-operation but to its worth as an expression of the needs of the parties as autonomous, individual entities.

By contrast, if the organisation of the modern family ought to express and promote organic solidarity, it seems that this is much more than an expression of the consensual meeting of the free wills of the individuals concerned or of the instrumental value of the marriage for the parties to it. Durkheim's opposition to divorce by mutual consent makes clear that if the value of the marriage is to set relations of organic solidarity in place this is a value that can be asserted even against the wills of the individuals concerned. Society, not the parties to the relationship, decides how the value is to be satisfied. Indeed, Durkheim seems to think that precisely because the family is becoming more and more a temporary means by which the instrumental purposes of the parties are satisfied, and less and less an enduring, transgenerational institution, its significance in the schema of social organisation and regulation is becoming reduced.[14] Yet it remains a vital focus of affective relationships. But how do these relationships relate to organic solidarity?

Finally, as noted earlier, it seems that ties of locality, for Durkheim, have decreasing significance in the realm of organic solidarity.[15] We have considered his views on the nation state as a territorially defined source of regulation.[16] While he makes clear that he thinks it will, as a practical matter, retain its dominance among the providers and enforcers of society's regulation, this does not seem to be a position that he asserts

12. See pp. 209–12, above.
13. See pp. 131–3, above.
14. See pp. 146 and 179, above.
15. W. S. F. Pickering (1984: 17) even suggests that he considered 'regional loyalty to be divisive'.
16. See pp. 194–5, above.

with particular enthusiasm. The nation state deserves patriotic allegiance, not on the basis of some traditional territorial basis of loyalty but only in so far as it upholds principles that fit it to take its place in a wider international community of humanity. In modern conditions the trajectory of development should, it seems, be towards internationalism: in his terms, towards Europe as a supranational entity and humanity as a world ideal; in more specifically legal terms, towards international human rights and other forms of regulation not necessarily bounded by the nation-state jurisdictions. What is it then that is to be made cohesive and interdependent through organic solidarity? What, ultimately, is the society or social group which is to be the focus of solidarity? No answer is given. Indeed, Durkheim does not even pose these questions.

As regards ethnicity and traditional cultural allegiances, evidence of Durkheim's thinking is limited. But he seems to attach little significance to them as foci of modern solidarity. It is surely significant that he rejected or 'quietly laid on one side' much of his own inherited Jewish culture, including its specific religious belief system (Pickering, 1984: 18), and argued passionately for individual rights that would ensure that groups (such as cultural or ethnic groups) could not repress the individuality and personal freedom of their members (Durkheim, 1969b). Again, he largely refused to be drawn into discussions of matters such as anti-semitism, which he saw not as relating to problems of cultural identity and its denial but, at least in France, merely as a symptom of structural problems in society as a whole (Durkheim, 1975a: II, 252–4). It seems that, for Durkheim, if there is to be a culture of beliefs, traditions and values worth taking account of in the organisation of modern society, it can only be one that glorifies the abstract individual, not particular groups.

The point of drawing these various matters together here is to suggest that when Durkheim thinks of solidarity as an object and justification for regulation he is touching on many different kinds of relationships that are governed by different kinds of moral imperatives. In general, he does not theoretically distinguish and show the connections between these kinds of relationships. Hence while his proposal for a legal pluralism based on a division of regulatory tasks between the state and 'corporations' is a pointer in the right direction towards recognising the necessity for regulatory diversity and co-ordination in modern societies, and the variety of social sources of law and regulation, it does not have the theoretical resources to carry these insights far.

Using the illustrations above of regulatory situations and group relationships discussed in Durkheim's work it is, however, possible to make some important demarcations. Four entirely distinct categories of solidarity that are in issue in these situations and relationships can be identified. Since the term 'solidarity' is so laden with Durkheim's own emphases and interpretations and the distinctive overtones of his own moralistic perspective, however, I prefer to refer to these four categories as types of community (Cotterrell, 1997), treating 'community' as an abstract idea (like solidarity in this sense) rather than an empirically recognisable social group of some kind.

Types of Community
①

Thus, one kind of community is associated with habitual or traditional forms of interaction; that is, the often accidental circumstance that people find themselves coexisting in a shared environment. This might be called *traditional community*. It includes what sociologists call local community – the coexistence of people in a defined geographical space such as a neighbourhood. But a similar kind of community is produced by the sharing of experiences, customs, history or language. A linguistic community, in ordinary terminology, is a group of people who share a common language or dialect. Of course, local and linguistic groups often reinforce each other. Secondly, community may be associated with a convergence of interests among a group. This can be called ② *instrumental community*, or community of interest. Its closest empirical correlate is a typical business community linked by trade relationships or agreements for co-operation. Thirdly, community may refer to a sharing of beliefs or values. This can be termed *community of belief*. ③ Religious congregations, churches or sects most obviously approximate this type. Finally, the uniting of individuals by their mutual affection may be thought of in terms of community. This type can be called ④ *affective community*. Its basis is in a sense of fiduciary responsibility for others, or of mutual care and concern for individuals. Family and friendship groups may most obviously approximate to it.

This classification, indirectly developed from themes in Weber's sociology (Cotterrell, 1997: 81), distinguishes the entirely different kinds of relationships implicated in Durkheim's notion of solidarity as a basis and aim of legal regulation. His sociological perspective on law invites us to consider how communities can be ultimately the source of the law that regulates them. It ignores most problems that attach to the mechanisms of representation and decision by which this might be done. But it does focus on the kinds of moral values that law must reflect if it is to be capable of expressing the normative character of the communities it regulates, receiving allegiance from people linked by relations of community, and thus having guaranteed moral authority.

Durkheim's legal theory identifies, despite some ambiguity, the central value system, individualism, that must provide the moral spine of modern law, even though it does not elaborate fully the scope of this system. His legal theory properly affirms that no specialised or localised group regulation can be morally acceptable in complex modern societies if it denies individual dignity and respect to any member of its own group or of other groups. But at the same time the theory affirms, no less forcefully, that the moral distance between state and citizen in modern society must be overcome by recognising a diversity of sources of public regulation within the nation state (and perhaps beyond it, in 'Europe' or some wider organisation of 'humanity'). Thus, Durkheim's sociological perspective is important to legal theory in two vital respects. First, it explains why and in what sense individualism is the value system that unites modern society and has to be affirmed by law; secondly, it explains why, alongside this universalistic law of individualism, pluralistic structures of regulation are needed to provide moral meaning in conditions of modern social complexity.

Durkheim, however, conceptualises this pluralistic regulation as a posited social fact, whereas it is surely more productive to see it as the activity of negotiating, compromising, rule-setting, rule interpretation and decision making that takes place in various kinds of group relationships. And it is certainly necessary to recognise that the kind of group Durkheim identifies as a potential source of regulation – that is, the occupational group – is only one potential locus of regulation alongside others. In contemporary society, group memberships are usually fluid, overlapping, transient and invariably multiple. Individuals regularly make and break links with others, and engage simultaneously in many different kinds of groups and associations. If we think in terms of community, as suggested above, this requires that we replace the idea of solidarity as social fact with that of community as a web of understandings about the nature of social relations. Then it becomes possible to see that these understandings can vary in different contexts and be represented legally in many different ways. The various contexts can be conceptualised in abstract terms in the four types of community postulated above.

Thus the kind of solidarity, or relations of community, entailed in a business contract may be very different, and imply different kinds of mutual trust between the parties, from those that spring from the shared beliefs of religious believers. Again, the ideal solidarity or community that one might hope to find in affective family ties may be entirely different. And ties of solidarity arising from a shared environment, traditions or common language may, again, have very different characteristics.

This is not the place to explore these matters further. They are raised here to suggest limitations as well as strengths of Durkheim's sociological perspective. This perspective may make it possible to set inquiries on the right lines if we seek to examine where contemporary law can find its moral foundations. But the concepts he uses to develop this perspective are suggestive rather than adequate to the complexities of the task. I have claimed also that his positivist method is unhelpful for many (though not all) purposes and that a more interpretive approach is required. Such an approach would focus on the subjective meaning of social action (here, the interaction of individuals in various types of relationships of community).

Because this interpretive approach is classically associated in sociology with Weber's work, a single statement might summarise the programme advocated here. Putting the matter very broadly and generally, sociology of law should pursue Durkheim's aspirations using methods inspired by Weber. More precisely, the effort to analyse law in a moral domain (which is certainly the aim of Durkheim's legal theory) has to involve an effort to understand in interpretive terms the moral meaning of law for the diverse categories and groups of individuals who encounter it and participate in it. It may be that, in terms of the four types of community referred to above, contemporary legal and social analysis, with its strong and appropriate focus on relations of instrumental community, has not so far sufficiently examined modern law's actual or potential role in supporting traditional, affective or belief-based relations of community as they manifest themselves in complex combinations in different empirical contexts.

Messages from the past

One final aspect of Durkheim's sociological perspective is specially relevant to the assessment of his legal theory. Considering it here takes us full circle in this study of his work. Earlier, in several contexts, the problematic way in which he uses historical evidence has been noted.[17] But we have not finally resolved the general issue of the place of historical experience in his view of law. In looking at the legal evolution thesis – in many ways the most famous aspect of Durkheim's legal theory – I suggested that history has a strangely subordinate role in a thesis that seems to be entirely about historical change. When Durkheim took evidence of ancient law from the texts of Henry Maine or the great nineteenth-century German legal historians, or from Tacitus or the Bible, it is hard to imagine that he thought that he was himself recording legal history. Surely he was seeking, in the experience of the distant past, illustration of the diverse ways in which, in the most varied circumstances throughout history, people have tried to express principles of coexistence through law.

This orientation of his work explains what seems initially to be a remarkably cavalier approach to methodology which allowed the Durkheimians to use almost interchangeably, as their sources for

17. See generally Chapter 6 and pp. 81, 141–2, above.

analysis, material from the history of ancient civilisations as well as from then recent ethnographic studies of tribal societies of Melanesia, North America and elsewhere. Simple societies of the present and the recent past on the one hand, and ancient civilisations on the other, are treated, in much Durkheimian writing, often as almost identical and mutually reinforcing sources of evidence.

The explanation must be that a concern with chronology is never really central to Durkheim's legal theory. The inquiries are much more timeless than they purport to be. Durkheimian sociology dresses its claims in historical description. But the most important messages it attempts to convey are about the moral dilemmas in which mankind has always found itself. The past is a repository of messages to help make sense of the present. For this reason, sometimes the most ancient past is specially useful to the Durkheimian project. In this context, history joins with myth. And myth, far from being valueless as a source for the study of legal and social life, may hold clues to some of its foundations, hidden from view in more sophisticated societies that are better able to rationalise their collective beliefs, fears and lack of self-knowledge.

In one obvious sense, Durkheim's own work is a message from the past. It speaks to us from a century ago. One might well ask how his claims that society is a moral phenomenon, that solidarity is a normal state for social life and that law can be thought of as an expression of morality can survive the lessons of what, for him, was the unknown tomorrow but, for us, is the unforgettable past. Can his moralistic legal theory speak through the din of violence from two world wars and many other conflicts, the Holocaust and numerous other horrors of the century that divides him from us? (cf. Baumann, 1989: 170–5.) I believe it still can. Durkheim's agenda for legal theory has to be considered a narrow one. It refuses to address many issues that must not remain unaddressed in the sociological study of law. But it keeps a sharp moral vision before it, one that affirms the overriding worth of each individual human being and the necessity of an open and diverse yet co-operative and solidary community, dedicated to the mutual support of its members. This moral vision is explained and justified sociologically. Durkheim fails to consider important aspects of the moral domain of modern law and leaves only ambiguity in addressing some others. Nevertheless, he presents a clear position on the way law should be conceptualised, in general terms, if something morally worthwhile is to be made of it. And he provides detailed arguments as to how this moral worth of law might be assessed.

Durkheim's agenda remains a focus of optimism in a contemporary world that often forgets what an important product of history law is, if it is seriously and consistently informed by the values he tried to express as the cult of the individual. The worst legacy of Durkheim's legal theory would be complacency about law's weaknesses and injustices, the adoption of a romantic moralism that cannot see law's blatant immoralities and cruelties, or its innumerable, mundane inadequacies as an agent of social solidarity. The best legacy would be to inspire critical analyses of law to explore in new ways how to make legal ideas and practices morally meaningful to the regulated; in other words, to help to change legal regulation and its environments so as to make Durkheim's 'focal' view of law seem less partial and more comprehensive as a perspective on legal reality in contemporary society.

Notes and further reading

Sources included in the bibliography of text references are cited in the following notes (as in the text) by author's name and publication date only.

Chapter 1 A sociological project

SOCIOLOGY'S AMBITION

For discussion of Durkheim's role in the founding of sociology see T. N. Clark, *Prophets and Patrons: The French University and the Emergence of the Social Sciences* (1973: ch. 6); Weisz (1983); V. Karady, 'Durkheim, les sciences sociales et l'université' (1976) 17 *Revue française de sociologie* 267; Karady, 'The Durkheimians in academe: a reconsideration', in Besnard (ed.) (1983). For the work of Durkheim's collaborators see Besnard (ed.) (1983); Clark (1968); Y. Nandan, *The Durkheim School: A Systematic and Comprehensive Bibliography* (1977).

A CAREER

Lukes (1973) is the standard, very comprehensive intellectual biography. For an outline of Durkheim's life in the context of his times see H. Peyre, 'Durkheim: the man, his time and his intellectual background', in Wolff (ed.) (1960). See also G. Davy, 'Émile Durkheim' (1960) 1 *Revue française de sociologie* 3; Davy, 'In memoriam: Émile Durkheim' (1957–8) *Année sociologique*, 3rd ser., vii (noting Durkheim's unfulfilled plan to write a book on law).

LAW IN SOCIOLOGY, SOCIOLOGY IN LAW

Apart from the major monographs and posthumously published lectures, convenient sources in French of Durkheim's essays and other writings are Durkheim (1969a, 1975a and 1987). His minor writings for the *Année sociologique* are translated in Y. Nandan (ed.) *Émile Durkheim: Contributions to L'Année sociologique* (1980). English translations of his essays are published in Bellah (ed.) (1973), Traugott (ed.) (1978), Pickering (ed.) (1975 and 1979), Wolff (ed.) (1960), Lukes and Scull (eds) (1983), A. Giddens (ed.) *Durkheim on Politics and the State* (1986) and Giddens (ed.) *Émile Durkheim: Selected Writings* (1972). Lukes (1973) includes a comprehensive bibliography of Durkheim's writings.

Modern studies of the place of law generally in Durkheim's sociology include: Vogt (1993); Lenoir (1994); Chazel (1991); Lukes and Scull (1983); Lukes (1973: ch. 13); Pearce (1989: ch. 5); A. Hunt, *The Sociological Movement in Law* (1978: ch. 4); R. Reiner, 'Crime, law and deviance: the Durkheim legacy', in Fenton (1984); Clarke (1976); Cotterrell (1977); Cotterrell (1995: ch. 9); R. Lenoir, 'Le droit et ses usages', in Besnard et al. (eds) *Division du travail et lien social: la thèse de Durkheim un siècle après* (1994); U. Bullasch, *Rechtsnorm und Rechtssystem in der Normentheorie Emile Durkheims* (1988); A. E. Ves Losada, 'Emile Durkheim y la Sociologia del Derecho' (1991) *Anuario de Filosofia Juridica y Social* 33.

FUNCTIONAL ANALYSIS

See A. Pierce, 'Durkheim and functionalism', in Wolff (ed.) (1960); R. T. Hall, *Émile Durkheim; Ethics and the Sociology of Morals* (1987: ch. 7). For a discussion of Durkheim's legal sociology emphasising its functional approach see A.-J. Arnaud and J. F. Dulce, *Introduction à l'analyse sociologique des systèmes juridiques* (1998: 48–53).

POSITIVISM

On the concept of social fact see Durkheim (1982a); Lukes (1973: 8–15); Giddens (1977: 291–6); M. Gilbert, 'Durkheim and social facts', in W. S. F. Pickering and H. Martins (eds) *Debating Durkheim* (1994); M. Gane, *On Durkheim's Rules of Sociological Method* (1988); P. Q. Hirst, *Durkheim, Bernard and Epistemology* (1975: 90–103). For advocacy of the objective study of law as social fact see Carbonnier (1994: 155–9); Black (1976); K. Olivecrona, *Law as Fact*, 2nd edn (1971). Davy, who always stressed the links between Durkheim's philosophical and sociological concerns, quotes Durkheim's 1911 letter in both of his memoirs listed in 'A career', above. For the view that Durkheimian sociology 'self-consciously attempted to overcome the object–subject distinction' characteristic of positivist method see S. G. Mestrovic, 'Durkheim's concept of anomie considered as a "total" social fact' (1987) 38 *British Journal of Sociology* 567.

THE PHILOSOPHICAL VOCATION OF SOCIOLOGY

On relationships between philosophy and sociology see Durkheim (1982a: 236ff.). Wallwork (1972: 7), who also emphasises Durkheim's philosophical contribution, argues that the positivist ideal that he programmatically sets out 'only slightly resembles his actual method'. Robert Hall (*Durkheim, op. cit.*, p. 75) writes that, as Durkheim gradually came to emphasise ideas as controlling forces in social change, he saw the philosopher's role as that of preparing 'the way for moral change on the level of beliefs and ideals' by systematising ideas and aspirations emerging in society.

Chapter 2 A moral mission

THE MALADY OF THE INFINITE

On Durkheim's views of anomie and regulation see Besnard (1993); B. Lacroix, 'Régulation et anomie selon Durkheim' (1973) 55 *Cahiers internationaux de sociologie* 265; R. B. Ginsberg, *Anomie and Aspirations* (1980); S. G. Mestrovic and H. M. Brown, 'Durkheim's concept of anomie as dérèglement' (1985) 33 *Social Problems* 81 (on anomie as a painful psychological state of derangement); and Mestrovic, 'Durkheim's concept of anomie considered as a "total" social fact', *loc. cit.*

On Durkheim's view of human nature see M. J. Hawkins, 'A re-examination of Durkheim's theory of human nature' (1977) 25 *Sociological Review* n.s. 229 (showing the development of Durkheim's thought towards a recognition of the sociological significance of biological aspects of human motivation); Hall, *Durkheim, op. cit.*, ch. 10.

ASPECTS OF BIOGRAPHY

On Durkheim's personality, Davy (1919) is a valuable source; see also Davy's two memoirs listed under 'A career', above. On Durkheim's Jewish background in relation to his social thought see, for example, Pickering (1994); Pickering (1984: 14–18); J.-C. Filloux, 'Il ne faut pas oublier que je suis le fils de rabbin' (1976) 17 *Revue française de sociologie* 259. I. Strenski, *Durkheim and the Jews of France* (1997) firmly and properly rejects any attempt to explain Durkheim's work in terms of his Jewishness, but sets it in the context of the Jewish intellectual life of his particular time and place. On Durkheim's early life and the influence of his father see L. M. Greenberg, 'Bergson and Durkheim as sons and assimilators' (1976) 9 *French Historical Studies* 619; cf. Pickering (1984: 13–14). On his change of view around 1895 on the importance of religion see Pickering (1984: 60–2). Durkheim attributed the change in his thinking particularly to his reading of the work of W. Robertson Smith: see Pickering (1984: 62–70). Cf. Alexander (1982: 484–8) (arguing that Durkheim's 'new' view of religion predated his reading of Smith). See also R. A. Jones, 'Robertson Smith, Durkheim and sacrifice' (1981) 17 *Journal of the History of the Behavioral Sciences* 184.

THE POLITICAL CONTEXT

On the Durkheimians' political allegiances and commitments see W. P. Vogt, 'Political connections, professional advancement and moral education in Durkheimian sociology' (1991) 27 *Journal of the History of the Behavioral Sciences* 56. For general background see, for example, J. A. Scott, *Republican Ideas and the Liberal Tradition in France, 1870–1914* (1951); J. P. Mayer, *Political Thought in France from the Revolution to the Fifth Republic* (1961: ch. 4); Hayward (1960). On the Dreyfus affair see, for example, J.-D. Bredin, *The Affair: The Case of Alfred Dreyfus* (1986).

ECONOMY AND SOCIETY

On Durkheim's thesis on the division of labour see, for example, W. Pope and B. D. Johnson, 'Inside organic solidarity' (1983) 48 *American Sociological Review* 681; P. M. Blau and R. L. Milby, 'Faits sociaux et structure sociale', in Besnard et al. (eds) *Division du travail, op. cit.*; Barnes (1966). On the concept of solidarity in French political and social thought see J. E. S. Hayward, 'Solidarity: the social history of an idea in nineteenth-century France' (1959) 4 *International Review of Social History* 261; Hayward, 'The official social philosophy of the French Third Republic: Léon Bourgeois and solidarism' (1961) 6 *International Review of Social History* 19; Scott, *Republican Ideas, op. cit.*, pp. 157–86; G. Gurvitch, *L'idée du Droit social* (1932: 567–89).

CURING SOCIETY'S MALADY

On Durkheim and Marx: A. Cuvillier, 'Durkheim et Marx' (1948) 4 *Cahiers internationaux de sociologie* 75. On Durkheim and Comte: F. Pécaut, 'Auguste Comte et Durkheim' (1921) 28 *Revue de métaphysique et de morale* 639; J. Heilbron, 'Ce que Durkheim doit à Comte', in Besnard et al. (eds) *Division du travail, op. cit.* On Durkheim and Spencer: M. Borlandi, 'Durkheim lecteur de Spencer', in Besnard et al. (eds) *Division du travail, op. cit.*; P. A. Corning, 'Durkheim and Spencer' (1982) 33 *British Journal of Sociology* 359; R. A. Jones, 'Durkheim's response to Spencer' (1974) 15 *Sociological Quarterly* 341; R. G. Perrin, 'Durkheim's misrepresentation of Spencer' (1975) 16 *Sociological Quarterly* 544 (and reply by Jones).

Chapter 3 A legal environment

LAW AS INDEX

Use of the 'index thesis': in a recorded discussion in 1906 Durkheim (1953a: 77) returns to the question of how 'moral reality' may be observed by the social scientist, stating that many moral maxims are accessible to study because they are 'condensed in legal formulas'. 'In law the greater part of domestic morality, the morality of contract and obligation, all the ideas relating to the great fundamental duties, are translated and reflected.' But he does not claim, as he had in 1893, that legal rules are an index of the moral nature of society: 'I do not deny that there are duties and moral ideas that are not formulated in law, but these must be reached by other methods.'

For a strong version of the claim that positivist measurement of law is central to legal sociology see Black (1976) which, however, treats law not as rules but as governmental behaviour. Theodor Geiger's legal sociology relies on a somewhat similar positivism while rejecting functional analysis as a general sociological method. See R. Mayntz (ed.) *Theodor Geiger on Social Order and Mass Society* (1969: 57–60). Black associates law with an absence of (the sense of) community (1976: 135) and Geiger with an absence of trust in social life (*op. cit.*, pp. 73, 74). Recognising the insufficiency of the positivist view of law shared by Durkheim, Black and Geiger seems a prerequisite for any theoretical view that law can be the collective product of an active community (rather than merely imposed on it), contributing to bonds of trust between its members. See Chapters 13 and 14, below.

REACHING OUT TO LAWYERS

On sociology of law as a focus for Durkheim's co-workers see Vogt (1983); Arnaud (1981: 113–18); Carbonnier (1994: 103–4, 105–6); Chazel (1991). In referring to Durkheim's collaborators in this book, I exclude (to make the scope of discussion manageable) scholars later influenced by him, but not co-workers on the *Année sociologique* under his editorship. For a detailed account of the *Année* group organised around Durkheim see P. Besnard, 'The *Année sociologique* team', in Besnard (ed.) (1983). A prominent Durkheimian legal scholar excluded by my self-limitation is Henri Lévy-Bruhl, a contributor to the social history of early Roman law: see Arnaud (1981: 145–7) and Carbonnier (1994: 106). Among the writers mentioned in the text, Huvelin's work is discussed in Chapters 6 and 8, Davy's and Mauss' in Chapter 8, and Lévy's in Chapter 12, below.

LEGAL SCHOLARSHIP AND SOCIAL CHANGE

On Gaston Richard (1860–1945) see Pickering (1984: 343–59). On the reception of sociology in French law faculties see Carbonnier (1994: 114–18); and on Durkheimian sociology's attitudes to legal studies in the law faculties see P. Lascoumes, 'Le droit comme science sociale: La place de É. Durkheim dans les débats entre juristes et sociologues à la charnière des deux derniers siècles (1870–1914)', in F. Chazel and J. Commaille (eds) *Normes juridiques et régulation sociale* (1991).

SOCIOLOGY IN LEGAL PHILOSOPHY

On Hauriou (1856–1929) see A. Broderick (ed.) *The French Institutionalists* (1970: part 1) – extracts from his writings, with commentary; D. Salas, 'Droit et institution: Léon Duguit et Maurice Hauriou', in P. Bouretz (ed.) *La force du droit* (1991); Y. Tanguy, 'L'institution dans l'œuvre de Maurice Hauriou' (1991) 107 *Revue du droit public* 61.

On Duguit (1859–1928) see Hayward (1960: part 2); E. Pisier-Kouchner, 'La sociologie durkheimienne dans l'œuvre de Duguit' (1977) 28 *Année sociologique*, 3rd ser., 95 (emphasising Duguit's partial use and rigid interpretation of Durkheim's ideas); Pisier-Kouchner (1972); Salas, 'Droit et institution', *loc. cit.*; W. Friedmann, *Legal Theory*, 5th edn (1967: 228–36); H. J. Laski, 'M. Duguit's conception of the state' in A. L. Goodhart et al. (eds) *Modern Theories of Law* (1933); J.-F. Perrin, 'Duguit et la "science du droit"', in Chazel and Commaille (eds) *Normes juridiques*, *op. cit.*; L. Sfez, 'Duguit et la théorie de l'État' (1976) 21 *Archives de philosophie du droit* 111. On Duguit's sociology seminar, which predated the publication of Durkheim's *Division of Labour*, see Chazel (1991: 27–8).

LEGAL INFLUENCES IN SOCIOLOGY

On the early, general influence of the German historical school of jurisprudence on Durkheim see Wallwork (1972: 23–5); and on his reaction to jurists' ideas generally see Lenoir, 'Le droit et ses usages', *loc. cit.*

Chapter 4 Law, morality, belief

A FOCUS OF BELIEF

On the nature and development of Durkheim's sociology of religion see Pickering (1984); N. J. Allen et al. (eds) *On Durkheim's Elementary Forms of Religious Life* (1998); R. A. Jones, 'Durkheim, Frazer and Smith' (1986) 92 *American Journal of Sociology* 596; Jones, 'Durkheim and *La Cité antique*', in Turner (ed.) (1993); Jones, 'Robertson Smith, Durkheim and sacrifice', *loc. cit.*; E. Wallwork, 'Durkheim's early sociology of religion' (1985) 46 *Sociological Analysis* 201 (on Durkheim's pre-1895 writings on religion in relation to his later work).

MORALITY, RELIGION AND LAW

On the collective consciousness: G. Gurvitch ('Le problème de la conscience collective dans la sociologie d'Émile Durkheim' in Gurvitch, 1963) suggests that Durkheim's conceptualisation of collective beliefs deterred him from recognising subjective aspects of morality. Gurvitch's view is criticised in Alexander (1982: 488), in my view justifiably given Durkheim's later understanding of morality and penal responsibility, discussed in this and the following chapter. See also G. Namer, 'La sociologie de la connaissance chez Durkheim et chez les durkheimiens' (1977) 28 *Année sociologique*, 3rd ser., 41 (on the evolution of Durkheimian conceptions of the collective consciousness and collective representations); P. Birnbaum, 'Cadres sociaux et répresentations collectives dans l'œuvre de Durkheim: l'exemple du *Socialisme*' (1969) 10 *Revue française de sociologie* 3 (on the development of Durkheim's view of the causal significance of collective representations). See also the acute brief discussion in D. LaCapra, *Émile Durkheim: Sociologist and Philosopher* (1972: 89–92); and P. Bohannon, 'Conscience collective and culture', in Wolff (ed.) (1960). On the concept of collective representations see Lukes (1973: 6–8); Pickering (1984: 283–90); Cladis (1992: 80–1). On law's origins in relation to religion see notes on 'Religion and early law', below.

SOCIOLOGY AS A KEY TO MORALITY

On Durkheim's view that morality must be a matter of duties owed to society at large see Wallwork (1972: 178ff.). On his science of morality see Hall, *Durkheim*, op. cit.; Wallwork (1972: chs 2 and 3); and W. W. Miller, *Durkheim, Morals and Modernity* (1996).

THE NATURE OF MORAL RULES

On Durkheim's attempt to distinguish utility from morality in the context of his discussion of hygiene rules see also Giddens (1977: 295–6) (arguing that similar reasons often lie behind obedience to moral rules and hygiene rules). On moral obligation see Wallwork (1972: 33–41). Wallwork (1972: 166–70) argues that Durkheim puts forward a kind of rule-utilitarian theory of morality since he sees moral principles as justified by their utility in promoting the good of society as a whole by furthering solidarity. See 'A coherent view of morality?' in Chapter 13, below.

LEGAL RULES AS A CATEGORY OF MORAL RULES

On Durkheim's view of the relationship between legal and moral rules see F.-A. Isambert, 'Durkheim et la sociologie des normes', in Chazel and Commaille (eds) *Normes juridiques, op. cit.* On general problems of conceptualising law in early or simple societies see, for example, G. MacCormack, 'On the problem of law in primitive societies', in W. Krawietz et al. (eds) *Objektivierung des Rechtsdenkens* (1984).

LAW BEYOND MORALITY?

On the evolution of Durkheim's view of morality see Hall, *Durkheim, op. cit.*, chs 4–6. On the implications of this evolution for his view of law see Isambert, 'Durkheim et la sociologie des normes', *loc. cit.*

Chapter 5 Crime and punishment

CRIME AND COLLECTIVE SENTIMENTS

On the distinction between normal and pathological see Hall, *Durkheim, op. cit.*, ch. 12; Lukes (1973: 28–30); Hirst, *Durkheim, op. cit.*, pp. 115–22; Gane, *Durkheim's Rules, op. cit.* On the relationship between crime and the collective consciousness see Garland (1983); Garland (1990); Erikson (1966) (on relationships between social control and group beliefs); Hart (1967) (criticising the thesis that penal law's task is to express collective sentiments); W. J. Thomas, 'Social solidarity and the enforcement of morals revisited' (1994) 32 *American Criminal Law Review* 49 (on Hart's critique of Durkheim).

For other theories explaining punishment as the expression of collective sentiments see J. F. Stephen, *Liberty, Equality, Fraternity* (1873); P. Devlin, *The Enforcement of Morals* (1965) (and, for criticism, see H. L. A. Hart, *Law, Liberty and Morality* (1963) and Hart, *Punishment and Responsibility* (1968: 169–73)). K. J. M. Smith (*James Fitzjames Stephen* 1988: 59) suggests that Durkheim may have known of the work of Stephen who had a high reputation as a jurist in France. Compared with Stephen and Devlin, Durkheim offers clearer, more modest views of the role of punishment in modern society because his sociology presents the life, dignity and security of individuals as the sole values to be protected by modern criminal law (see 'The evolution of punishment' and Chapter 7, below).

Crime as a concern of Durkheim's early work: the main discussions are in Durkheim (1984, 1982a) and the essay 'Crime et santé sociale', dating from 1895 and translated in Lukes and Scull (eds) (1983) and Traugott (ed.) (1978). Punishment's role in enforcing morality is a central focus of Durkheim's early work, but, significantly, in *The Division of Labour* this is presented as of declining relative importance among law's functions. As Durkheim's view of morality moves from its early stress on coercion and duty to its later equal concern with attachment to groups and individual autonomy, law is presented as facilitative and liberating rather than repressive. As discussed later in the text of this chapter, this emphasis even colours Durkheim's later writings on punishment. Thus, his perspective on law is, in general, non-authoritarian and relatively non-censorious (even seeking some value in certain kinds of crime). In this respect it contrasts strongly with other moralistic legal theories, such as Stephen's and Devlin's, that seek to specify what law must prohibit to fulfil its moral function. For discussion of Durkheim's ideas on punishment and responsibility at various stages of his career see J.-L. Génard, 'Responsabilité et normativité dans l'école et la pensée de Durkheim', in P. Robert et al. (eds) *Normes,*

normes juridiques, normes pénales (1997), vol. 2; LaCapra, *Durkheim, op. cit.*, pp. 92–103.

THE PROBLEM OF REGULATORY OFFENCES

On perceptions of the nature of regulatory offences in relation to 'ordinary' criminal law see Cotterrell (1992: 270–2). On regulatory law generally see A. I. Ogus, *Regulation* (1994).

PUNISHMENT AND THE NATURE OF THE STATE

See F. R. Kellogg, 'Peins criminelles et évolution sociale' (1977) 28 *Année sociologique*, 3rd ser., 79 (defending Durkheim's arguments in the penal evolution essay as valid in essentials); Grabosky (1978) (claiming that Durkheim did not anticipate the modern trend towards use of non-custodial penal sanctions).

FUNCTIONS OF CRIME AND PUNISHMENT

See Garland (1990). On the normality of crime see also Durkheim's 'Crime et santé sociale', *loc. cit.*, written in response to criticism by the criminologist Gabriel Tarde. On the dispute between Durkheim and Tarde (which largely reflected the competition between sociology and psychology as modes of social explanation at the end of the nineteenth century) see Lukes and Scull (1983).

VARIATIONS IN PUNISHMENT

P. A. Sorokin, *Social and Cultural Dynamics* (1937), vol. 2, ch. 15 provides a remarkably ambitious study of changes in 'ethicojuridical mentality in criminal law' as reflected in the legal codes of France, Germany, Italy, Austria and Russia throughout the history of these nations. In Durkheimian fashion, he examines the presence or absence of 104 offences and their relative seriousness according to their official expression and concludes that 'ethicojuridical mentality' varies not in linear fashion but, in so far as definite trends are identifiable, in relation to general culture. See also N. Christie, 'Changes in penal values' (1968) 2 *Scandinavian Studies in Criminology* 161 (suggesting that changes in types of punishment may be best understood as adaptations of penal measures to changes in the value of things of which offenders can be deprived).

THE EVOLUTION OF PUNISHMENT

Spitzer (1975, 1979) is highly critical of Durkheim; Kellogg, 'Peins criminelles', *loc. cit.*, sees the modern trend towards individualisation of punishments as validating the central point of Durkheim's theory of penal evolution. T. A. Jones, 'Durkheim, deviance and development' (1981) 59 *Social Forces* 1009, argues that Durkheim was essentially correct in predicting that imprisonment (and fines) would become the sole means of punishment in industrialised society; his theory needs amendment but it is not necessary to discard its conceptual basis. For other general accounts of penal evolution see, for example, G. Rusche and O. Kirchheimer, *Punishment and Social Structure* (1939); M. Foucault, *Discipline and Punish* (1977); D. Melossi and M. Pavarini, *The Prison and the Factory* (1981); D. Garland, *Punishment and Welfare* (1985).

Chapter 6 Legal evolution

THE LEGAL EVOLUTION THESIS

On social morphology see H. F. Andrews, 'Durkheim and social morphology', in Turner (ed.) (1993); L. F. Schnore, 'Social morphology and human ecology' (1958) 63 *American Journal of Sociology* 620; Hirst, *Durkheim, op. cit.*, pp. 122–35.

LAW AS A SOCIOLOGICAL CONCEPT

Criticism of Durkheim's thesis as a representation of legal history: see Sheleff (1975); Sheleff (1997: part 2). For an interesting partial defence of Durkheim in the light of H. L. A. Hart's legal philosophy see E. Colvin, 'The sociology of secondary rules' (1978) 28 *University of Toronto Law Journal* 195, at pp. 203–5.

TESTING DURKHEIM

Generally critical of Durkheim's thesis on the relationship between legal and social development are R. K. Merton, 'Durkheim's *Division of Labor in Society*', in Nisbet (1965) (noting 'defective ethnographic data'); E. Faris, 'Book review' (1934) 40 *American Journal of Sociology* 376 ('the work accepts as accurate the crude misconceptions of the 1880s concerning the life of primitive man'); Barnes (1966); Schwartz and

Miller (1964); Schwartz (1974); Clarke (1976). See also Wimberley (1973); Schwartz, 'Social factors in the development of legal control' (1954) 63 *Yale Law Journal* 471. More supportive is S. F. Moore, 'Legal liability and evolutionary interpretation', in her *Law as Process* (1978). Conceptual problems are addressed in Baxi (1974); Cotterrell (1977); and G. Turkel, 'Testing Durkheim' (1979) 13 *Law and Society Review* 721.

USES OF HISTORY

On Durkheim's approach to history see LaCapra, *Durkheim, op. cit.*, ch. 5; R. N. Bellah, 'Durkheim and history', in Nisbet (1965). On the methods of Fustel de Coulanges' *La Cité antique* (1864), which strongly influenced Durkheim, see F. Hartog, 'Préface' to the Flammarion edition, noting the book's lack of concern with details of chronology and context. Hartog remarks: 'Is it even useful to point out that neither archaeology nor the ancient texts corroborate this vision of origins [of family property]?' (1864: xviii); Durkheim 'pondered with . . . [Fustel] and against him; in any case, from his starting point . . .' (1864: xxiii). Fustel saw history's true object of study as the human spirit, rather than material facts and institutions; history 'should aim to know what this spirit believed, thought, felt in different epochs of the life of the human race' (quoted pp. xxiii–xxiv). Perhaps, ultimately, Durkheim's (1982a: 211–28) view was not dissimilar. See, further, on Fustel, notes below on 'The evolution of property rights'. On Durkheim and history see also 'Messages from the past' in Chapter 14, below.

RELIGION AND EARLY LAW

See Mauss (1896) and Gernet (1951). On Maine's thesis on early law and religion see also A. S. Diamond, *Primitive Law, Past and Present* (1971: 47ff.); B. S. Jackson, 'Law and language', in A. Diamond (ed.) *The Victorian Achievement of Sir Henry Maine* (1991). On Maine's influence on French understandings of early law, see Carbonnier (1994: 88–9). The strongest direct influence on Durkheim's conviction that law and religion are intertwined in early society was probably Fustel de Coulanges, who taught him at the École Normale Supérieure. See Pickering (1984: 56–8). See also J. Carbonnier, 'La religion, fondement du droit?' (1993) 38 *Archives de philosophie du droit* 17.

THE BIRTH OF INDIVIDUAL RIGHTS

Huvelin (1873–1924) was a prolific and erudite scholar of early Roman law, and especially of the history of commercial law. His work on law, magic and religion is discussed in Mauss (1990: ch. 3) and Gurvitch (1963: ch. 9) (which considers various theories of the sources of law in magical practices). See also Gurvitch (1942); C. Faralli, 'Magie', in A.-J. Arnaud (gen. ed.) *Dictionnaire encyclopédique de théorie et de sociologie du droit*, 2nd edn (1993: 355–7); Duxbury (1989); P. de Tourtoulon, *Philosophy in the Development of Law* (1922: 179–92).

The writings of the jurist Karl Olivecrona show his awareness of Huvelin's work. In Olivecrona's view (much influenced by the philosopher Axel Hägerström's analyses of Roman Law):

> We relegate magic to the most primitive stages of civilisation. This is entirely wrong. Beliefs which are fundamentally magical play an important role in every society, including our own, not only in the religions but also in the legal field. So long as we do not see this, we are blinded to the supernatural element in the legal concepts of the Romans. (Olivecrona, *The Acquisition of Possession in Roman Law*, 1938, p. 3)

(See also Olivecrona, *Law as Fact*, *op. cit.*, treating modern ideas of legal rights and transactions as equivalent to, but different from, magical ideas.) But the assertion that magic has a role in relation to modern law dangerously confuses two ideas: first, the important idea that faith, of some kind, underpins the ultimate authority of modern, no less than early, law; secondly, the false idea that the doctrines and procedures of modern law may not, in all respects, require rational justification. Magical elements in early Roman law are rarely discussed in modern textbooks, presumably because the main justification for studying Roman law is now thought to lie in its character as a historical source of legal concepts embodying modern rationality.

On magic generally see D. O'Keefe, *Stolen Lightning* (1982); I. C. Jarvie and J. Agassi, 'The problem of the rationality of magic' (1967) 18 *British Journal of Sociology* 55; Agassi and Jarvie, 'Magic and rationality again' (1973) 24 *British Journal of Sociology* 236; M. Buchowski, 'The rationality of magic' (1988) 18 *Philosophy of the Social Sciences* 509; P. Blumberg, 'Magic in the modern world' (1963) 47 *Sociology and Social Research* 147; F. Graf, *La magie dans l'antiquité gréco-romaine* (1994); V. I. J. Flint, *The Rise of Magic in Early Modern Europe* (1991).

Chapter 7 Moral foundations of modern law

MODERN LAW: THE EARLY THESIS

The Division of Labour can be treated as the starting point for the development of Durkheim's legal theory because, taken alone, his work on law prior to the publication of that book is insufficient to justify attributing a legal theory to him. Nevertheless, *The Division of Labour* seems to modify earlier positions of Durkheim, for example on the nature of morality. For Jeffrey Alexander (1982: 296) and Mark Cladis (1992: ch. 2) the book shows Durkheim's 'temporary' move to a more deterministic and materialist explanation of morality, before returning to develop an earlier emphasis on the importance of ideal forms.

MODERN LAW: AN ALTERNATIVE LATER THESIS?

On Durkheim's changed view of law after publication of *The Division of Labour* see also Alexander (1982: 271–9); and Génard, 'Responsabilité', *loc. cit.*, pp. 20–1. On 'paradoxical claims' in Durkheim's early work that may have led to his changed outlook see Wallwork (1972: 81–2).

Fauconnet (1874–1938) was a key member of the *Année* group and eventually became professor of sociology at the Sorbonne. On his study of responsibility see Génard, 'Responsabilité', *loc. cit.*, pp. 28ff.; Piaget (1932: 314–28); P. Poncela, 'Autour de l'ouvrage de Paul Fauconnet' (1977) 22 *Archives de philosophie du droit* 131. On the balancing of subjective and objective elements in modern conceptions of responsibility see Hart, *Punishment and Responsibility*, *op. cit.*, pp. 152–7.

THE MORALITY OF RESTITUTIVE LAW

On the change of emphasis in Durkheim's work towards 'a more idealistic [in my terminology, ideational] conception of society' see also Wallwork (1972: ch. 3); and É. Benoit-Smullyan, 'The sociologism of Émile Durkheim and his school', in H. E. Barnes, *Introduction to the History of Sociology* (1948), noting (p. 510) 'a new and distinct phase' of Durkheim's work from around 1898. Jeffrey Alexander (1982: 230ff.) argues (in a detailed study of changes in Durkheim's thought) that structural inconsistencies in the arguments of *The Division of Labour* ensured that in later writings Durkheim would express views incompatible with these arguments. See also M. J. Hawkins, 'Continuity and change in Durkheim's theory of social solidarity' (1979) 20 *Sociological Quarterly* 155 (arguing that changes in Durkheim's ideas after publication of *The Division of Labour* amount to 'a theoretical re-orientation' of his approach to social solidarity; this, in turn, explains the neglect in his later work of concepts crucial to his first book); Pope and Johnson, 'Inside organic solidarity', *loc. cit.* (claiming that problems of Durkheim's first book can be avoided by discarding the concept of organic solidarity, and that Durkheim in fact did so in his later work). But the moral consequences of interdependence which the concept of organic solidarity implies surely remain a focus of all Durkheim's thought.

THE CULT OF THE INDIVIDUAL

See Giddens (1971); F.-A. Isambert, 'Durkheim et l'individualité', in Pickering and Miller (eds) (1993); J. Neyer, 'Individualism and socialism in Durkheim', in Wolff (ed.) (1960); Isambert, 'La naissance de l'individu', in Besnard et al. (eds) *Division du travail, op. cit.* W. W. Miller, 'Durkheim and individualism' (1988) 36 *Sociological Review* 647, argues (plausibly) that modern society generates both moral conflicts and unrealisable ideals, and Durkheim's sociology cannot show how society produces a single, appropriate, 'normal' morality of individualism, but it can show the social conditions under which moral values are chosen. Pope and Johnson, 'Inside organic solidarity', *loc. cit.*, argue that the cult of the individual is only one of four moral ideas that Durkheim sees as uniting complex societies, the others being the virtue of specialisation, the ideal of justice and the moral diversity of occupational groups. Cladis (1992) relates Durkheim's individualism to liberal and communitarian political philosophy. On the evolution of values of individual responsibility and dignity as central to modern law see P. Stein and J. Shand, *Legal Values in Western Society* (1974: ch. 5).

THE NATURE OF RIGHTS

On Durkheim and human rights see: J.-C. Filloux, 'Individualisme et éducation aux droits de l'homme chez Émile Durkheim', in Pickering and Miller (eds) (1993); Pickering (1993) (Durkheim's attempt to find a basis for human rights in the quasi-religious cult of the individual is self-defeating); but cf. Thompson (1993) (the idea of the cult of the individual with its sacred aura is important to human rights: 'it is only collective representations held as sacred that can promote moral community').

Chapter 8 Contract

TWO APPROACHES TO CONTRACT

For commentary on Durkheim's ideas on contract see Hunt, *Sociological Movement, op. cit.*, pp. 85–8; J.-C. Rouveyran, 'Contribution à une sociologie des contrats' (1977) 28 *Année sociologique*, 3rd ser., 115 (mapping the 'contractual universe' as a sociological field, drawing on the work of Durkheim, Mauss and Davy).

CONTRACT AND STATUS

For Maine's view of the evolution of contract see Maine (1861: ch. 9) and, for comparison of Maine's and Durkheim's views, Cocks (1988: 156–7).

SOCIAL ORIGINS OF CONTRACTUAL OBLIGATION

Davy (1883–1976) wrote on legal and political theory as well as sociology. For biographical information see J. Stoezel (1976) 17 *Revue française de sociologie* 157, and A. Girard (1976) 27 *Année sociologique*, 3rd ser., 5. On Davy's work on contract see MacCormack (1980); Aillet (1923: part 1). *La foi jurée* provoked fierce criticism from within the Durkheimian circle as soon as it was published. The book was attacked, among other reasons, for making the potlatch too central to its explanation of the evolution of contractual individualism and for under-emphasising the significance of the potlatch's mystical and ritual elements. Some of this criticism might be interpreted as suggesting that Davy should have paid much more attention to ideational rather than merely functional explanation, and that he was seeking to ground contract not in the general evolution of moral experience but in a very specific institution found in certain societies. On these controversies see P. Besnard, 'Un conflit au sein du groupe durkheimien' (1985) 26 *Revue française de sociologie* 247; and M. Fournier, *Marcel Mauss* (1994: 486–8). On the Kwakiutl potlatch, see H. Codere, *Fighting with Property* (1950); and P. Drucker and R. F. Heizer, *To Make My Name Good* (1967). On the problem of time in reciprocal obligations and the social emergence of the idea of credit see Gernet (1956: 138–46), discussing (in a Durkheimian context) law and 'pre-law' in Ancient Greece.

THE MORALITY OF RECIPROCITY

Mauss (1872–1950), Durkheim's nephew, was a close collaborator and an important contributor to the development of anthropology in France. See Mauss' own 'An intellectual self-portrait', in Besnard (ed.) (1983), where he notes: 'Guided by [Franz] Boas' admirable descriptions of the American Northwest that Durkheim brought to my attention, I was able to bring out an entire system of facts that are very widespread throughout most ancient civilisations. . . . From these facts, I drew out the at once religious, mythical and contractual idea of the gift' (p. 147). The best source (in French) on Mauss' life and work is Fournier, *Marcel Mauss, op. cit.*, a richly detailed intellectual biography. On Mauss's *The Gift* (1990) the literature is now extensive: see LaCapra, *Durkheim*, op. cit., pp. 105–11; M. Godelier, *L'énigme du don* (1996); B. Karsenti, *Marcel Mauss: le fait social total* (1994); J. Lacorse, 'Réciprocité positive et réciprocité negative' (1987) 83 *Cahiers internationaux de sociologie* 291 (on writings, since Mauss, suggesting that reciprocity is not necessarily a mechanism of social cohesion); G. MacCormack, 'Mauss and the "spirit" of the gift' (1982) 52 *Oceania* 286; M. Panoff, 'Marcel Mauss's "The Gift" revisited' (1970) 5 *Man* n.s. 60. For various approaches to a morality of reciprocity see, for example, A. E. Komter (ed.) *The Gift: An Interdisciplinary Perspective* (1996).

Génard, 'Responsabilité', *loc. cit.*, argues (p. 20) that Mauss' and Davy's work forced Durkheim to reconsider his early thesis of the lack of restitutive law in ancient and simple societies since he had associated reciprocity and exchange with restitutive law. But this is doubtful, partly because Durkheim's concept of restitutive law involves more than this (see Chapter 6, above) and partly because other problems forced Durkheim's changed emphasis in analysing modern law after the publication of *The Division of Labour* (see Chapter 7, above).

CONTRACT, INDIVIDUALISM AND SOLIDARITY

Just contracts: on Durkheim's idea of justice see C. J. Sirianni, 'Justice and the division of labour' (1984) 32 *Sociological Review* n.s. 449; E. Schoenfeld and S. Mestrovic, 'Durkheim's concept of justice and its relationship to social solidarity' (1989) 50 *Sociological Analysis* 111 (linking Durkheim's concept of justice to Jewish traditions, but for persuasive criticism see Strenski, *Durkheim*, op. cit.).

Chapter 9 Property, inheritance and family law

PROPERTY RIGHTS AND SOLIDARITY

On Durkheim's writings on property see Hunt, *Sociological Movement*, *op. cit.*, pp. 88–90. On 'negative solidarity': Niklas Luhmann rightly sees this idea as symptomatic of Durkheim's lack of interest in conceptualising social relations opposed to solidarity: see Luhmann, 'Durkheim on morality and the division of labour', in his *The Differentiation of Society* (1982). For a general account of property rights in French law see J. Bell et al., *Principles of French Law* (1998: ch. 9).

PROPERTY AND INDIVIDUALISM

For discussion of theories asserting a basis of the moral legitimacy of property in individualism see Waldron (1988: ch. 8); P. G. Stillman, 'Property, freedom, and individuality in Hegel's and Marx's political thought', in J. R. Pennock and J. W. Chapman (eds) *Property* (1980).

THE EVOLUTION OF PROPERTY RIGHTS

On the relation of Durkheim's work to that of Fustel de Coulanges see Jones, 'Durkheim and *La Cité antique*', *loc. cit.*; F. Héran, 'L'institution démotivée' (1987) 28 *Revue française de sociologie* 67.

The idea of the religious origins of property rights survives or is recreated in collective land claims of aboriginal peoples in many parts of the world. As Durkheim's analysis would suggest, the concept of property entailed in these claims, rooted in appeals to myths of origin or religious traditions, is often wholly different from (and not necessarily simpler than) that underlying modern property rights. The idea of property as a spiritual bond between human beings and their environment contrasts sharply with the concept of rights of ownership defining an asset that can be the object of exclusive possession, access or use, as well as an item of commerce. For generalisations about embryonic ideas of property, highlighting their frequent complexity and variety, see, for example, L. T. Hobhouse, 'The historical evolution of property in fact and in idea', in his *Sociology and Philosophy* (1966); R. Lowie, 'Incorporeal property in primitive society' (1928) 37 *Yale Law Journal* 551; Hoebel (1964: ch. 4).

INHERITANCE AND THE LIMITS OF PROPERTY

See also Fustel de Coulanges (1864: book 2, ch. 7).

FAMILY, MARRIAGE AND DIVORCE

On Durkheim's views of male–female relationships and of divorce some of the best sources are B. G. Cashion, 'Durkheim's concept of anomie and its relation to divorce' (1970) 55 *Sociology and Social Research* 72 (defending the value of Durkheim's analysis of divorce despite the inadequacies of his understanding of women's situation); M. Gane, 'Durkheim: woman as outsider', in Gane (ed.) *The Radical Sociology of Durkheim and Mauss* (1992) (on the place of women in Durkheim's sociology); Besnard (1973) (exploring 'a kind of incompatibility between Durkheimian sociology and women' arising from Durkheim's views). Divorce by mutual consent, which had existed for a period after the 1789 Revolution, was reintroduced in French law in 1975 (Civil Code Arts 230–6).

Chapter 10 The state and democracy

THE PLACE OF POLITICS

On the place of politics in Durkheim's sociological project see Favre (1983); L. A. Coser, 'Durkheim's conservatism and its implications for his sociological theory', in Wolff (ed.) (1960) (on his political outlook and attitude to social conflict). On Durkheim's political theory generally see Lacroix (1981); Müller (1993); Giddens (1972); M. Richter, 'Durkheim's politics and political theory', in Wolff (ed.) (1960); Pearce (1989: ch. 3); M. J. Hawkins, 'Émile Durkheim on democracy and absolutism' (1981) 2 *History of Political Thought* 369 (claiming that Durkheim's writings on politics do not form a coherent whole and lack a consistent theory of the state). F. Hearn, 'Durkheim's political sociology' (1985) 52 *Social Research* 151, argues that Durkheim's political sociology is compromised by its attempt to adhere both to the idea of a democracy of active, informed citizens and also to an idea of the corporatist state, which when put into practice denies this kind of democracy.

THE FUNCTION OF THE STATE

On Durkheim's conception of the state see P. Birnbaum, 'La conception durkheimienne de l'État' (1976) 17 *Revue française de sociologie* 247 (arguing that Durkheim provides no sociology of political facts, nor one that would show the links between the state and other social structures).

THE AUTHORITY OF THE STATE

See M. Bach, 'Individualism and legitimation' (1990) 31 *Archives européennes de sociologie* 187 (on political legitimacy as a Durkheimian concern).

DEMOCRACY

See Hawkins, 'Durkheim on democracy and absolutism', *loc. cit.* (arguing that Durkheim's idea of absolutism is confused and that he provides no clear criteria for distinguishing democracies from other kinds of state); I. Horowitz, 'Socialisation without politicisation' (1982) 10 *Political Theory* 353 (on Durkheim's view of the relation of the individual to the state); J. Prager, 'Moral integration and political inclusion: a comparison of Durkheim's and Weber's theories of democracy' (1981) 59 *Social Forces* 918 (claiming that Durkheim's work is important in providing a theory of values as a basis of democracy, although it ignores the need for institutional analysis of democratic structures).

Chapter 11 Making and interpreting law

THE LEGISLATIVE FUNCTION

For recent discussion of democracy as a form of collective deliberation see, for example, J. Bohman and W. Rehg (eds) *Deliberative Democracy* (1997); S. Benhabib, 'Toward a deliberative model of democratic legitimacy' and J. Cohen, 'Procedure and substance in deliberative democracy', both in S. Benhabib (ed.) *Democracy and Difference* (1996).

MAKING LAW, INTERPRETING LAW

Because Durkheim fails to analyse the criteria that should govern deliberation in lawmaking and legal interpretation his sociology is ambiguous as to how far the 'government consciousness' of legislator, judge or administrator should reflect the values of the collective consciousness, expressed in general social practices, and how far it should take the lead in guiding or refining collective representations. Durkheim claims that individual moral decisions may properly diverge from 'the prevailing moral opinion' of the public because the 'society that morality bids us desire is not the society as it *appears* to itself but the society as it is or is really becoming [presumably as revealed by sociology]. The consciousness which society may have of itself, . . . expressed in general opinion, may be an inadequate view of the underlying reality' (Durkheim, 1953d: 38; and see Piaget, 1932: 331ff.). It would seem, therefore, that the lawmaker's task is not to follow public opinion as such but to reason out law's appropriate stances in the light of sociology's explanations of the moral needs of society in its specific historical situation. An illustration might be the substantial abolition of capital punishment in advanced modern societies (for moral reasons discussed in Chapter 5, above), despite some strong public opinion in favour of its retention (on which see Kellogg, 'Peins criminelles', *loc. cit.*).

OFFICIALS, EXPERTS AND CITIZENS

On Durkheim's view of officials see Birnbaum, 'Conception durkheimi- enne de l'État', *loc. cit.* (the Durkheimian state is an instrument of rationality independent of social conflicts; thus, its officials must be apolitical). On his analyses of ritual see H. D. Duncan, 'The develop- ment of Durkheim's concept of ritual and the problem of social disre- lationships', in Wolff (ed.) (1960); H. Alpert, 'Durkheim's functional theory of ritual', in Nisbet (1965). And see S. Lukes, 'Political ritual and social integration', in his *Essays in Social Theory* (1977). On ritual and law see P. A. Winn, 'Legal ritual' (1991) 2 *Law and Critique* 207.

DEVOLUTION OF REGULATION

See M. J. Hawkins, 'Durkheim on occupational corporations' (1994) 55 *Journal of the History of Ideas* 461; T. V. Kaufman-Osborn, 'Émile Durkheim and the science of corporatism' (1986) 14 *Political Theory* 638; C. Gautier, 'Corporation, société et démocratie chez Durkheim' (1994) 44 *Revue française de science politique* 836; E. Reynaud, 'Groupes secondaires et solidarité organique' (1983) 33 *Année sociologique*, 3rd ser., 181; Cladis (1992: ch. 6); A. Supiot, 'Actualité de Durkheim: notes sur le néocorporatisme en France' (1987) 6 *Droit et Société* 177. For aspects of the wider political and legal debate to which Durkheim's ideas contributed in France see Hayward (1960). His ideas on the role of professional associations have been linked with English guild socialism and find echoes in recent conceptions of associational democracy. See Pearce (1989: 56). Hawkins, *loc. cit.*, notes important differences between Durkheim and the guild socialists (his rejection of class representation and less emphasis on democratic representation generally), and between Durkheim's ideas and corporatism (his insistence on the value of individualism as against any claims of *raison d'état*). For a careful discussion in historical context of the value and dangers of systems of functional representation see Bobbio (1987: ch. 2).

Chapter 12 Political action and political ideals

LAW AS AN OBSTACLE TO SOLIDARITY

For an interpretation of Durkheim's work presenting the themes of anomie and of the oppressive aspects of modern life as central to it see S. R. Marks, 'Durkheim's theory of anomie' (1974) 80 *American Journal of Sociology* 329. Cuvillier, 'Durkheim et Marx', *loc. cit.*, argues (p. 79) that Durkheim sees economic injustice as being overcome through 'a purely mechanical process', because he always thinks in terms of society as a whole, rather than in terms of social groups interacting.

A CONTEXT OF LAW REFORM

The social upheavals inspiring the rethinking of nineteenth-century legal ideas were sometimes referred to as a 'revolt of [social] facts' against law, an odd and worrying idea from a Durkheimian viewpoint, in which law's moral nature depends on it being in conformity with social facts, especially as related to the needs of solidarity. See Chazel (1991: 35–6); Arnaud (1975: ch. 2).

A CRY OF MISERY

On Durkheim's view of socialism see also J.-C. Filloux, *Durkheim et le socialisme* (1977); Birnbaum, 'Cadres sociaux', *loc. cit.*; D. Pels, 'A fellow-traveller's dilemma' (1984) 19 *Acta Politica* 309, portraying Durkheim's position as that of 'the sympathetic but reticent outsider ... rationalised into a posture of scientific detachment' (p. 326); M. Gane, 'Institutional socialism and the sociological critique of communism', in Gane (ed.) *Radical Sociology, op. cit.*

A RADICAL JURIST IN DURKHEIM'S WORLD

Emmanuel Lévy (1871–1944): Lévy's whole career was marked by his political commitment and the fierce, sometimes bitter, controversy that surrounded him. He began his teaching in Algiers at the time of the anti-semitic agitation there in 1897–8 and his lecture room was the focus of some of its early, violent manifestations. Later he combined his academic position in the Lyons law faculty with prominent service in local government, holding the position of deputy mayor of the city for many years. Very active in socialist politics, he addressed much of his writing to fellow socialists and workers, rather than jurists. This, and the aphoristic style and undeveloped nature of some of his work, as well as its polemical character, no doubt contributed to the controversy it raised among lawyers: see especially G. Ripert, 'Le socialisme juridique d'Emmanuel Lévy' (reprinted in Lévy, 1933) which is extremely critical. In general, juristic commentary hardly treated Lévy kindly.

His integrity and originality, however, brought him loyal supporters. Mauss warmly defended him: see 'Emmanuel Lévy, juriste, socialiste, et sociologue' in Mauss, *Écrits politiques* (1997). After his death, Paul Roubier wrote: 'To those who have been his disciples or colleagues he will always appear as a figure filled with the richest gifts, pride, spirit and heart' (*Annales de l'Université de Lyon 1943–4*, 1945: 62). Dean Jean Carbonnier commented (letter to the author, 28 April 1998, translated): 'I have met, among my generation, people from Lyons who were Lévy's students in civil law. I have always been struck by the fact that, even if they firmly distanced themselves from sociology and socialism, they held an extremely warm memory of their professor and his intellectual and moral authority.' See also E. Lambert, 'Préface' in Lévy (1926); P. Hebey, *Alger 1898* (1996: 96–8).

THE CREDIT RIGHT OF LABOUR

Among the most fully argued of Lévy's studies is Lévy (1909). Some of his work is collected, often in abbreviated or re-edited form, in Lévy (1926 and 1933). The most detailed discussion of his ideas is Gurvitch (1934). There is a brief, dense summary in the same author's *Éléments de sociologie juridique* (1940: 109–14) (very inadequately translated into English in Gurvitch (1947: 105–9)). Useful commentary can be found in Arnaud (1975, 1981). Chazel (1991: 36–7) notes perceptively that Duguit and Lévy develop, in parallel ways, opposite tendencies in Durkheim's work. Duguit applies Durkheim's positivism and functionalism to remove all subjective elements from legal analysis, which he then purports to base only on observation of material social conditions (social solidarity as a social fact). By contrast, Lévy proposes an analysis of law as removed from material conditions and grounded entirely in shared beliefs or convictions. For Chazel this 'changes Durkheim's thought to the point of misrepresenting it' (p. 37). For reasons given in the text, however, I think Lévy's approach can be seen as developing, in radical directions, implications clearly present in Durkheim's work. In broad terms, Duguit draws on the early purely functional view of law developed in *The Division of Labour,* while Lévy's approach relates to the ideational thesis about the nature of modern law developed in Durkheim's later work.

L. Frobert, 'Sociologie juridique et socialisme réformiste: note sur le projet d'Emmanuel Lévy' (1997) 3 *Durkheimian Studies* (n.s.) 27, proposes three distinct phases of Lévy's work. In the first phase (1896–9), Lévy identified the foundation of law in collective convictions. The second phase (1900–14) was concerned with examining the legal destiny of capital confronted by organised labour. The third (through the inter-war years) focused on the role of law in securing a balance between competing collective claims or expectations and so securing social peace. Frobert's thoughtful paper was not available to me in time for account to be taken of its argument in the text. However, Lévy's own integration and collation (in his 1926 and 1933 books) of writings from all periods of his career, with much cross-referencing, suggests that he saw his work, through all its phases, very much as a unity.

LEGAL ALLEGIANCE TO WHAT?

On the nation state as a focus of allegiance see M. M. Mitchell, 'Émile Durkheim and the philosophy of nationalism' (1931) 46 *Political Science Quarterly* 87 (very strongly emphasising Durkheim's national focus); J. R. Llobera, 'Durkheim and the national question', in Pickering and Martins (eds) *Debating Durkheim, op. cit.* (seeking to redress the balance). On conflicting foci of allegiance see Wallwork (1972: 174–5). LaCapra, *Durkheim, op. cit.,* claims (p. 93) that Durkheim, in his First World War propagandist writings, 'without hesitation placed the humanistic *conscience collective* of modern society [that is, the cult of the individual] above legal duties to the state. Had he lived longer Durkheim would in all probability have extended his theory of value and obligation to include a more inclusive and nonpartisan investigation of civil disobedience.' But this is speculation.

Chapter 13 The moralistic perspective

TWO VIRTUES

Durkheim's moralistic perspective: in some respects Ronald Dworkin's work (*Law's Empire*, 1986) is reminiscent of Durkheim's thought – particularly its emphasis on law as the elaboration of principle, values and shared beliefs, rather than as the expression of utilitarian calculation. Dworkin also locates the source of law in the moral life of a community, and assumes law and morality to be interdependent and elaborated through deliberative political processes. But he rejects any positivist conception of law as social fact, such as Durkheim's, and his work lacks the sociological perspective on law and morality which is a primary virtue of Durkheim's legal theory. The same absence of sociological foundation vitiates Patrick Devlin's argument (*Enforcement of Morals, op. cit.*) that (English) law's task is to reinforce shared moral beliefs, although Devlin's thesis has been compared with Durkheim's: see Hart (1967).

Natural law theory, claiming that law's essence, authority or validity derives directly from morality, also tends to lack such a foundation. It typically proclaims certain moral principles underlying law as 'natural' in the sense of self-evident, grounded in human nature, revealed by the intuitions of conscience, or derived from the natural conditions of all human life or of any social existence. Durkheim's approach, by contrast, insists that morality varies with historical context and social experience and hence its validity is rooted in the particular circumstances in which people live, as well as in prevailing shared beliefs. Yet, as Wallwork (1972: 164–5) and others have noted, some of Durkheim's thinking assumes the existence of universal moral values (for example, the value of solidarity).

INDIVIDUALISM AND RIGHTS

For a defence of Durkheim's analysis of individualism, linking it to current debates in political philosophy, see Cladis (1992). On the evolution of human rights discourse in relation to individualism see M.-B. Dembour, 'Human rights talk and anthropological ambivalence', in O. Harris (ed.) *Inside and Outside the Law* (1996).

POWER AND FORCE

On the relationships between legal regulation and the resolution of conflicts of interest see V. Aubert, *Continuity and Development in Law and Society* (1989: ch. 3). Aubert argues that law turns conflicts of interests into conflicts over values or beliefs (that is, conflicts as to which norms apply or as to the circumstances existing to which norms must be applied). Thus, like Durkheim, Aubert sees law as objectifying conflicts, removing them from the personal interests of the parties and making them matters for society at large, to be addressed normatively rather than by *ad hoc* compromise. As Aubert puts it (and the words could be Durkheim's): 'A bargain struck leaves no mark upon the normative order' (p. 103). In Durkheim's terms, law is not mediation but the structure of society's fundamental norms and the process of their formulation.

A FOCAL MEANING OF LAW

On Weber's legal theory see generally Kronman (1983). On the relationship (or lack of one) between Durkheim's and Weber's work see A. Giddens, 'Weber and Durkheim: coincidence and divergence', in W. J. Mommsen and J. Osterhammel (eds) *Max Weber and His Contemporaries* (1987); E. Tiryakian, 'A problem for the sociology of knowledge: the mutual unawareness of Émile Durkheim and Max Weber' (1966) 7 *Archives européennes de sociologie* 330; but cf. Lukes (1973: 397). Reinhard Bendix remarks (in his *Max Weber: An Intellectual Portrait*, 1966: 493) that it is difficult to see how Weber 'could have known Durkheim's work without taking direct issue with it' because (as exemplified in their respective analyses of law) Durkheim 'persistently mixed the approaches of science and ethics which Weber sought to separate as clearly as possible.' Bendix's comment highlights the difficulty in attaching the label 'positivist' to Durkheim's work as a whole: see Chapter 14, below.

A COHERENT VIEW OF MORALITY?

On the relationship of voluntas and ratio in law see Cotterrell (1995: chs 13 and 15).

CAN WE BELIEVE IN LAW?

The basis of law's legitimacy: Bach, 'Individualism and legitimation', *loc. cit.*, argues that the problem of legitimation is fundamental in Durkheim's political writings; legitimation is, for Durkheim, based in traditions that embody definitions of dominant cultural values. For discussion of how far the cult of the individual (and presumably its legal expressions) can be seen as a modern object of faith see Pickering (1993); Thomson (1993); J.-C. Filloux, 'Personne et sacré' (1990) 69 *Archives de sciences sociales des religions* 41; J. A. Prades, 'La religion de l'humanité', *ibid.* 55; W. S. F. Pickering, 'The eternality of the sacred: Durkheim's error?', *ibid.* 91; and F.-A. Isambert, 'Une religion de l'homme?' (1992) 33 *Revue française de sociologie* 443 (discussing Filloux's, Prades' and Pickering's papers).

Chapter 14 The sociological perspective

POSITIVISM AND ITS DISCONTENTS

For comparison of sociological positivism and legal positivism in relation to competing 'interpretive' approaches see Cotterrell (1992: 8–14). On legal positivism generally see, for example, Hart (1958); Austin (1832); Hart (1994). John Austin's positivistic legal philosophy, while insisting on an analytical separation of law and morality, affirms, like Durkheim's sociology, the possibility of positive sciences of both law and morality. See Austin (1832: 126–7). At the end of his life, Austin, like Durkheim, saw positive law and positive morality as 'the inseparably-connected parts of a vast organic whole' (Austin, *Lectures on Jurisprudence*, 1873: 17).

On the interpretive nature of law see, for example, generally A. Marmor, *Interpretation and Legal Theory* (1992); Marmor (ed.) *Law and Interpretation* (1995).

Positivism as useful for some purposes but not others: for legal philosophers, legal positivism is usually an all-or-nothing matter, to be adopted or rejected; the same is usually true for sociologists as regards sociological positivism. But law can always be seen from a variety of participant perspectives and participants vary their perspectives depending on their shifting concerns with law. Legal theory's task is surely to understand and integrate these perspectives. Positivism is important for some perspectives, unhelpful or misleading for others. It is important to identify law objectively and uncontroversially (positivistically) as 'in existence' or 'in force' in order to advise a client (as a lawyer), plan lawful projects and assert rights (as a citizen), or identify certain phenomena for study as 'law' (as a social scientist). But this partial legal perspective is often hard to maintain consistently in practice since positivism gives little aid in understanding practices of creation, interpretation, enforcement, alteration or abolition of positive law (Cotterrell, 1989: ch. 8). Hence, lawyers, lay citizens and legal sociologists (even including Durkheim to some extent) often alternate

– perhaps hardly noticing the shift – between positivistic and 'inter-pretive' perspectives on law. See also Cotterrell, 'Why must legal ideas be interpreted sociologically?' (1998) 25 *Journal of Law and Society* 171.

THE ORGANISATION OF ORGANIC SOLIDARITY

See H.-P. Müller, 'Social differentiation and organic solidarity' (1994) 9 *Sociological Forum* 73 (arguing that Durkheim could not show why the division of labour produces organic solidarity; yet he correctly noticed key characteristics of modern society – its integration and social differentiation, individualist values, welfare state, mixed economy and problems of anomie); Reynaud, 'Groupes secondaires', *loc. cit.*, argues that, while Durkheim recognises that secondary groups can create their own regulation in their own sphere, he does not see that this conflicts with the idea of a uniform social participation directed towards society as a whole. Pope and Johnson ('Inside organic solidarity', *loc. cit.*) see the concept of organic solidarity as confused and the basis of this soli-darity as unclear in Durkheim's analysis.

VARIETIES OF COMMUNITY

See generally Cotterrell, 'Law and community: a new relationship?' (1998) 51 *Current Legal Problems* 367; Cotterrell (1997); Cotterrell (1995: ch. 15); A. P. Cohen, *The Symbolic Construction of Community* (1985). For a sample of literature mapping the parameters of the types of community referred to in the text see B. Anderson, *Imagined Communities* (1991); J. W. Chapman and I. Shapiro (eds) *Democratic Community* (1993); V. Van Dyke, 'Justice as fairness: for groups?' (1975) 69 *American Political Science Review* 607; W. Kymlicka (ed.) *The Rights of Minority Cultures* (1995); M. McDonald, 'Should commu-nities have rights?', in An Na'im (ed.) (1992); A. N. Ancheta, *Race, Rights and the Asian American Experience* (1998); D. E. Ager, *Language, Community and the State* (1997); J. A. Fishman, *Reversing Language Shift* (1991); G. Salaman, 'Some sociological determinants of occupa-tional communities' (1971) 19 *Sociological Review* n.s. 53; Y. Dezalay and B. Garth, *Dealing in Virtue* (1996); M. S. Granovetter, 'The strength of weak ties' (1973) 78 *American Journal of Sociology* 1360; R. N. Morris, 'The assimilation of strangers in a small residential community' (1963) 11 *Sociological Review* n.s. 5; G. Simmel, 'The stranger', in K. H. Wolff (ed.) *The Sociology of Georg Simmel* (1950); Merry (1991); B. Yngvesson, *Virtuous Citizens, Disruptive Subjects* (1993); G. Frug, 'Decentering decentralization' (1993) 60 *University of Chicago Law*

Review 253; Frug, 'The geography of community' (1996) 48 *Stanford Law Review* 1047.

MESSAGES FROM THE PAST

Durkheim clothes his claims in the terminology of science. But it may be that he seeks 'truths' about humanity that can merely be illustrated (not validated) by the interpretation of collected data. If his project is seen (partly) in this light, history may provide for it an infinity of circumstances any of which can be a focus for considering timeless issues of the individual's relation to society, and perhaps of the very nature of human existence. In Durkheim's time, 'primitive societies' were of interest 'as being nearest the presumed original condition of humanity' (E. S. Hartland, *Primitive Law*, 1924: 200). But the idea of such an 'original condition' is, of course, an escape from any constraint of historical chronology. To recognise that, at this level, inquiries tend to become studies of the meaning of documented myths or empirically informed speculations beyond anything positivist science could approve is not necessarily to denigrate them (see P. Veyne, *Did the Greeks Believe in Their Myths?*, 1988). It may be to accept the need for the eventual fusion of sociology and philosophy that Durkheim envisaged. See Davy, 'In memoriam', *loc. cit.*

References

Dates (in round brackets) are those of the original publication of the edition or translation cited. Dates of first publication in French of works cited in English translation are also given [in square brackets] where these are directly relevant to the careers of Durkheim or his associates.

Aillet, G. (1923) 'Droit et sociologie', 30 *Revue de métaphysique et de morale* 97–119, 451–76.

Alexander, J. C. (1982) *Theoretical Logic in Sociology. Vol. 2: The Antinomies of Classical Thought: Marx and Durkheim.* London: Routledge & Kegan Paul.

An-Na'im, A. A. (ed.) (1992) *Human Rights in Cross Cultural Perspectives: A Quest for Consensus.* Philadelphia: University of Pennsylvania Press.

Arnaud, A.-J. (1975) *Les juristes face à la société du XIXe siècle à nos jours.* Paris: Presses Universitaires de France.

——(1981) *Critique de la raison juridique 1. Où va la Sociologie du droit?* Paris: Librairie Générale de Droit et de Jurisprudence.

Atiyah, P. S. (1981) *Promises, Morals, and Law.* Oxford: Clarendon.

Austin, J. (1832) *The Province of Jurisprudence Determined,* reprinted in J. Austin, *The Province of Jurisprudence and the Uses of the Study of Jurisprudence,* pp. 1–361. London: Weidenfeld & Nicolson, 1955.

Barnes, J. A. (1966) 'Durkheim's *Division of Labour in Society*', 1 *Man* (n.s.) 158–75.

Barnett, R. E. (1986) 'A consent theory of contract', 86 *Columbia Law Review* 269–321.

Bauman, Z. (1989) *Modernity and the Holocaust.* Cambridge: Polity.

Baxi, U. (1974) 'Durkheim and legal evolution', 8 *Law and Society Review* 645–51.

Bellah, R. N. (1973) 'Introduction', in Bellah (ed.) (1973), pp. ix–lv.

——(ed.) (1973) *Émile Durkheim on Morality and Society: Selected Essays.* Chicago: University of Chicago Press.

Besnard, P. (1973) 'Durkheim et les femmes ou le *Suicide* inachevé', 14 *Revue française de sociologie* 27–61.

——(ed.) (1983) *The Sociological Domain: The Durkheimians and the Founding of French Sociology.* Cambridge: Cambridge University Press.

——(1993) 'Anomie and fatalism in Durkheim's theory of regulation', in Turner (ed.) (1993), pp. 169–90.

Black, D. (1976) *The Behavior of Law.* New York: Academic Press.

——(1989) *Sociological Justice*. New York: Oxford University Press.

Bobbio, N. (1987) *The Future of Democracy: A Defence of the Rules of the Game*, trans. R. Griffin. Cambridge: Polity.

Bolgar, V. (1953) 'Why no trusts in the civil law?', 2 *American Journal of Comparative Law* 204–19.

Bouglé, C. (1935) *Bilan de la sociologie française contemporaine*. Paris: Alcan.

Carbonnier, J. (1994) *Sociologie juridique*, 2nd edn. Paris: Presses Universitaires de France.

Chazel, F. (1991) 'Émile Durkheim et l'élaboration d'un "programme de recherche" en sociologie du droit', in F. Chazel and J. Commaille (eds) *Normes juridiques et régulation sociale*. Paris: Librairie Générale de Droit et de Jurisprudence, pp. 27–38.

Cladis, M. S. (1992) *A Communitarian Defense of Liberalism: Émile Durkheim and Contemporary Social Theory*. Stanford, CA: Stanford University Press.

Clark, T. N. (1968) 'The structure and functions of a research institute: the *Année Sociologique*', 9 *Archives européennes de sociologie* 72–91.

Clarke, M. (1976) 'Durkheim's sociology of law', 3 *British Journal of Law and Society* 246–55.

Cocks, R. C. J. (1988) *Sir Henry Maine: A Study in Victorian Jurisprudence*. Cambridge: Cambridge University Press.

Cohen, M. R. (1933) *Law and the Social Order: Essays in Legal Philosophy*. Hamden, CT: Archon reprint 1967.

Collins, H. (1986) 'Democracy and adjudication', in N. MacCormick and P. Birks (eds) *The Legal Mind: Essays for Tony Honoré*. Oxford: Clarendon Press, pp. 67–82.

Cotterrell, R. (1977) 'Durkheim on legal development and social solidarity', 4 *British Journal of Law and Society* 241–52.

——(1989) *The Politics of Jurisprudence: A Critical Introduction to Legal Philosophy*. London: Butterworths.

——(1992) *The Sociology of Law: An Introduction*, 2nd edn. London: Butterworths.

——(1993) 'Trusting in law: legal and moral concepts of trust', 46 *Current Legal Problems* 75–95.

——(1995) *Law's Community: Legal Theory in Sociological Perspective*. Oxford: Clarendon Press.

——(1997) 'A legal concept of community', 12 *Canadian Journal of Law and Society* 75–91.

Cuklanz, L. M. (1996) *Rape on Trial: How the Mass Media Construct Legal Reform and Social Change*. Philadelphia: University of Pennsylvania Press.

Daube, D. (1973) 'The self-understood in legal history', 18 *Juridical Review* (n.s.) 126–34.

Davy, G. (1919) 'Émile Durkheim: 1 – L'homme', 26 *Revue de métaphysique et de morale* 181–98.

——(1920) 'L'idéalisme et les conceptions réalistes du Droit', 45 *Revue philosophique* 234–76, 349–84.

——(1922) *La foi jurée – étude sociologique du problème du contrat: La formation du lien contractuel*. New York: Arno reprint 1975.

——(1957) 'Introduction', in Durkheim (1957), pp. xiii–xliv.

De Tourtoulon, P. (1908) *Les principes philosophiques de l'histoire du droit*, vol 1. Paris: Alcan.

Diamond, A. S. (1935) *Primitive Law*. London: Watts reprint 1950.

——(1951) *The Evolution of Law and Order*. London: Watts.

Duguit, L. (1919) *Law in the Modern State*, trans. F. and H. Laski. New York: Fertig reprint 1970 [originally published in French in 1913].

——(1921) 'Objective law' (Parts 1–4), 20 *Columbia Law Review* 817–31, 21 *Ibid.* 17–34, 126–43, 242–56.

Durkheim, É. (1887) 'La science positive de la morale en allemagne', reprinted in Durkheim (1975a), vol. 1, pp. 267–343.

——(1890) 'Les principes de 1789 et la sociologie', reprinted in Durkheim (1987), pp. 215–25.

——(1893a) *De la division du travail social*. Paris: Presses Universitaires de France, Quadrige reprint 1986.

✗——(1893b) 'Définition du fait moral', reprinted in Durkheim (1975a), vol. 2, pp. 257–88.

——(1895) *Les Règles de la méthode sociologique*. Paris: Flammarion reprint 1988.

——(1897) 'Gaston Richard, *Le socialisme et la science sociale*' [Review], reprinted in Durkheim (1987), pp. 236–44.

——(1898) 'La prohibition de l'inceste et ses origines', reprinted in Durkheim (1969a), pp. 37–101.

——(1900a) 'La sociologie et son domaine scientifique', reprinted in Durkheim (1975a), vol. 1, pp. 13–36.

——(1900b) 'La sociologie en France au XIXe siècle', reprinted in Durkheim (1987), pp. 111–36.

——(1900c) 'Notes critiques' [Comment on Neukamp, 'Das Zwangsmoment im Recht . . .'], reprinted in Durkheim (1975a), vol. 3, pp. 319–21.

——(1903) 'Notes critiques' [Review of Huvelin (1900)], reprinted in Durkheim (1969a), pp. 463–4.

——(1904) 'Notes critiques' [Review of Lambert, *La fonction du droit civil comparé*], reprinted in Durkheim (1975a), vol. 3, pp. 266–71.

——(1906a) 'Notes critiques' [Review of Dereux, *De l'interpretation des actes juridiques privés*], 9 *Année sociologique* 418–20.

——(1906b) 'Le divorce par consentement mutuel', reprinted in Durkheim (1975a), vol. 2, pp. 181–94.

——(1907) 'Notes critiques' [Review of books by Fouillée, Belot and Landry], reprinted in Durkheim (1969a), pp. 568–84.

——(1909) 'Sociologie et sciences sociales', reprinted in Durkheim (1987), pp. 137–59.

——(1912) *Les formes élementaires de la vie religieuse*. Paris: Presses Universitaires de France, Quadrige reprint 1985.

——(1915) *The Elementary Forms of the Religious Life*, trans. by J. W. Swain of Durkheim (1912). London: Allen & Unwin reprint 1976.

——(1925) *L'éducation morale*. Paris: Presses Universitaires de France, Quadrige reprint 1992.

——(1928) *Le socialisme*. Presses Universitaires de France, Quadrige reprint 1992.

——(1950) *Leçons de sociologie: physique des mœurs et du droit*. Paris: Presses Universitaires de France, Quadrige reprint 1995.

——(1952) *Suicide: A Study in Sociology*, trans. J. A. Spaulding and G. Simpson. London: Routledge & Kegan Paul [originally published in French in 1897].

——(1953a) *Sociology and Philosophy*, trans. D. F. Pocock. New York: Free Press reprint 1974.

——(1953b) 'Individual and collective representations', in Durkheim (1953a), pp. 1–34 [originally published in French in 1898].

——(1953c) 'Value judgments and judgments of reality', in Durkheim (1953a), pp. 80–97 [originally published in French in 1911].

——(1953d) 'The determination of moral facts', in Durkheim (1953a), pp. 35–62 [originally published in French in 1906].

——(1957) *Professional Ethics and Civic Morals*, trans. by C. Brookfield of Durkheim (1950). London: Routledge & Kegan Paul.

——(1958) *Socialism and Saint-Simon*, trans. by C. Sattler of Durkheim (1928). New York: Collier reprint 1962.

——(1960a) 'Sociology and its scientific field', trans. by K. H. Wolff, in Wolff (ed.) (1960), pp. 354–75 [originally published in Italian in 1900].

——(1960b) 'The dualism of human nature and its social conditions', trans. by C. Blend, in Wolff (ed.) (1960), pp. 325–40 [originally published in French in 1914].

——(1961) *Moral Education*, trans. by E. K. Wilson and H. Schnurer of Durkheim (1925). New York: Free Press.

——(1969a) *Journal sociologique*, ed. J. Duvignaud. Paris: Presses Universitaires de France.

——(1969b) 'Individualism and the intellectuals', trans. by S and J. Lukes, reprinted in Pickering (ed.) (1975), pp. 59–73 [originally published in French in 1898].

——(1973a) 'Sociology in France in the nineteenth century', trans. by M. Traugott of Durkheim (1900b), in Bellah (ed.) (1973), pp. 3–22.

——(1973b) 'Two laws of penal evolution', trans. by T. A. Jones and A. Scull, reprinted in M. Gane (ed.) *The Radical Sociology of Durkheim and Mauss*. London: Routledge, 1992, pp. 21–49. [originally published in French in 1901].

——(1975a) *Textes*, 3 vols, ed. V. Karady. Paris: Les Éditions de Minuit.

——(1975b) 'Contribution to discussion: "religious sentiment at the present time"' in Pickering (ed.) (1975), pp. 181–9 [originally published in French in 1919].

——(1978a) 'Sociology and the social sciences', trans. of Durkheim (1909), in Traugott (ed.) (1978), pp. 71–87.

——(1978b) 'Course in sociology: opening lecture', in Traugott (ed.) (1978), pp. 43–70 [originally published in French in 1888].

——(1978c) 'Introduction to the sociology of the family', in Traugott (ed.) (1978), pp. 205–28 [originally published in French in 1888].

——(1979) 'Review: Lévy-Bruhl, *La morale et la science des mœurs*', in Pickering (ed.) (1979), pp. 29–33 [originally published in French in 1904].

——(1982a) *The Rules of Sociological Method and Selected Texts on Sociology and Its Method*, trans. by W. D. Halls of Durkheim (1895) and other texts. London: Macmillan.

——(1982b) 'Marxism and sociology: the materialist conception of history', in Durkheim (1982a), pp. 167–74 [originally published in French in 1897].

——(1982c) 'Debate on explanation in history and sociology', in Durkheim (1982a), pp. 211–28 [originally published in French in 1908].

——(1983a) 'Gaston Richard's *Essai sur l'origine de l'idée de droit*', trans. by A. Scull, in Lukes and Scull (eds) (1983), pp. 146–54 [originally published in French in 1893].

——(1983b) 'The origins of penal law', trans. by S. Lukes and W. D. Halls, in Lukes and Scull (eds) (1983), pp. 154–7 [originally published in French in 1905].

✗——(1984) *The Division of Labour in Society*, trans. by W. D. Halls of Durkheim (1893a). London: Macmillan.

——(1987) *La science sociale et l'action*, ed. J.-C. Filloux, 2nd edn. Paris: Presses Universitaires de France.

Durkheim, É. and Fauconnet, P. (1982) 'Sociology and the social sciences', in Durkheim (1982a), pp. 175–208 [originally published in French in 1903].

Duvignaud, J. (1965) *Durkheim: sa vie, son œuvre, avec un exposé de sa philosophie*. Paris: Presses Universitaires de France.

Duxbury, N. (1989) 'Foundations of legal tradition: the case of Ancient Greece', 9 *Legal Studies* 241–60.

Eisenmann, C. (1968) 'Duguit, Léon', in D. Shills (ed.) *International Encyclopedia of the Social Sciences*. New York: Free Press, vol. 4, pp. 305–8.

Erikson, K. (1966) *Wayward Puritans: A Study in the Sociology of Deviance*. New York: Wiley.

Fauconnet, P. (1928) *La responsabilité: étude de sociologie*, 2nd edn. Paris: Alcan.

Favre, P. (1983) 'The absence of political sociology in the Durkheimian classifications of the social sciences', in Besnard (ed.) (1983), pp. 199–216.

Fenn, R. K. (1982) *Liturgies and Trials: The Secularisation of Religious Language*. Oxford: Blackwell.

Fenton, S. (1984) *Durkheim and Modern Sociology*. Cambridge: Cambridge University Press.

Filloux, J.-C. (1993) 'Inequalities and social stratification in Durkheim's sociology', in Turner (ed.) (1993), pp. 211–28.

Finnis, J. (1980) *Natural Law and Natural Rights*. Oxford: Clarendon Press.

Fishkin, J. S. (1991) *Democracy and Deliberation: New Directions for Democratic Reform*. New Haven, CT: Yale University Press.

Fitzpatrick, P. (1992) *The Mythology of Modern Law*. London: Routledge.

Fried, C. (1981) *Contract as Promise: A Theory of Contractual Obligation*. Cambridge, MA: Harvard University Press.

Friedman, L. M. and Percival, R. V. (1976) 'A tale of two courts: litigation in Alameda and San Benito Counties', 10 *Law and Society Review* 267–301.

Fukuyama, F. (1992) *The End of History and the Last Man*. London: Hamish Hamilton.

Fustel de Coulanges, N. D. (1864) *La Cité antique: étude sur le culte, le droit, les institutions de la Grèce et de Rome*. Paris: Flammarion reprint 1984.

Garfinkel, H. (1956) 'Conditions of successful degradation ceremonies', 61 *American Journal of Sociology* 420–4.

Garland, D. (1983) 'Durkheim's theory of punishment: a critique', in D. Garland and P. Young (eds) *The Power to Punish: Contemporary Penality and Social Analysis*. London: Heinemann, pp. 37–61.

——(1990) *Punishment and Modern Society: A Study in Social Theory*. Oxford: Clarendon Press.

George, R. P. (ed.) (1992) *Natural Law Theory: Contemporary Essays*. Oxford: Clarendon.

Gernet, L. (1951) 'Droit et prédroit en Grèce ancienne', reprinted in Gernet (1982), pp. 7–119.

——(1956) 'Le temps dans les formes archaïques du droit', reprinted in Gernet (1982), pp. 121–56.

——(1982) *Droit et institutions en Grèce antique*. Paris: Flammarion.

Gewirth, P. (1988) 'Aeschylus' law', 101 *Harvard Law Review* 1043–55.

Giddens, A. (1971) 'The "individual" in the writings of Émile Durkheim', reprinted in Giddens (1977), pp. 273–91.

——(1972) 'Durkheim's political theory', reprinted in Giddens (1977), pp. 235–72.

——(1975) 'The high priest of positivism: Auguste Comte', reprinted in A. Giddens, *Profiles and Critiques in Social Theory*. London: Macmillan, 1982, pp. 68–75.

——(1977) *Studies in Social and Political Theory*. London: Hutchinson.

Grabosky, P. N. (1978) 'Theory and research on variations in penal severity', 5 *British Journal of Law and Society* 103–14.

Gray, K. (1991) 'Property in thin air', 50 *Cambridge Law Journal* 252–307.

Grey, T. C. (1980) 'The disintegration of property', in J. R. Pennock and J. W. Chapman (eds) *Property*. New York: New York University Press, pp. 69–85.

——(1984) 'The Constitution as scripture', 37 *Stanford Law Review* 1–25.

Gross, H. (1979) *A Theory of Criminal Justice*. New York: Oxford University Press.

Gurvitch, G. (1934) 'Les fondements et l'évolution du droit d'après Emmanuel Lévy', reprinted in Gurvitch (1935), pp. 170–99.

——(1935) *L'expérience juridique et la philosophie pluraliste du droit*. Paris: Pedone.

——(1942) 'Magic and law', 9 *Social Research* 104–22.

——(1947) *Sociology of Law*. London: Routledge & Kegan Paul reprint 1973.

——(1963) *La Vocation actuelle de la sociologie. Vol. 2 – Antécédents et perspectives*, 2nd edn. Paris: Presses Universitaires de France.

Gusfield, J. R. (1963) *Symbolic Crusade: Status Politics and the American Temperance Movement.* Urbana: University of Illinois Press.
Gutteridge, H. C. (1933) 'Abuse of rights', 5 *Cambridge Law Journal* 22–45.
Hägerström, A. (1953) *Inquiries into the Nature of Law and Morals,* trans. C. D. Broad. Stockholm: Almqvist & Wiksell.
Hamnett, I. (1975) *Chieftainship and Legitimacy: An Anthropological Study of Executive Law in Lesotho.* London: Routledge & Kegan Paul.
Hart, H. L. A. (1958) 'Positivism and the separation of law and morals', reprinted in Hart (1983), pp. 49–87.
——(1967) 'Social solidarity and the enforcement of morality', reprinted in Hart (1983), pp. 248–62.
——(1983) *Essays in Jurisprudence and Philosophy.* Oxford: Clarendon Press.
——(1994) *The Concept of Law,* 2nd edn. Oxford: Clarendon Press.
Hauriou, M. (1970) 'The theory of the institution and the foundation: a study in social vitalism', trans. M. Welling, in A. Broderick (ed.) *The French Institutionalists: Maurice Hauriou, Georges Renard, Joseph T. Delos.* Cambridge, MA: Harvard University Press, pp. 93–124. [originally published in French in 1925].
Hayward, J. E. S. (1960) 'Solidarist syndicalism: Durkheim and Duguit', 8 *Sociological Review* 17–36, 185–202.
Hepworth, M. and Turner, B. S. (1982) *Confession: Studies in Deviance and Religion.* London: Routledge & Kegan Paul.
Hoebel, E. A. (1964) *The Law of Primitive Man: A Study in Comparative Legal Dynamics.* Cambridge, MA: Harvard University Press.
Holmes, Jr, O. W. (1881) *The Common Law.* New York: Dover reprint 1991.
Honoré, T. (1960) 'Ownership', reprinted in T. Honoré, *Making Law Bind: Essays Legal and Philosophical.* Oxford: Clarendon Press, 1987, pp. 161–92.
Huvelin, P. (1900) 'Les tablettes magiques et le droit romain', reprinted in P. Huvelin, *Études d'histoire du droit commercial romain,* ed. H. Lévy-Bruhl. Paris: Librairie du Receuil Sirey, 1929, pp. 219–71.
——(1907) 'Magie et droit individuel', 10 *Année sociologique* 1–47.
Ireland, P., Grigg-Spall, I. and Kelly, D. (1987) 'The conceptual foundations of modern company law', 14 *Journal of Law and Society* 149–65.
Joas, H. (1993) 'Durkheim's intellectual development: the problem of the emergence of new morality and new institutions as a leitmotif in Durkheim's oeuvre', in Turner (ed.) (1993), pp. 229–45.
Kellough, G. (1996) *Aborting Law: An Exploration of the Politics of Motherhood and Medicine.* Toronto: University of Toronto Press.
Kelsen, H. (1991) *General Theory of Norms,* trans. M. Hartney. Oxford: Clarendon Press.
Kronman, A. (1983) *Max Weber.* London: Edward Arnold.
Lacroix, B. (1981) *Durkheim et le politique.* Montréal: Presses de L'Université de Montréal.
Lawson, F. H. and Rudden, B. (1982) *The Law of Property,* 2nd edn. Oxford: Clarendon Press.

Lenman, B. and Parker, G. (1980) 'The state, the community and the criminal law in early modern Europe', in V. A. C. Gatrell, B. Lenman and G. Parker (eds) *Crime and the Law: The Social History of Crime in Western Europe Since 1500*. London: Europa, pp. 11–48.

Lenoir, R. (1994) 'Mœurs, morale et droit chez Durkheim', 19 *Droits* 23–36.

Levinson, S. (1988) *Constitutional Faith*. Princeton, NJ: Princeton University Press.

Lévi-Strauss, C. (1945) 'French sociology', in G. Gurvitch and W. E. Moore (eds) *Twentieth Century Sociology*. New York: Philosophical Library, pp. 503–37.

Lévy, E. (1909) *Capital et travail*. Paris: Librairie du Parti Socialiste.

——(1926) *La vision socialiste du droit*. Paris: Giard.

——(1933) *Les fondements du droit*. Paris: Alcan.

Luhmann, N. (1985) *A Sociological Theory of Law*, trans. E. King and M. Albrow. London: Routledge & Kegan Paul.

Lukes, S. (1973) *Émile Durkheim: His Life and Work: A Historical and Critical Study*. London: Allen Lane.

——(1982) 'Introduction', in Durkheim (1982a), pp. 1–27.

Lukes, S. and Scull, A. (1983) 'Introduction', in Lukes and Scull (eds) (1983), pp. 1–32.

——(eds.) (1983) *Durkheim and the Law*. Oxford: Martin Robertson.

Lyons, D. (1984) *Ethics and the Rule of Law*. Cambridge: Cambridge University Press.

MacCormack, G. (1980) 'Georges Davy and the origin of contract', 15 *Irish Jurist* 166–76.

MacCormick, D. N. (1974) 'Law as institutional fact', 90 *Law Quarterly Review* 102–29.

——(1982) 'Voluntary obligations', in D. N. MacCormick, *Legal Right and Social Democracy: Essays in Legal and Social Philosophy*. Oxford: Clarendon Press, pp. 190–211.

——(1992) 'Natural law and the separation of law and morals', in George (ed.) (1992), pp. 105–33.

Maine, H. S. (1861) *Ancient Law*. London: Dent reprint 1977.

Malinowski, B. (1926) *Crime and Custom in Savage Society*. London: Routledge & Kegan Paul reprint 1978.

Mauss, M. (1896) 'La religion et les origines du droit pénal d'après un livre récent', reprinted in M. Mauss, *Œuvres*. Paris: Les Éditions de Minuit, 1969, vol. 2, pp. 651–98.

——(1958) 'Introduction to the first edition', in Durkheim (1958), pp. 32–6.

——(1972) *A General Theory of Magic*, trans. R. Brain. London: Routledge & Kegan Paul [originally published in French in 1904].

——(1979) *Seasonal Variations of the Eskimo: A Study in Social Morphology*, trans. J. J. Fox. London: Routledge & Kegan Paul [originally published in French in 1906].

——(1990) *The Gift: The Form and Reason of Exchange in Archaic Societies*, trans. W. D. Halls. London: Routledge [originally published in French in 1925].

Merry, S. E. (1991) *Getting Justice and Getting Even: Legal Consciousness Among Working-Class Americans.* Chicago: University of Chicago Press.

Mestrovic, S. G. (1988) *Émile Durkheim and the Reformation of Sociology.* Totowa, NJ.: Rowman & Littlefield.

Miller, W. W. (1993) 'Durkheim: liberal-communitarian', in Pickering and Miller (eds) (1993), pp. 82–104.

Müller, H.-P. (1993) 'Durkheim's political sociology', in Turner (ed.) (1993), pp. 95–110.

Nisbet, R. A. (1965) *Émile Durkheim.* Englewood Cliffs, NJ: Prentice-Hall.

——(1966) *The Sociological Tradition.* London: Heinemann reprint 1976.

Pearce, F. (1989) *The Radical Durkheim.* London: Unwin Hyman.

Piaget, J. (1932) *The Moral Judgment of the Child*, trans. M. Gabain. Harmondsworth: Penguin reprint 1977.

Pickering, W. S. F. (1975) 'A note on the life of Gaston Richard and certain aspects of his work', in Pickering (ed.) (1975), pp. 343–59.

——(ed.) (1975) *Durkheim on Religion: A Selection of Readings with Bibliographies*, trans. J. Redding and W. S. F. Pickering. London: Routledge & Kegan Paul.

——(ed.) (1979) *Durkheim: Essays on Morals and Education*, trans. H. L. Sutcliffe. London: Routledge & Kegan Paul.

——(1984) *Durkheim's Sociology of Religion: Themes and Theories.* London: Routledge & Kegan Paul.

——(1993) 'Human rights and the cult of the individual: an unholy alliance created by Durkheim?', in Pickering and Miller (eds) (1993), pp. 51–76.

——(1994) 'The enigma of Durkheim's Jewishness', in W. S. F. Pickering and H. Martins (eds) *Debating Durkheim.* London: Routledge, pp. 10–39.

Pickering, W. S. F. and Miller, W. W. (eds) (1993) *Individualism and Human Rights in the Durkheimian Tradition.* Oxford: British Centre for Durkheimian Studies.

Pisier-Kouchner, E. (1972) *Le service public dans la théorie de l'état de Léon Duguit.* Paris: Librairie Générale de Droit et de Jurisprudence.

Raz, J. (1980) *The Concept of a Legal System: An Introduction to the Theory of Legal System*, 2nd edn. Oxford: Clarendon Press.

——(1994) *Ethics in the Public Domain: Essays in the Morality of Law and Politics.* Oxford: Clarendon Press.

Sanders, J. (1990) 'The interplay of micro and macro processes in the longitudinal study of courts: beyond the Durkheimian tradition', 24 *Law and Society Review* 241–56.

Schumpeter, J. A. (1952) *Capitalism, Socialism and Democracy*, 5th edn. London: Allen & Unwin reprint 1976.

Schwartz, R. D. (1974) 'Legal evolution and the Durkheim hypothesis: a reply to Professor Baxi', 8 *Law and Society Review* 653–68.

Schwartz, R. D. and Miller, J. C. (1964) 'Legal evolution and societal complexity', 70 *American Journal of Sociology* 159–69.

Sheleff, L. S. (1975) 'From restitutive law to repressive law: Durkheim's *The Division of Labour in Society* revisited', 16 *European Journal of Sociology* 16–45.

——(1997) *Social Cohesion and Legal Coercion: A Critique of Weber, Durkheim and Marx.* Amsterdam: Rodopi.

Shils, E. (1991) 'Henry Sumner Maine in the tradition of the analysis of society', in A. Diamond (ed.) *The Victorian Achievement of Sir Henry Maine: A Centennial Reappraisal.* Cambridge: Cambridge University Press, pp. 143–78.

Silverstein, H. (1996) *Unleashing Rights: Law, Meaning and the Animal Rights Movement.* Ann Arbor: University of Michigan Press.

Spitzer, S. (1975) 'Punishment and social organisation: a study of Durkheim's theory of penal evolution', 9 *Law and Society Review* 613–37.

——(1979) 'Notes toward a theory of punishment and social change', in R. J. Simon and S. Spitzer (eds) *Research in Law and Sociology: A Research Annual.* Greenwich, CT: JAI Press, vol. 2, pp. 207–29.

Thompson, K. (1993) 'Wedded to the sacred: response to W. S. F. Pickering', in Pickering and Miller (eds) (1993), pp. 77–81.

Traugott, M. (ed.) (1978) *Émile Durkheim on Institutional Analysis,* trans. M. Traugott. Chicago: University of Chicago Press.

Turner, S. P. (ed.) (1993) *Émile Durkheim: Sociologist and Moralist.* London: Routledge.

Tyler, T. R. (1990) *Why People Obey the Law.* New Haven, CT: Yale University Press.

Vogt, W. P. (1983) 'Obligation and right: the Durkheimians and the sociology of law', in Besnard (ed.) (1983), pp. 177–98.

——(1993) 'Durkheim's sociology of law: morality and the cult of the individual', in Turner (ed.) (1993), pp. 71–94.

Waldron, J. (1988) *The Right to Private Property.* Oxford: Clarendon Press.

Wallwork, E. (1972) *Durkheim: Morality and Milieu.* Cambridge, MA: Harvard University Press.

Watson, A. (1985) *The Evolution of Law.* Oxford: Blackwell.

——(1988) *Failures of the Legal Imagination.* Edinburgh: Scottish Academic Press.

Weber, M. (1948) 'Science as a vocation', in H. H. Gerth and C. W. Mills (eds and trans.) *From Max Weber: Essays in Sociology.* London: Routledge & Kegan Paul, pp. 129–56.

——(1968) *Economy and Society: An Outline of Interpretive Sociology,* trans. E. Fischoff et al. Berkeley: University of California Press reprint 1978.

Weisz, G. (1983) 'The republican ideology and the social sciences: the Durkheimians and the history of social economy at the Sorbonne', in Besnard (ed.) (1983), pp. 90–119.

Wimberley, H. (1973) 'Legal evolution: one further step', 79 *American Journal of Sociology* 78–83.

Wolff, K. H. (ed.) (1960) *Essays on Sociology and Philosophy by Émile Durkheim et al.* New York: Harper & Row reprint 1964.

Index